Alison Pargeter is a writer and analyst specialising in the Middle East and North Africa. She has held academic positions at the University of Cambridge and Kings College, London, and is a senior associate at Menas Associates, an international consultancy firm. Her other publications include *Libya: The Rise and Fall of Qaddafi* and *The New Frontiers of Jihad: Radical Islam in Europe*.

'Alison Pargeter has established a reputation as one of the best current analysts of Islamic radicalism. This book – detailed, authoritative, sober, perceptive and meticulously researched – shows why. It is an important contribution to our understanding both of the Muslim Brotherhood itself, to the controversies that surround the movement and to the broader phenomenon of political Islam. A must read for scholars, students and anyone interested in the Middle East.'
Jason Burke, author of *Al-Qaeda: The True Story of Radical Islam*

'A tour de force ... This well-written and much-needed book admirably traces the origins and development, internal debates and frictions, geographical spread – and abiding contradictions – of a movement that, despite its ambiguities and shortcomings, remains very much a force to be reckoned with.'
Alan George, University of Oxford

'This highly lucid and approachable analysis of the Brotherhood offers a welcome degree of clarity. Alison Pargeter offers a global picture of the trajectories the movement has taken in the Arab world and in Europe. Based on important internal documents, and, crucially, a remarkable array of on-the-record interviews with senior Brotherhood personnel, Pargeter allows the Brothers to do much of the talking.'
Richard Phelps, *Perspectives on Terrorism*

'Highly recommended, especially t(
Jihadism, Wahhabism, Salafism and
and all equally to be feared.' *New Stat*

Alison Pargeter

THE MUSLIM BROTHERHOOD

From Opposition To Power

SAQI

This paperback edition published by Saqi Books 2013

First published in hardback by Saqi Books 2010

Copyright © Alison Pargeter 2010

ISBN 978-0-86356-859-6
eISBN 978-0-86356-746-9

Alison Pargeter has asserted her right under the Copyright, Designs
and Patents Act, 1988, to be identified as the author of this work.

This book is sold subject to the condition that it shall not, by way of trade or otherwise,
be lent, resold, hired out, or otherwise circulated without the publisher's prior consent in
any form of binding or cover other than that in which it is published and without a
similar condition including this condition being imposed on the subsequent purchaser.

A full CIP record for this book is available
from the British Library.

Printed and bound by CPI Group (UK) Ltd, Croydon, CR0 4YY

Saqi Books
26 Westbourne Grove
London W2 5RH

www.saqibooks.com

Contents

Introduction   7

1. Conflicting Currents: The Egyptian Ikhwan in Opposition   15

2. From Diplomacy to Arms and Back to Diplomacy: The Evolution
   of the Syrian Ikhwan   65

3. The International *Tanzeem*: Myth or Reality?   103

4. A School of Thought: The Ikhwan in Europe   136

5. The Ikhwan and Violence   179

6. The Arab Spring: From Opposition to Power   211

Conclusion: The Challenges Ahead   245

Acknowledgements   259

Notes   260

Bibliography   287

Index   293

Contents

Introduction

One of the unforeseen consequences of the Arab Spring has been the catapulting of the Muslim Brotherhood (*al-Ikhwan al-Muslimeen*) – one of the longest surviving and most controversial of all political Islamist movements – from the underground to the forefront of the Middle Eastern political arena. Despite the fact that the popular uprisings that gripped parts of the Arab world in 2011 were largely non-ideological in nature, driven largely by youth who came together with no political agenda other than to oust the authoritarian regimes that had gripped the region more or less since independence, it was the Brotherhood that was to reap the advantages of the revolutions. In Egypt, the Brotherhood through its political arm, the Freedom and Justice Party, emerged triumphant in both parliamentary and presidential elections; in Tunisia, An-Nahda, which although not officially part of the Brotherhood follows its broad ideological orientation, won the largest majority in the elections to the constituent assembly and went on to lead the government; in Libya, the Brotherhood's Justice and Construction Party may not have triumphed in the elections to the General National Congress but it still became part of the government as well as a key political player; in Syria, meanwhile, the Brotherhood is playing a major role in the opposition platforms that have sprung up and looks set to have a stake in the country's future. The Arab Spring, therefore, turned out to be a triumph for the forces of reformist political Islam.

This turn of events is all the more paradoxical given that the Brotherhood has always been a movement that has shunned revolutions and that repeatedly declared itself not to be interested in taking power. It preferred to work from the bottom up, or so it proclaimed, educating society Islamically in order to prepare it for the eventual establishment of an Islamic state. Yet when it came to it, the Brotherhood rushed at the opportunity to get to power. The movement mobilised its resources on an unprecedented level to manoeuvre its way through the transition and to dominate the emergent political arena.

To those familiar with the Brotherhood, the movement's behaviour during the Arab Spring was not all that surprising. The Brotherhood has always been a movement of controversy and contradiction that has proved near impossible to pin down. Indeed, it has always represented a conundrum to those trying to fathom it. It is a social movement that also functions as a political entity; it is a transnational organisation that emphasises the independence of its national branches; it projects itself as pacific yet some of its branches have been directly involved in violent action; it broadly rejects the West and Western values yet is increasingly anxious to be seen in Western eyes as a moderate organisation that upholds progressive inclusive values. It is also a movement that has been cloaked in ambiguity and that has comprised so many different strands and currents that it has struggled to articulate a single stance on many key issues including violence, the role of women and the role of non-Muslim minorities. It is easy to understand, therefore, why observers and policymakers have found it difficult to develop a coherent policy towards the movement. It is also easy to understand why the Brotherhood's shift into the political mainstream following the Arab Spring has created such a challenge for policymakers, particularly those in the West.

Yet now, it seems, is the Brotherhood's time. It has certainly been a long wait. The movement was first established in Egypt in 1928 where it emerged partly as a response to the colonialist presence in the country, but also to the end of the last caliphate, the Ottoman Empire. The Brotherhood came within the tradition of the reformist school that emerged in Egypt in the late nineteenth century through scholars such as Rashid Rida and Muhammad Abdu who believed that the only way the Islamic world could meet the challenges posed by Westernisation and modernisation was to return to the 'uncorrupted' values of the Islamic past. The movement soon gathered momentum and by the 1950s had also developed into a reaction against the modernising secular forces of Arab nationalism that threatened to unseat traditional conservative religious values. As a result, the Brotherhood drew much of its support from the classes that feared change, namely the petty bourgeoisie and the trading and artisan classes. Indeed, since its beginnings, it has been a largely reactionary movement, preoccupied by issues of public morality and the preservation of traditional values.

Although the Brotherhood originated in Egypt as a result of a specific set of social and political conditions, its ideology soon spread and branches began to spring up in other countries. Syria and Jordan were perhaps the most important branches in the early days but it was not long before most of the countries of the Middle East had their own branch or equivalent of the Brotherhood. It was able to spread in this way because it offered a simple ideology that corresponded with the mood of the time and that seemed to represent a reassuring beacon of constancy during a period of immense upheaval in the region. Indeed, its slogan said it all: 'Islam is the solution.'

Whilst it had started out primarily as a social and cultural movement, the Brotherhood came to take on more of a direct political role and by the 1950s had evolved into one of the most powerful opposition currents in the region. Like many other groups operating at the time, its politics became increasingly radical in the 1960s and 1970s, largely as a response to repression by the regimes in the region, which viewed it as a potential challenge to their own hegemony. In the 1970s, caught up in the current of Islamic revivalism that swept the Islamic world, the Ikhwan came to articulate its demands ever more forcefully. Perhaps the most extreme example is that of the Syrian branch, which got involved in a bloody conflict with the Ba'athist regime culminating in the deaths of thousands of its members and supporters. As a result of this increasingly antagonistic relationship to the state, a number of Ikhwani were pushed out of their home countries. Some sought refuge in Saudi Arabia whilst others went to Europe.

The push into Europe broadened the scope of the Brotherhood setting in motion the beginnings of its transnational ambitions through its international organisation. However, as it became clearer that returning home would be impossible, Europe-based Ikhwani began to establish their own organisations in the continent. As a result, the Brotherhood succeeded in crafting a network of branches and organisations across Europe, the Middle East and beyond, becoming perhaps the most influential Islamist opposition movement in the world.[1] From its various centres, it worked to further the cause of Islam in the hope that it would one day come to power and realise its dream of creating an Islamic state.

The events of 9/11 were to alter the Brotherhood's situation dramatically. As the world woke up to the bombings in the United States, political Islamist groups suddenly came under the harsh glare of a new spotlight. Attention inevitably focused on the Ikhwan. In some quarters the movement was simply considered part and parcel of the al-Qa'ida phenomenon, whilst others accused it of acting as an incubator for militancy on the grounds that some of those who formed part of the global jihadist network had spent their formative years with the movement. In the end, the Brotherhood escaped being branded as an international terrorist organisation. Nonetheless, the threat of being made a proscribed group continued to hang over the Ikhwan and its members found themselves in the position of having to prove their 'moderate credentials' to the world. However, the Brotherhood remained a potent force both in the Middle East and beyond, able to capture and articulate the forces of conservative Islam and to posit itself as a 'pure' and authentic alternative to the regimes in power.

Yet for all its strength, after almost eight decades in opposition, by the 2000s the Brotherhood was coming to resemble somewhat of a spent force. Bogged down in stasis and in-fighting, exhausted by the years of oppression and seemingly resigned to the unchanging nature of the political landscape of the Middle East, the Brotherhood looked to be resigned to its fate. In addition, it was finding itself increasingly challenged by the growing power of the Salafist currents that were expanding into its own constituencies and attracting the youth in particular. As such the Brotherhood was coming to look as much part of the creaking furniture of the Middle East as the very regimes it sought to challenge.

The Arab Spring was to change all that. The uprisings breathed new life into the Brotherhood that finally saw its chance to realise the ambitions that had eluded it for so long. Drawing on its years of experience and its organisational skills, as well as its trademark pragmatism, the Brotherhood (and its counterpart, An-Nahda) moved skilfully to outmanoeuvre the other players on the political scene. However, the Brotherhood's coming to power was not solely down to the way in which it played the transition period. It was also because the movement succeeded in reaching out to the masses and offering them a credible alternative.

This book analyses the evolution of the Ikhwan from its inception in Egypt in 1928 to its emergence into the political mainstream. It examines the aims and strategies of the movement and assesses why, prior to the Arab Spring, the Brotherhood seemed to be stuck in a rut, unable to move beyond its own traditions and history or to engage in reform in any meaningful way. It also analyses how the movement responded to the uprisings of the Arab Spring and how, in the Egyptian case in particular, it manoeuvred itself into power. It looks, too, at the complex dynamics between national and international concerns as expressed through the relationship between the mother branch in Cairo and the rest of this transnational movement.

First published in 2010, much of the material in this book is based upon research conducted in 2007 and 2008 thanks to the generous support of the Smith Richardson Foundation. It includes material drawn from interviews with key members of the Brotherhood, past and present, and with those in the wider Islamist movement, as well as from literature produced by the Ikhwan itself. This updated edition includes a new chapter that deals with the Brotherhood and the Arab Spring, focusing in particular on the Egyptian Ikhwan. This edition also addresses some of the key challenges that the Brotherhood and its Tunisian counterpart, An-Nahda, are grappling with now that they are in power.

Chapter One deals with the Egyptian Ikhwan, the mother branch of the entire Muslim Brotherhood movement. Tracing its evolution from the days of its founder, the chapter explores how the Egyptian brothers became so hampered by their own traditions that they struggled to resolve their own internal contradictions. Chapter Two looks at what was in its heyday the other major Middle Eastern branch, the Syrian Ikhwan. This chapter examines the Syrian Brotherhood's shift into violence in the 1980s and its subsequent return to diplomacy, something that makes it arguably one of the most progressive Ikhwani branches today. Chapter Three deals with the highly controversial subject of the Brotherhood's international organisation. Whilst many Ikhwani deny it even exists, this mysterious body has played a major role in the Brotherhood's evolution, especially during the 1980s. Its importance may have declined in recent years, but it still has a role to play within the Ikhwan's international structures. Chapter Four examines the Brotherhood in Europe, looking specifically at the UK, French and German branches and at the various Ikhwani-oriented organisations and institutions that have been established there. It assesses the challenges facing these organisations given the fact that they are minority communities with limited influence living in a secular society. Chapter Five offers an assessment of the Ikhwan's relationship to violence. It explores the attitudes within the movement towards the ideology of violence through key scholars such as Sayyid Qutb and to jihad, including examining the role that the Ikhwan played in the war in Afghanistan during the 1980s. Chapter Six offers an examination of the Brotherhood's shift from opposition movement to mainstream political actor during the Arab Spring. Focusing primarily on Egypt, it looks at how the Brotherhood responded to the revolution and worked its way into power. Finally the conclusion addresses some of the key challenges facing the Brotherhood now that power has finally become a reality.

Conflicting Currents

The Egyptian Ikhwan in Opposition

The Egyptian Ikhwan has always been considered to be the heart and the soul of the entire Muslim Brotherhood. Not only is it the founding branch of the transnational movement – something that gives it a particular historical legitimacy – its Murshid (Supreme Guide) is spiritual guide to the Brotherhood as a whole. Decisions made in Cairo reverberate around the movement's other branches with special significance and still carry a certain moral authority. Indeed, the Egyptian branch is considered to be the vanguard of the entire Brotherhood movement.

In many ways, the Egyptian brothers have lived up to this role. They weathered the storm of the many decades of sustained and brutal repression at the hands of the Egyptian state and despite being banned for almost a century, succeeded in maintaining a substantive grass roots following across the country. The Egyptian Ikhwan also succeeded in making its presence felt on the political scene, manoeuvring itself into parliament without even having a political party and dominating many of the country's professional associations. The Brotherhood proved successful on the financial front too, creating its own Islamic financing networks that sustained the movement throughout the years of hardship. As such, the Egyptian Brotherhood had established itself to such an extent that by the time the Arab Spring reached Egypt, the Brotherhood was poised to step out of the wings and into power.

Yet despite all these achievements, in the years leading up to the 2011 revolution, the Egyptian Ikhwan looked to be a movement in stasis. It was utterly bogged down in introspection and indecision, unable to take a clear stance on many issues, not least the extent to which it should reform. Indeed, the Brotherhood seemed to have got itself caught between an awareness of the need to meet the challenges of a changing world and the need to remain true to its founding principles. Thus, whilst in the years before the revolution, it adopted a more reformist discourse that was fully in keeping with the spirit of the times, at the same time it seemed unwilling to move very far from the core principles established by the movement's founder Hassan al-Banna in the 1920s.

This basic contradiction manifested itself in an often ambiguous discourse and a basic unwillingness to spell out policies on more controversial issues, something that brought charges from within Egypt and beyond that the movement was playing a political game in order to further its own interests. Indeed, the contradictory signals that have emerged from the Ikhwan's executive body, the Guidance Office, meant that any gains the movement made were often reversed by its own undoing.

One of the reasons the Ikhwan was so unable to articulate a more cohesive strategy is that it was forced to operate under extremely difficult conditions. Any move they made had to be a careful calculation of risk, weighing up the potential cost not only to the movement as a whole but also to individual members, who have repeatedly found themselves in prison. However, whilst state repression was certainly a factor in the Ikhwan's inability to reform, it cannot be considered the sole cause of this failing.

Internal wrangling within the movement between those of a conservative bent and those who wished to become more engaged in the political process also played its part. Commentators often portrayed this division as a clash of generations with the conservative old guard pitted against the younger reformist faction, themselves in late middle age. Whilst such a divide certainly existed and continues to exist, it is perhaps misleading to overplay the generational factor. The group known as the reformists, which comprised figures such as Issam al-Ariyan and Abdul Moneim Aboul Fotouh, was a specific set of individuals who came to the Brotherhood in the 1970s as students and who were more overtly political than their predecessors. Indeed, rather than a reformist current, it is perhaps more accurate to talk about reformist figures or individuals. Their bid to push the movement to take a more progressive stance came up against repeated resistance from the more conservative elements within the leadership. That this wrangling was at times played out in the public domain only served to strengthen the impression that the Ikhwan was lacking in direction.

However, this conflict of views is not sufficient to explain the dichotomy in which the Egyptian Ikhwani found themselves. The problem was always far more complex than a simple clash of views within the leadership. Rather it was a result of the Ikhwan's need to play to several different constituencies simultaneously and its desire to be all things to all men. As a movement, the Egyptian Ikhwan always sought to appeal to as broad a base as possible in order to challenge the regime of the day, hence the all-encompassing slogan 'Islam is the solution'. Whilst this wide popular base was always one of the Ikhwan's key strengths, it restricted how far it could stray from the original ideology of its founder. Many of the movement's supporters and sympathisers backed the Ikhwan precisely because they considered that it held on to traditions such as calling for the implementation of Sharia law. Moreover some of the movement's supporters considered the Ikhwan to be representing

Islam itself, a view that the Brotherhood was not averse to promoting over the years. It is this amalgamation of the political and the religious that has always given the Ikhwan its potency. As such the extent to which it was able to reform was always limited by the movement's need to remain anchored in its own traditions.

However, like other Islamist groups, the Ikhwan was always anxious to demonstrate that it could be considered as a trusted political partner and that it was not seeking to overturn the state through revolution. Rather, the brothers asserted that they wanted whoever rules Egypt to do so in a proper Islamic manner, seemingly indicating that they would like to take the role of moral arbiters of the state.

Whilst the pressure to be seen as a moderate progressive organisation was exacerbated after 9/11, this tension between the need to reform and the need to hold fast to tradition was present from the very beginnings of the movement. Hassan al-Banna struggled to strike a balance between engaging with the country's establishment and appeasing his followers, many of whom were anxious for the Ikhwan to take a more radical stance. This remained a constant pressure for the Brotherhood. Whilst other Ikhwani branches, such as the Syrians, were able to shake themselves up and put forward programmes that strayed further from the original tenets of the movement, the Egyptians repeatedly failed to break free of their own traditions.

Al-Banna: The Man and the Myth

If the Murshid is held up as the main spiritual reference for the Muslim Brotherhood worldwide, Hassan al-Banna is revered as the leader of all leaders and has attained near iconic status within the movement. Yet it is in Egypt that the figure of al-Banna looms largest and where his memory is ever present. This reverence for al-Banna is not only related to the fact that in 1928 he founded the Muslim Brotherhood;

by extension, he sowed the seeds of the contemporary political Islamist movement that would play such a major role in the history of the twentieth and twenty-first centuries.

Yet a kind of personality cult has evolved around the figure of al-Banna, wherein stories about his character seem to overshadow discussions of his ideas. The Ikhwan's website, full of descriptions of al-Banna's personal qualities and his dedication to the cause, is testimony to this. One article on the website cites the reason for the movement's expansion as 'the enthusiastic and marvellous nature of al-Banna'.[1] It goes on to describe him as a man with an almost superhuman capacity for hard work, stating, 'He visited every village in the Upper Egypt in twenty days, sometimes he would be in Bai-Swaif in the morning, have lunch in Beba, in al-Wasta in the evening and stay the night in al-Fayoom ... he regarded the Call for Allah first and foremost.'[2]

There is a tendency within the Brotherhood if not to equate al-Banna with the Prophet, then at least to depict him as more than merely mortal. For example, one of the founding members of the Brotherhood, Mahmoud Abdelhalim, describes al-Banna as 'less than the Prophet. Nevertheless al-Dawa preoccupied him ... and the likes of Hassan al-Banna are the heirs of the Prophet'.[3]

There are several reasons why discussions of al-Banna tend to focus more on his personal attributes than his ideology. Firstly, such descriptions reflect the fact that he appears to have been blessed with a particularly forceful personality and a special charisma. He certainly had the personal touch and those who knew him relate that he made them feel as though he had an intimate connection to them. Farid Abdel Khaliq, who went on to become al-Banna's personal secretary, has described meeting al-Banna for the first time. From that night, he followed him everywhere he went to preach, explaining: 'The way he spoke allowed you to see the whole sky through a keyhole.'[4] Similarly, former Murshid Omar al-Tilimsani used near metaphysical terms to describe al-Banna, noting, 'In the presence of al-Banna I was like a dead man in the hands of someone washing my corpse.'[5] Another Egyptian Ikhwani, Musa Ishaq Al-Husayni, has also commented, 'His mastery over his followers was complete and inclusive, almost approaching sorcery.'[6]

Secondly, it is probably fair to say that al-Banna's personal qualities were more impressive and left a greater impression than his ideology. Although he was able to tap into the grievances of a generation, he can hardly be considered to have been a major intellectual force or even a scholar. His ideology was drawn primarily from the great reformist Islamist thinkers of the nineteenth century such as Rashid Rida and Jamal al-Din al-Afghani, and as Egyptian philosopher Hassan Hanafi has argued, 'he came to complete the project of al-Afghani'.[7] As Hanafi goes on to comment, 'To say the truth, the ideas of Hassan al-Banna probably may not amount to much: an Islam that is simple and clear ... The Qur'an, The Hadiths etc ... His ideas were very clear, very pure and there was no ideological complexity, but ... as an organizing power ... he was something else.'[8]

Hanafi's comments are probably a little harsh: whilst al-Banna may not have been a scholar in the conventional sense, he did succeed in establishing a movement that was able to present itself as something progressive and modern despite upholding traditional values, and which clearly had a broad appeal. Through the simple message that Islam was a means of regulating every aspect of life, he skilfully tapped into people's concerns about the eroding of tradition and the increasing Westernisation of the Egyptian elite, along with the seemingly quiescent attitude of the official religious establishment. (Some scholars at Al-Azhar University seemed almost willing to adopt the secularist ideas that were openly propagated by some of the intelligentsia. Ali Abd al-Raziq, for example, denied that Islam was in any way connected to politics.)

Al-Banna articulated the anxieties of a generation who were struggling to deal with the encroaching modernisation that had accompanied the colonial presence and which the Egyptian elite seemed more than willing to accept. Although al-Banna did not reject the West in itself, he certainly had major concerns about the impact of Western culture on his own society, asserting: 'Western civilization has invaded us by force and with aggression on the level of science and money, of politics and luxury, of pleasures and negligence, and of various aspects of a life that are comfortable, exciting and seductive.'[9] His assertion of the comprehensiveness of Islam seemed therefore to offer certainties in an increasingly uncertain world.

He also saw the Brotherhood as a champion of anti-imperialism, and his strong views about the British colonial presence certainly increased his movement's appeal. Al-Banna and the Muslim Brotherhood came to present themselves as the guardians of the native popular culture against the distortions of foreign and secularist ideologies.[10] Yet rather than retrenching himself in the traditions of the past, al-Banna was able to present his ideas and his desire for action as something new and exciting and it was for this reason that many of his adherents were drawn from the younger generations. As Brynjar Lia has argued in his excellent study *The Society of the Muslim Brothers in Egypt*, the fundamental appeal of the Ikhwan was 'its ability to link issues which were usually associated with reactionism and backwardness, such as Islamic laws and strict public morality, to the national issues of independence and development'.[11]

Yet, as Hanafi correctly identifies, it was al-Banna's ability to mobilise and organise people that enabled him to turn his organisation into such a significant force. Farid Abdel Khaliq has argued that al-Banna 'wasn't about absolute ideas. He was an organisational thinker ... He translated theoretical ideas into reality.'[12] Even al-Banna himself seems to have concurred with this assessment of his qualities, once telling his followers, 'I might have not left a lot of books with you but my job is to write men rather than to write books.'[13] He also responded to one suggestion that he write a book thus: 'In the time that I would waste in writing a book, I could write one hundred young Muslims. Every one of them would be a living, speaking influential book.'[14]

Another reason for this near mythical status is that no other leader within the movement has come close to having the calibre of its founder. It is striking that in spite of being at the forefront of such an important worldwide organisation, the Egyptian Ikhwan has failed to produce any Murshid, or, indeed, any thinker, who can match the talents and qualities of al-Banna. Although certainly well respected within Islamist circles, successive Murshids such as Omar al-Tilimsani or Hassan al-Hodeibi have left no real long-lasting impression beyond the confines of the movement. The only other Murshid or Egyptian Ikhwan who has come close to having the same aura or legacy as Hassan al-Banna was the more controversial figure Sayyid Qutb, although there is ongoing debate about the extent to which Qutb reflected the views of the Ikhwan. Qutb himself seems to have been as disappointed in this lack of intellectual ability within the Ikhwan's leadership and is alleged to have complained to a fellow member of the Brotherhood that his experience in prison had revealed to him the shallowness of the thinking of the Ikhwan's leaders.[15]

On account of these factors, al-Banna's hold is such that his ideas, conceived over eight decades ago in response to a set of very specific conditions inside Egypt, have been almost untouchable. His legacy means that altering the fundamental principles of the movement that he established has been almost unthinkable for many of the Ikhwan – and he will be forever held up as an almost 'divine' leader.

Yet this image of the movement's founder as a flawless leader is at odds with the true picture. In reality al-Banna was a shrewd political operator whose ultimate goal was the survival of his movement at what some would argue was almost any cost. In addition the Brotherhood under al-Banna was as riven with factions and rivalry as it is today. In spite of his best attempts to impose rigid obedience on his followers, al-Banna struggled for many years to appease the various competing factions within his support base, setting in motion the above cited contradiction within the Ikhwan between the political realities of the day and traditional Islamic principles.

The Roots of Pragmatism

Al-Banna's image of devout purity and humility notwithstanding, what ensured the success and survival of his movement was his extreme pragmatism. He repeatedly proved his willingness to be flexible in his principles for the good of the greater cause. This flexibility held as true in his personal relations as it did in his political dealings. Farid Abdel Khaliq has related his shock at how, in the spirit of practicality, al-Banna once reassured a rich man that he did not need to perform his ablutions before praying after the man told him he bathed twice a day and considered himself to be clean enough.[16] Within this ethos, al-Banna was acutely aware of how to project an image in order to win people over to his cause. Even his choice of clothes was a calculated decision designed to achieve maximum impact and he wore a different garb to fit each occasion, be it a suit, a jelaba or a fez.[17]

It was not only on the personal level that al-Banna displayed his willingness to demonstrate expediency. He also proved an adept and shrewd political operator, who was not averse to the idea of becoming part of the political establishment in order to further the goals of the Ikhwan – even though this directly contradicted his own teachings and ideology. Whilst he was explicit in his condemnation of political parties in Egypt, referring to those that existed as 'the parasites of the people' and the 'greatest threat to our development',[18] at one point he proposed that the Ikhwan join Hizb al-Watani (the Nationalist Party). His motivations for doing so were because he believed the party's immense popularity would assist his own movement.[19] The proposal was ultimately rejected, yet al-Banna's willingness to join forces with an established political party demonstrates just how far he was prepared to go in order to bolster his movement and gain political leverage. In spite of all the teachings advocating the need to educate the population from below, it sometimes seemed as though playing a part in the politics of the day was the ultimate and more pressing ambition.

Al-Banna was always aware that in order for his movement to survive, he needed to come to an understanding with the powers that be, even if he considered their rulings un-Islamic. A detailed account of the political ins and outs of the al-Banna period is outside the scope of this study and there are already a number of excellent works on the subject.[20] However, it is clear that al-Banna was, in the words of Farid Abdel Khaliq, 'very keen to have a kind of understanding between himself and the rulers'.[21] He focused a great deal of energy avoiding antagonising the Palace and was also keen to come to an understanding with the government of the day. In March 1942, disregarding his condemnation of multiparty politics, al-Banna (with the support of the Guidance Office) decided to field seventeen candidates in the parliamentary elections. He put himself forward to stand for Ismailia and focused his election campaign around Islamic and moral issues. However, he came under intense pressure from the government to withdraw the Ikhwan's candidacies and to make a written statement declaring his loyalty to the government and the 1936 Anglo-Egyptian Treaty, which was the legal foundation for the British presence in Egypt. This was quite a demand given that in 1938–9 the Ikhwan, as part of its anti-imperialist stance, had demanded the amendment of this treaty. Nonetheless, even though the Ikhwan's Guidance Office decided that he should reject these demands, al-Banna acted unilaterally and decided instead to cut his own deal with the government of the day. In return for publishing an open letter supporting the treaty and withdrawing from the elections, he extracted a promise from Prime Minister Mustafa Pasha al-Nahas that the government would allow the movement to operate freely and that it would take action against the sale of alcohol and prostitution.

Clearly al-Banna was intent on doing his utmost to ensure the survival of the Brotherhood, even if that meant entering into deals with a regime that it considered un-Islamic.

Moreover, for all that al-Banna extolled the virtues of *shura* (consultation), he did not always live by its principles. As Dr Abdelaziz Kamel, a member of the Ikhwan, has commented, al-Banna didn't believe in the principle of *shura* because for him *shura* wasn't obligatory for the Murshid himself. Al-Banna repeatedly made unilateral decisions, completely bypassing the Guidance Office and infuriating many within it in the process. This held true when he was selecting candidates to high-ranking appointments or deciding where to channel funds. His insistence on total obedience resulted in his acquiring a reputation for being authoritarian.[22] This judgement is probably a little unfair; rather than being dictatorial, al-Banna seems to have had his own vision of what he wanted his movement to be. To this end he pushed ahead with his own policies, unwilling to see this vision thwarted by others within the organisation, even if that alienated some of his followers.

Clearly the roots of the Ikhwan's trademark pragmatism were established at the very beginnings of the movement through al-Banna's personal style. However, such willingness to co-operate with the authorities, as well as al-Banna's autocratic style, provoked intense criticism from inside the movement as more radical elements considered al-Banna's stance to be too moderate and accommodationist. Resistance to his leadership really began to gather momentum in the late 1930s, when a group of Ikhwani became increasingly frustrated at al-Banna's gradual and what they considered to be passive approach. This group appears to have been led at one point by Ahmed Rifat, who accused the Ikhwan of dealing with the government rather than confronting it for its failure to rule by the Qur'an. They also accused the Ikhwan of not doing enough to assist the Palestinians, who were rising up against the British and the Jews, and of not being forceful enough over the issue of women. At one point they even proposed that all Ikhwani should carry bottles of ink to throw at those women who did not wear correct Islamic attire. [23]

Although these more militant elements are often portrayed as nothing more than a handful of hot heads, there was quite a sizeable current within the Ikhwan who resented al-Banna's non-confrontational approach and his willingness to co-operate with whatever political partners he deemed fit. According to Mahmoud Abdelhalim, who was a high-ranking member of the Brotherhood at this time, many senior Ikhwan actually supported Ahmed Rifat. Abdelhalim describes a meeting in which Rifat began verbally insulting al-Banna and explains that although many of the Ikhwani from Cairo were horrified at Rifat's manner, by the end of the meeting he had succeeded in attracting even greater support among those brothers who came from outside Cairo. [24] It seems that some parts of the Ikhwan were waiting for a man like Rifat to come along: 'A large number of Ikhwani gave Ahmed Rifat's call their full attention and they responded quickly. As soon as they heard Ahmed Rifat they found in his language echoes of what was going on inside themselves.' [25]

But in his bid for the movement to be all things to all men, rather than expelling this group al-Banna instead tried to convince and somehow accommodate them. Some of the other Ikhwani were furious that their leader chose to protect them. [26] Yet al-Banna's way of handling this group came to be symptomatic of the way in which he dealt with the more militant currents that continued to evolve inside his movement, especially among the youth. For him, containment was the most appropriate solution. Therefore whilst al-Banna continued to advocate a peaceful approach and continued dealing with the powers of the day, he also began adapting his leadership style to try to appease those who were calling for more direct action.

In May 1938 he adopted a more hawkish rhetoric, declaring that if the authorities failed to implement the Ikhwan's programmes the movement would consider itself 'at war with every leader, every party and every organisation that does not work for the victory of Islam!'[27] However, he was still unwilling to actually put these words into action. As a result his attempts to contain these more militant elements failed and a group of them, which included a number of senior brothers and which by the late 1930s had formed their own group under the name 'Mohamed's Youth', seceded from the Brotherhood.[28] In 1942 Mohamed's Youth issued a communiqué in which it accused al-Banna of deviating from true Islamic principles by declaring that the success of the Islamic mission was 'dependent on pleasing the rulers and working under their party banner'.[29]

However, the secession of Mohamed's Youth should not be read as a rejection by al-Banna of the principle of the use of military means to effect change. His reputation for moderation notwithstanding, in the late 1930s he set up a secret military unit known as the Nizam al-Khass under the leadership of Saleh Ashwami.[30] Although the Brotherhood has argued that this military wing was set up in direct response to the situation in Palestine and that its main objective was to provide military assistance to the Palestinians, it was in line with al-Banna's vision for the movement right from its inception. One of the founding members of the Nizam al-Khass explained:

> The image that al-Ustath [the Master] had in his mind since he started his *dawa* in Ismailia about that [military] aspect of *dawa* activity was ... of a military group that would encapsulate the idea of jihad in Islam ... He was so keen to emphasise military activity in order to demonstrate the idea of jihad. But he was frightened that these kinds of things might be used against him.[31]

Al-Banna was so keen to set up some kind of military arm that he had established scout units to provide physical training for the young cadres in preparation for the later military phase without drawing suspicion on the part of the authorities. However, the creation of the Nizam al-Khass was also a useful way to relieve some of the pressure from the more ardent activists within his organisation. As Lia has argued, 'There can be little doubt that strong internal pressure from radical members was the major factor behind the formation of the military wing.'[32] Although this assertion may be a little overstated, such pressure certainly contributed to pushing al-Banna into setting up something that was already in his mind and the Palestinian cause provided him with the opportunity to kill several birds with one stone.

The Nizam al-Khass may have a troubled history, but like its founder it still has a special place in the hearts of many Ikhwani and is considered as something glorious. The former Supreme Guide Mehdi Akef still describes this group as 'the pride of the Muslim Brotherhood'.[33] Yet at the time its establishment sowed yet further dissent within the Ikhwan's ranks. Whilst some were happy with the military dimension, others were less comfortable with it and found it to be outside of the movement's traditional sphere of activity. Some brothers believed the whole project to be downright bizarre. Mahmoud A'asaf, one time Information Secretary of the Ikhwan, related how one day in 1944 he and another leading member of the Ikhwan Dr Abdelaziz Kamel were called to give *baya* (oath of allegiance) to the Nizam al-Khass in a house in the Al-Saliba district of Cairo:

> ... we entered a dark room and an unidentifiable person was there although his voice was very well known to us. It was the voice of Saleh Ashwami and in front of him was a low table at which he was sitting cross-legged. On the table there was a Qur'an and a pistol. He asked both of us to put our right hands on the Qur'an and the pistol and to give baya and obedience to the Nizam al-Khass and to work for the triumph of Islamic *dawa*. That was very strange and spread foreboding in us.[34]

Similarly, Farid Abdel Khaliq, one of the most devoted of al-Banna's followers, described his displeasure at being called to join the Nizam al-Khass and at having to undergo a special test in which he was asked to take a bag to a certain address.[35] Upon realising that the bag contained explosives, he refused to participate any further.

As well as alienating some of his more moderate followers by the establishment of the Nizam al-Khass, al-Banna struggled to contain his own creation. In the late 1940s, the Nizam al-Khass, by this point under the control of the ambitious Abdel Rahman al-Sanadi, was responsible for a series of acts of political violence including attacks on British forces. Of course such violence was in line with the times, as various groups including the nationalists began to adopt more militant tactics against their foes.[36] In January 1948 Egyptian forces discovered caches of arms and explosives in the hills outside Cairo and clashes between the police and a number of young Ikhwani, led by a member of the Nizam al-Khass who had been training in the hills, ensued. Later in the same year the group was responsible for the killing of an Egyptian judge, Ahmed al-Khazindar Bey, who had handed down a prison sentence to a member of the Ikhwan for attacking British soldiers. It seems that after al-Banna had made a passing comment declaring that he wished to be rid of the judge, Abdel Rahman al-Sanadi took him at his word. Al-Sanadi explained, 'When *al-Ustath* says that he wishes to get rid of al-Khazindar, his desire to get rid of him is an order.'[37] However, in the row that ensued al-Banna refused point blank to take any responsibility for the killing.

The extent of al-Banna's responsibility for the actions of the Nizam al-Khass is still a matter of debate given that as Murshid he was overall leader and insisted on obedience as one of the core principles of the secret apparatus. Regardless of whether he can be held responsible it is noteworthy that, after the assassination, al-Banna did not expel al-Sanadi. Instead he took steps to take further control of the Nizam al-Khass himself. Yet the Ikhwan's growing militarisation along with the increasing tensions and popular unrest within Egypt in the run up to the 1952 nationalist revolution put the authorities on high alert, and they began to prepare the ground for the Brotherhood's dissolution. The assassination of Prime Minister Nuqrashi in December 1948 by a young Ikhwani veterinary student and a bomb attack attempt on a Cairo courthouse by a member of the Nizam al-Khass were the last straw. Al-Banna, shaken by events, was by this point desperately trying to make his peace with the government and wrote a public letter declaring that those who had perpetrated the acts of violence were 'neither brothers, nor are they Muslims'.[38]

Al-Banna's willingness to distance himself from those within his movement who had taken action was a miscalculation on his part, for it prompted uproar and anger within the ranks of the Brotherhood. Moreover, it failed to win over the authorities; instead, al-Banna resorted to writing a pamphlet titled *Qawl Fasl* in which he asserted that all the charges against the brothers were fabrications or distortions, and that the only reason the movement possessed arms was in order to assist the Palestinians. To little avail: al-Banna's assassination in February 1949 was followed by mass arrests and the military trials of scores of Ikhwani.

Therefore even though al-Banna has always been held up as a beacon of moderation and as the traditional face of the Brotherhood, he was always willing to accommodate more militant elements within his movement. Yet it appears that in trying to meet the demands of all the different constituencies he needed to keep on side, he ultimately lost control. One could argue that al-Banna was essentially a simple man with a belief that all answers lie in Islam and that in spite of all his pragmatism he had bitten off more than he could chew, getting himself caught up in a situation that was ultimately to prove too complex for him. It seems that he was never able to reconcile his desire to adopt a cautious approach with his bid to be seen as defending Islam and capable of mounting a challenge to established order. In the language of

Mahmoud Abdelhalim, he did not want his *dawa* to become cold prey for his enemies.[39] Al-Banna's failure to balance these two conflicting requirements has not been unique to him; as discussed above, this problem is one of the core issues that has continued to characterise the Ikhwan and that remains unresolved today.

Internal Wrangling and the Triumph of the Nizam al-Khass

The death of al-Banna served to bring the various tensions that had been simmering for years well and truly to the fore. Whilst al-Banna had struggled to contain the different elements within the Ikhwan, his charisma, as well as his having founded the movement, had enabled him to have some sort of authority over the organisation. However, he left no natural heir to the Brotherhood, which meant that after his death competing factions sought to claim leadership of the Ikhwan. Two distinct camps emerged at this time. The first consisted of those who believed that a successor should be appointed from within al-Banna's own family and the second comprised the Nizam al-Khass, who considered themselves to be the elite of the Ikhwan and as such the rightful successors to the top post. But this battle was about more than just who was to be leader; it was about charting the future course and character of the movement as a whole.

The division between these two competing camps over who should lead the Brotherhood was so intense that in the end the only solution was to bring in a compromise figure to take up the post. The choice was Hassan al-Hodeibi, who although not actually a member of the Ikhwan had been very close to al-Banna for many years. A judge, al-Hodeibi was well connected to the establishment, especially to the upper echelons of the Palace. Fathi al-Asal, who was the General Inspector of the Ikhwan's Headquarters at the time, said of al-Hodeibi, 'He was the Murshid of the Palace, not the Murshid of the Brotherhood.'[40]

Al-Hodeibi himself, who appears to have been an organiser as much as anything else, was initially reluctant to take up the post on account of the bitter internal divisions within the Guidance Office.[41]

His appointment turned out to be a victory for the Nizam al-Khass. One of the reasons they accepted him was because he was weak and could therefore be subject to manipulation; furthermore, he could act as a useful more neutral figurehead for the movement given its own difficulties with the authorities. Indeed, the Nizam al-Khass made it clear to the new Murshid that they expected him to be little other than a front man and that they intended to be the real arbiters of power within the movement. Upon assuming the post al-Hodeibi is reported to have been told, 'We want nothing from you; you need not even come to the headquarters. We will bring the papers for you to sign or reject as you will ... We only want a leader who will be a symbol of cleanliness.'[42]

Despite al-Hodeibi's best attempts to prevent the Nizam al-Khass from dominating the movement, he was, as they had predicted, no match for them. Part of his problem was that he was living in the shadow of al-Banna, who for all his faults was still hailed as the ultimate leader. As such, al-Hodeibi was never able to muster the same respect or loyalty as his predecessor. Moreover, al-Hodeibi's open objections to both secrecy and violence – the two elements that distinguished the Nizam al-Khass from the rest of the movement – meant that from the beginning he was set on a path that would bring him into conflict with these powerful figures. More importantly, he condemned the violent acts that the Nizam al-Khass had been involved in, calling them acts of 'extravagation ... and deviation from the original duty of the Brotherhood organisation'.[43] This not only infuriated the Nizam al-Khass, it also discredited the nobility of purpose with which these events were viewed and challenged some traditional views in the society on both means and ends.[44] According to Maimoun al-Hodeibi, Hassan al-Hodeibi's son, who was himself later to become the Murshid, his father 'did not have al-Banna's charisma.

This created a sense of confusion within the group, especially when the paramilitary wing ... did not accept his authority as leader, weakening the Brotherhood. As a result, there were only a few people within the movement that he really trusted, and he never had complete control over the paramilitary wing.'[45]

His lack of control was such that he even proved unable to discover exactly who all of the Nizam al-Khass's members were. He made an attempt in 1953 to expel a number of key figures and to dissolve the unit but this proved fruitless, as for many the idea of the Ikhwan without the Nizam al-Khass was unthinkable, and he was pressurised into retracting. At this time he appointed his own man, Yousef Talat, to be the new head of the unit, hoping he would be able to bring it within the formal structures of the Brotherhood. However, even this was not sufficient to bring the unit under his true control.

Yet it was not just the Nizam al-Khass that al-Hodeibi struggled to direct. The new Murshid proved unable to harness the movement as a whole and as a result the Ikhwan became paralysed under his leadership. As its membership began to dwindle and dissent among the ranks increased, al-Hodeibi was accused of turning the Ikhwan into a movement of words not action.[46] Yet while al-Hodeibi was weak, he cannot be blamed as entirely responsible for the movement's demise. It was also a reflection of the changing political environment in Egypt.

Shortly after al-Hodeibi's appointment as Murshid, President Gamal Abdel Nasser came to power in his nationalist revolution of 1952. Given that the Brotherhood had maintained good relations with the nationalists before they had come to power, the Ikhwani had high hopes for their future and expected to be given space in which to operate under the new regime. Some brothers were overjoyed at Nasser's coming to power, as they believed that he would move to bring about Islamic rule. However, as it became increasingly apparent that Nasser had no intention of applying Islamic law, they became increasingly disillusioned and fierce disagreements occurred within the Guidance Office over the extent to which the movement should be prepared to work with the regime. Around the same time, Nasser began to view the Ikhwan as an irritant, not least because it was resisting some of his policies. In January 1954 the new cabinet plunged the Ikhwan into disaster by dissolving the Muslim Brotherhood.[47] It also launched an aggressive press campaign against the movement and arrested scores of brothers, provoking yet further discord among the Ikhwan's ranks.

It was in such extreme circumstances that the Nizam al-Khass seemed to come into their own, as if they had been given the opportunity to act and to assert their domination. They took it upon themselves to issue threatening letters to members of the Brotherhood who had escaped arrest, deeming their lack of persecution an indication that they had been colluding with the regime.[48] They also began to push for the Ikhwan to take some sort of public action against the government. Al-Hodeibi's attempts to act as peacemaker fell on deaf ears and his unwillingness to act – especially in the face of Nasser's signing an evacuation treaty with the British that many Ikhwani considered to be tantamount to 'giving away the nation' – prompted some elements within the Nizam al-Khass to initiate a more radical plan.

On 26 October 1954 as Nasser gave a speech in Cairo to celebrate the British evacuation treaty, he was shot at eight times, but escaped unharmed. The truth of who exactly was involved in this plot aside from the supposed assassin, Mahmoud Abdel Latif, a tinsmith from Imbaba, and how much the Ikhwan's leadership knew about it, is still not clear. However, the consequences for the Brotherhood were severe: the regime retaliated by hanging six men and arresting thousands of Ikhwani, essentially crushing the organisation.

Thus al-Hodeibi had proved even more inept than his predecessor at managing the different strands within the Ikhwan. His failure to rein the more activist elements in resulted in a fallow period for the Brotherhood and the movement was effectively stymied during the second half of the 1950s and throughout the 1960s due to the fact that so many Ikhwani had been imprisoned. However, rather than diminishing these more militant elements' appetite for action, their spell in prison only hardened them and made them even more determined to challenge the Nasser regime. Despite the organisational stasis, there were a number of ideological developments during this time that served to bolster these more hardline elements. These developments, arguably the first since the movement's inception, came through the figure of Sayyid Qutb, whose more radical ideas began to take hold and gather a momentum of their own. As has been well documented by numerous scholars, Qutb came to advocate that the leaders of Egypt and Egyptian society could be considered as part of *jahiliya* (pre-Islamic ignorance) and were therefore legitimate targets in the struggle to create an Islamic order. In a movement so dominated by organisers and so parched of thinkers, Qutb's ideas came to breathe new life into the organisation. For those of a more militant persuasion it would seem that it was in Qutb that they found a real successor to al-Banna, a man whose ideas could provide the intellectual justifications for the action they so craved.

By the mid-1960s, the Qutbists had formed their own movement within the Ikhwan, which became known as Organisation 1965. It is not clear how much support this group had from al-Hodeibi, who was under house arrest at this time. He seems to have accepted the development, perhaps aware that he could not stop such a powerful current. One analyst argues:

> Because Qutb's ideological development was not a secret, we can also conclude that al-Hodeibi was aware of the ideological foundation of Organisation 1965. In any case, al-Hodeibi made no effort to object to the group or Qutb's theories, and it can be assumed that he chose to tacitly accept, if not support the activities of Organisation 1965.[49]

However, once the regime began to clamp down on this group, accusing it of plotting to overthrow the state and executing a number of those involved – including Qutb himself, who was hanged in 1966 – as well as arresting many brothers, al-Hodeibi moved quickly to distance himself from the group.

This provoked yet another internal crisis within the movement, with different strands in the Ikhwan unable to agree on what their stance towards the state should be. Many of those who had followed Qutb, including Mustafa Shukri who went on to establish the militant Takfir wal Hijra group, could not stomach the idea of taking a conciliatory approach towards the state and split off from the Brotherhood to follow an ultimately self-destructive path. Meanwhile, al-Hodeibi tried to set the Ikhwan back on a course of moderation. As part of this process, he published his famous text, *Preachers Not Judges*, which is widely regarded as an indirect refutation of Qutb's ideas, although it was as much a rejection of the ideas of Indian theologian Abu Ala Maududi as it was of Qutb's. Indeed, the text is broadly a dismissal of extremist thought and the concept of pronouncing others as *kufar* (apostate). Although serious questions have been raised as to whether al-Hodeibi was pressurised into writing the book by the regime, or whether he wrote it at all, it is used by the Ikhwan today as evidence of his peaceful stance and his re-channelling the movement back to its original moderate direction as conceived by al-Banna.

The breakaway by the more militant Qutbist elements within the Ikhwan and al-Hodeibi's reassertion of the Ikhwan's non-confrontational stance did not bring an end to the divisions. The 1970s were to lay the foundations for another major split that would occur later on, which symbolised the Ikhwan's never-ending conundrum over how to place themselves *vis-à-vis* the rulers of the day. The whole conflictual scenario was beginning to seem like a perpetual cycle of indecision and disagreement that increasingly came to paralyse the Ikhwan.

The Dilemma of the New Generation

The 1970s began with the promise of an era of golden opportunity for the Ikhwan. Shortly after coming to power in October 1970, President Sadat sought to reconcile with the Islamists and set about releasing members of the Brotherhood. Among those released were a group of hawkish members of the Nizam al-Khass including Mustafa Mashour, Ahmed al-Malat, Kamel Sananiri, Ahmed Hassanein and Hosni Abdelbaqi. They took it upon themselves to wrestle control of the Ikhwan away from Hassan al-Hodeibi once and for all. These figures soon gained a reputation for being tough; one former Ikhwani has described them as being 'like steel'.[50] Another observed, 'When they left prison they were very young and they were very practical and the most activist. They took control of the movement in Egypt.'[51] They appointed themselves as members of the Guidance Office at this time, giving themselves the reins of power.

This group's primary task was to try to rebuild the Ikhwan, which had by this point become so weak and fragmented that it was more the shell of a movement than a force in itself. This group, hardened by their prison experience, sought to turn the Ikhwan into a body fit to pose a real and robust challenge to the state. Whilst on the one hand they focused their energies on trying to re-establish some sort of legal recognition by the state, the main push was to try to recruit new members to fill the Ikhwan's empty ranks. The most obvious place to begin recruiting was on the university campuses that had by this point become key centres of political activism, both left-wing and Islamist. This new political consciousness among the country's student population was in part fuelled by international events such as the humiliating defeat of the Arabs against Israel in 1967, but was also a reflection of the failings of the nationalist state that had not lived up to expectations. The rise of the Islamist current was also due to the fact that Sadat had allowed space for Islamist groups to operate on the campuses, ostensibly in a bid to act as a counterweight to the Nasserists and leftists that were a potential challenge to his rule. As a result numerous Islamist groups and cells, each with their own emir, had sprung up on campuses across the country. Gradually they grouped themselves under the umbrella name of al-Jama'at al-Islamiya. Among the leaders of these groups were figures such as Abdul Moneim Aboul Fotouh, Issam al-Ariyan, Abu Ala Madhi and Mahmoud Ghazlan, all names that were to loom large in the Brotherhood. These figures had all benefited from the democratisation of education that had come about with the Nasser regime and came mostly from modest backgrounds.

Although these groups were politicised and opposed to what they considered to be the un-Islamic nature of the Egyptian regime, they were predominantly preoccupied with enforcing Islamic morals and behaviour within their own milieu. They focused their attentions on issues such as encouraging female students to wear the hijab, ensuring there was sufficient segregation of the sexes within the university campuses and seeing that lectures were stopped in order for students to be able to pray. Their slogans at this time were 'all for Sharia and all against atheism and nudism' and 'neither East nor West, but for Qur'anic Islam'.[52]

These groups, with their call for a return to traditional conservative values, were able to capture the student mood of the day and they spread with remarkable speed. They also succeeded in taking control of the student unions; in the late 1970s al-Jama'at al-Islamiya led the unions in eight out of the twelve universities including in Cairo, Minya and Alexandria. By the end of the 1970s, they had become so strong that they were able to take their activism beyond the campuses, organising public prayers and gatherings that attracted thousands and that were attended by famous Islamic scholars such as Sheikh Yusuf al-Qaradawi and Sheikh Mohamed al-Ghazali. In short, al-Jama'at al-Islamiya had become the most effective populist Islamist movement in Egypt, able to achieve what had always eluded the Ikhwan – mass popular support.

Although these student groups had no one specific religious reference at the time, they were particularly influenced by Salafist teachings as well as by literature that was flooding in from Saudi Arabia and that was provided free of charge. However, these students were also attracted to the ideas of the Muslim Brotherhood, especially through the works of Sayyid Qutb that were circulating. It is true that the al-Jama'at al-Islamiya had certain reservations about the Ikhwan's less rigid approach to Islamic codes – such as the fact that its members did not have beards or wear the traditional jalaba, and were willing to hang pictures in their houses or listen to music – but they felt a certain affinity with this historic movement and shared its conviction that 'Islam is the solution'.

More important than the Ikhwan's ideology was the fact that some of the leaders of the al-Jama'at al-Islamiya began having personal contacts with members of the Brotherhood. These contacts first came about in the early 1970s before the Nizam al-Khass group had even been released from prison. President Sadat began allowing some of the Brotherhood prisoners to be given medical treatment at the Qasr al-Aini Hospital in Cairo, where they were visited by some of the student activists. Al-Ariyan describes it:

> It was a dream for me to meet the Sheikhs of the Ikhwan as we used to hear stories that were full of terror and fear about them. But when we saw them and talked with them we found them to be different people. We found mujahideen who sacrificed themselves for the sake of al-Dawa. They refused to compromise even though their fate was prison and torture and sometimes death.[53]

It seemed to these young Islamists that whilst they had been engaged in student politics these Brotherhood stalwarts had been living the real experience.

Those members of the Nizam al-Khass who started leaving prison in the early 1970s decided to build on these contacts, seeing in these young students an opportunity to breathe new life into their own failing movement. They began actively recruiting these student leaders. Abu Ala Madhi recounts how Mustafa Mashour used to visit him at home in order to convince him to join the movement.[54] Similarly Kamel Sananiri used to summon these young student activists to try to persuade them to join the Ikhwan's ranks. As Aboul Fotouh, a student union leader at that time, recounts, 'Sananiri was for me a symbol of a preacher and a mujahid that we needed to take as an example.' He went on to observe, 'The characters of the leaders captured us and had the biggest impact in our desire to join their group.'[55]

One of the reasons the student leaders were so attracted to these characters was because of their more militant stance, which was in tune with the student radicalism of the day. They felt much closer to the ideas of the Nizam al-Khass than they did to the more traditional Ikhwani school, as represented by its more moderate currents. As Aboul Fotouh has said:

> Our ideas and our methodology was close to the methodology and the way of thinking of the Organisation 1965 ... Even more than that I see in the brothers of the Nizam al-Khass such as Mustafa Mashour, Kamel Sananiri, Hosni Abdelbaqi, Ahmed Hassanein and Ahmed al-Malat that their methodology was close to us and when they left prison they were carrying the same ideas as us. Therefore they were closer to us at that time than the older generation of Ikhwan who were brought up at the time of al-Banna.[56]

This distinction was so great that Aboul Fotouh also declared:

It was one of life's good coincidences that we met the people of the Nizam al-Khass, the fundamentalists, before we met other more moderate leaders. If the first contact had been with those moderates such as Omar Tilimsani and those who were close to him, we would have decided not to join the group.[57]

However, in spite of their reverence for these Ikhwani legends, the al-Jama'at al-Islamiya leaders were undecided about which group should absorb which. As far as the Ikhwani leaders were concerned, being the older and more experienced organisation, they would not countenance anything other than the younger body's being absorbed into their own ranks. As Kamel Sananiri told Issam al-Ariyan, the Ikhwan would not consider accepting the al-Jama'at al-Islamiya joining as a group but only as individuals.[58]

After a year of dialogue and debate, the al-Jama'at al-Islamiya, bowing to age and experience, accepted the idea of becoming part of the Ikhwan. Among those who moved from the al-Jama'at al-Islamiya to the Ikhwan at this time were not only Aboul Fotouh and al-Ariyan, but also Abu Ala Madhi, Mahmoud Ghazlan, Usam Hashish, Sana Abu Zeid and Mohamed Abdelatif among many others. Key to this process appears to have been Aboul Fotouh, one of the most prominent leaders at the time. Abu Ala Madhi claims that if not for Aboul Fotouh, he would not have joined the Ikhwan at all.[59]

Although organisational links were established between the two movements in 1975, with the agreement to join forces coming around a year later, the merger was not made public until 1980. Part of the reason for this secrecy was because the al-Jama'at al-Islamiya was a loose affiliation comprising different tendencies, including those of jihadist or a more purely Salafist orientation, that were hostile to the Brotherhood. More importantly, the Ikhwan decided it would be more advantageous to get the student leaders to recruit under the al-Jama'at al-Islamiya banner as they believed this would bring more people to the cause. This was especially the case in the Al-Said and Al-Minya regions, which were dominated by the jihadist current and where the Ikhwan had almost no presence.

After news of the merger leaked out the more militant elements, angered by the deception, broke away to form their own groups such as al-Jihad. Some of these more militant elements also kept the name al-Jama'at al-Islamiya and like al-Jihad proved willing to employ violence to achieve their objectives. Yet it would be wrong to assume that these student activists who had joined the Ikhwan were averse to the principle of violence. Many of them were fully accepting of the idea of using force to achieve their objectives. Where they differed from the other groups was in their views on when and how it should be used. As Aboul Fotouh explains: 'Our rejection of violence wasn't on principle … violence was acceptable and the difference [with the others] was only in its timing and utility.'[60] This way of thinking was of course directly in line with that of those more militant elements within the Brotherhood. Aboul Fotouh also acknowledges that there was a current within the Ikhwan which shared this position until 1984 when the Brotherhood had a major reassessment and decided to condemn the use of violence. Yet it is notable that even though the Brotherhood leadership, which had by this point passed to Omar al-Tilimsani, was opposed to violence, it was prepared to take in these young student cadres as a means of bolstering the organisation.

And bolster it they did. Through this highly strategic move the Ikhwan succeeded in bringing a whole new base into the movement that had until that point consisted primarily of a leadership with no one to lead. Aboul Fotouh clarifies: 'We were an organisation before we delivered it to the Ikhwani and they became the leaders of it. The Ikhwan was a house that the young of al-Jama'at al-Islamiya filled and pumped new blood into.'[61] Some of the young students who joined the Ikhwan at this time were astonished to discover just how empty a shell the Brotherhood was. Abu Ala Madhi says: 'When we joined we were shocked to find it was hollow inside. The leaders had cheated us and told us they were the biggest *jama'a* [group] and had their traditions but when we joined we found it to be empty. In the Al-Minya governate when we joined we discovered there wasn't a single member of the Ikhwan in it.'[62]

It is perhaps because of the fact that they were already leaders in their own right and because they had built up such a large populist movement – which essentially saved the Ikhwan – that this group somehow retained a sense of their own importance and a belief that they had a major stake in deciding the Ikhwan's future. As Abu Ala Madhi declares: 'Our generation did a big favour to the Brotherhood and without us it would have died.'[63] As a result this group had a sense of their own importance and it made them less willing to adopt the blind obedience that had so characterised the Brotherhood under al-Banna.

In addition, this group were far more politicised than the former cadres of the Ikhwan and they gave the Brotherhood a new sense of urgency. This urgency was of course fuelled by the 1979 Iranian revolution, which had proved that an Islamic state was possible, and by the growing tide of Islamic consciousness that was sweeping the Islamic world. Furthermore, this generation was used to working openly and was unconstrained by the same sense of secrecy and fear that characterised those leaders who had spent so many years in prison. As one analyst describes: 'Their experience was different from that of the sheikhs of the Nizam al-Khass who had grown up in hiding, in the ritual of secrecy and in detention.'[64] They also differed from their predecessors in that they sought to take the Ikhwan in a new direction, moving away somewhat from ideological and theological issues to focus more on practical socio-economic challenges such as poverty or corruption. Aboul Fotouh became an ardent critic of the Sadat regime publishing outspoken criticisms not only of its lack of Islamic values but also of its corruption and its inability to meet the everyday needs of the population. This group were essentially political players for whom the excitement of the political scene appears to have been as important as the religious dimension.

Having gained direct political experience through their involvement in student unions, this group saw an opportunity in the unions and professional syndicates. Aboul Fotouh, Abu Ala Madhi and al-Ariyan all became well-known activists in the professional syndicates during the 1980s. This highly pragmatic group proved willing to enter what were ostensibly secular organisations through elections in order to consolidate their influence. Their dominance of these institutions enabled the Ikhwan to address the concerns of the middle classes more directly, attracting greater numbers to the cause.[65] They also began reaching out to people more directly by offering welfare services such as setting up free clinics to provide medical treatment to students plugging the gaps where the state was so woefully inadequate.

As the 1980s progressed this group began pushing for more direct participation in the political system. Although they had started out sharing the more hawkish ideology of the Nizam al-Khass, by the early 1980s it seems that they had become convinced by the arguments of Omar al-Tilimsani. Although al-Tilimsani, appointed as Murshid in 1977, was originally conceived as a front man for the Ikhwan behind whom the Nizam al-Khass would pull the strings, it appears that he was able to impose himself on the organisation more than Hassan al-Hodeibi was ever able to do. Al-Tilimsani brought back more traditionalist figures such as Farid Abdel Khaliq into the Guidance Office, where they acted as a counterweight to figures such as Mustafa Mashour. The Murshid also seems to have been able to bring people around to his way of thinking and his belief that the best means of achieving the movement's goals was through participating in the political arena. According to Barot, 'He attracted a great number of those who are now in the reformist current of the group including ...

Abu Ala Madhi and Aboul Fotouh. This generation brought the group [Brotherhood] to the core of Egyptian political life despite the fact that it was still illegal.'[66] A similar view was expressed by Egyptian brother and former head of the Al-Taqwa bank, Youssef Nada, who remarked, 'Omar al-Tilimsani brought the Ikhwan back to life.'[67]

Ironically the Murshid's task of steering the movement down a more moderate path was made easier by the fact that after President Mubarak came to power in 1981 following Sadat's assassination, the regime carried out a major clampdown of the Ikhwan, resulting in a number of key figures from the Nizam al-Khass (including Mustafa Mashour) fleeing abroad. The removal of this more militant group from the scene enabled these reformist characters to seek a greater and more direct engagement with the practical issues of politics. As one member of the Ikhwan recalls, 'By the 1980s the demand for Sharia had receded and was replaced by calls for freedom to establish political parties and join elections and have newspapers etc.'[68] Of course these calls were in part a response to the prevailing political conditions of the day and the fact that the new President made it clear that the only way to play a part in the country's political life would be to join in the system of political parties. Mubarak's Electoral Law of 1983, which ruled that political activism would be restricted to the realms of political parties that had been sanctioned by the Parties' Committee, forced the Ikhwan to think in a different way. This posed a serious dilemma for the Brotherhood. In line with the ideology of al-Banna, they were essentially averse to the idea of party politics. Moreover, they were all too aware that their strength on the popular level at least had always derived from the fact that they were about more than just politics. Indeed, they were so successful because they were a *jama'a* (group) that blended politics with being a religious and cultural social movement. The leadership had further to consider the repercussions of such a move outside of Egypt, given that they were leading an international organisation that looked to them for guidance and example. Local concerns could never be entirely disassociated from the restraints of the international arena. Perhaps even more importantly, the Ikhwan knew that it was highly unlikely that the powers would countenance the establishment of such a party.

Yet the Ikhwan felt that somehow it was time to enter the political arena that was opening up. As a result, in 1983 at a large meeting in Cairo, Omar al-Tilimsani mooted the idea of establishing a political party that would not eclipse the *jama'a* but that would work alongside it. However, his suggestion was roundly rejected. Mehdi Akef recounts: 'I told al-Tilimsani that my understanding of the Brotherhood was that it was a comprehensive organisation ... and therefore would not accept or agree to its abolition or replacement by a political party regulated by the Parties Law.'[69] In spite of this rejection al-Tilimsani pushed ahead and established a special committee to draw up drafts for a party manifesto. At the same time the leadership looked for an alternative way to enter the political system.

Proving just how pragmatic it could be, in 1984 the Ikhwan decided to take part in the parliamentary elections by allying itself with the al-Wafd party – a secular nationalist party – and gaining eight seats. It also used the same approach in the 1987 elections, this time allying with Amal and Ahrar parties and winning thirty-six seats, which made it the largest opposition group in parliament. Although it boycotted the elections of 1990, the Ikhwan contested them again in 1995, putting forward 170 candidates as independents and also fielding a few others with the al-Wafd. But whilst this course of action brought the Ikhwan some degree of political leverage, it also left it open to accusations of having taken a contradictory and vague stance.

This willingness to engage in such partnerships certainly drew disapproval from some of the hardliners within the Ikhwan. Mustafa Mashour, who was outside of the country at the time, is reported to have criticised the 1984 alliance:

The aim of the Brotherhood is not to gain the support of he who votes for us on the ballot, but of he who enlists himself and his assets for Allah ... We are asking for the student of the next world rather than government and earthly posts as they exist in political parties. We are asking for those who work in the field of *dawa* with the fear of Allah, piety, and loyalty to the goal of establishing the Islamic government. This does not mean that we reject politics. We are aware of its role and importance, but allocate it the proper weight without overshadowing other activities.[70]

Nonetheless, the pull of politics proved stronger for this reformist generation and they sought to capitalise on the advances they had made. But in the perpetual cycle of push and pull between the different currents within the Ikhwan, their bid to travel further down the line of political participation was brought to an abrupt halt.

The al-Wasat Affair

The death of Omar al-Tilimsani in May 1986 was to mark yet another watershed moment for the Ikhwan. Al-Tilimsani had somehow championed the reformist current, working closely with them to try to achieve change through a more open approach, and his death came as a major blow. As Abu Ala Madhi describes, 'We tried to reform the Ikhwan from the inside but the death of al-Tilimsani killed all types of internal reform.'[71] Similarly Issam Sultan, another reformist figure, described how when Omar al-Tilimsani died it wasn't only his person that disappeared, but also 'his mentality, his culture and his openness'.[72] These comments may reflect a tendency within the Ikhwan to overemphasise al-Tilimsani's role, for in spite of his obvious ability to win over those within the reformist current, the movement was still essentially in the grip of the Nizam al-Khass group, who acted like back room operators. This was the view of Egyptian al-Qa'ida ideologue Ayman al-Zawahiri:

> The Muslim Brotherhood had a peculiar organisational structure. The overt leadership was represented by General Guide Omar al-Tilimsani, who was the leader in the eyes of the population and the regime. Actually the real leadership was in the hands of the Special Order Group [Nizam al-Khass] that included Mustafa Mashour, Dr Ahmad al-Malat, may he rest in peace, and Kemal Sananiri, may he rest in peace.[73]

Indeed, one of the reasons al-Tilimsani had been able to achieve such success during his time as Murshid was because so many of the Nizam al-Khass were forced abroad at the time, weakening their control of the day-to-day running of the movement. However, his death coincided with the return to Egypt of a number of key members of the old guard who during their time away had been busy building up the Ikhwan's international networks. These figures included Mustafa Mashour who returned from Germany, Maimoun al-Hodeibi from Saudi Arabia, Mahmoud Izzat from Yemen and Khairet al-Shater from Yemen and London. Their reappearance on the scene was to herald a new era of rigidity within the movement. Whilst Mashour had long been a key figure, it was Maimoun al-Hodeibi who really came to dominate the Ikhwan during this period. Many have argued that al-Hodeibi, who unlike his father was a real hardliner, came to be the de facto leader of the Brotherhood at this time.

Just as they had done with Hassan al-Hodeibi, this group engineered the appointment of a successor to al-Tilimsani who would act as a front man whilst they held on to the reins of power. The new appointee was Mohamed Hamed Abu Nasser, a man who had not even finished secondary school. Of all the Ikhwan's leaders, he left perhaps the least impression of all. Yet he served the purpose of the Nizam al-Khass group who immediately took steps to curb the activities of the younger reformists within the organisation. According to Abu Ala Madhi, 'After the return of this group we saw there was an attempt by them to restrict this generation that was leading the real work inside the Ikhwan.'[74]

This old guard were so entrenched in their own ideology that they could not accept the reformists' willingness to engage with other parts of the Egyptian opposition. In 1992 some of the Ikhwan ran a forum to which they invited a number of influential Egyptian figures and intellectuals from outside of the Brotherhood. During the meeting Maimoun al-Hodeibi, displaying an extraordinary arrogance and lack of understanding about the nature of open political debate, began questioning whether these guests were qualified to speak given that they were individuals and unlike him did not have movements behind them.[75] Al-Hodeibi's intervention prompted many of these influential individuals to leave the meeting, provoking an extreme embarrassment among the reformist Ikhwani who were hosting the forum. The following year the reformist current were chastised by al-Hodeibi for holding a forum in the Ramses Hilton in Cairo that brought together the various strands of the opposition ranging from communists to Nasserists and to jihadists. They were also admonished for supporting the National Pact which had been agreed upon by the opposition and that the Ikhwan's leadership refused to sign. Such opposition to engaging in the politics of the day led one member of the reformist current to bemoan, 'They simply are not politicians, they are spiritual leaders.'[76]

At the same time, this reformist group were getting increasingly frustrated that in spite of all the years they had been part of the Ikhwan they were repeatedly prevented from taking up senior positions within the movement. One reformist explained, 'The Brotherhood taught us that the government was corrupt and needed to be brought down, but we found through our experience that decisions were taken by a small group of people in the Brotherhood ... it was something that made us very uneasy.'[77] The group were crushingly disappointed in 1995 when the Ikhwan's internal elections resulted in no change at all to the membership of the Guidance Office, a result that according to Issam Sultan the core of the movement had paved the way for.[78]

They were even more outraged in January 1996 when during the burial of Mohamed Hamed Abu Nasser, rather than follow the Brotherhood's correct procedure for electing a new leader, Maimoun al-Hodeibi simply appointed Mustafa Mashour as the new Murshid to whom all those present gave their *baya* (oath of allegiance). This incident, which became known as the graveside pledge, was to sow further resentment among the young activists. Afterwards Sultan went to Mashour and asked him why he had been chosen in this unorthodox manner. Mashour, who claimed he had been surprised by al-Hodeibi's choosing him, told Sultan: 'Allah has chosen for al-Jama'a. Allah chose Hassan al-Banna and then Allah chose Hassan al-Hodeibi and then Omar al-Tilimsani, then Hamed Abu Nasser and then the poor slave [i.e. himself].'[79] Clearly such sentiments did not wash with the likes of the reformist current, who could only see a leadership that was blocking all possibility of reform and that was entrenched in the mentality of the 1950s.

As their frustration grew, this group became more overt about their disappointment with the leadership, bringing the disunity into the public sphere. In January 1995 Salah Abd al-Karim, the editor of the *Engineers Union* magazine, wrote an article criticising the domination of the old guard within the Ikhwan and calling on party elders to restrict themselves to the role of advisers.[80] Similarly, at a meeting of brothers in the unions one of the Ikhwan gave a speech in which he criticised the old guard for being too narrow-minded and inward-looking and insufficiently open to other political and social forces outside the movement.[81] By the mid-1990s the reformist current had come to the conclusion that, in the words of one of them, 'We are something and they are something else and it is impossible for these two seas to meet. One of them was fresh water and the other salty.'[82]

After concluding that there was no scope to change the Ikhwan from inside, one group of reformists decided to push ahead with their own project to establish a political party. This group was led by Abu Ala Madhi with the support of around seventy young reformists including Issam Sultan and the journalist and member of the Engineers Syndicate Council, Salah Abd al-Maqsud. A striking number of those involved were from the engineering sector including Abu Ala Madhi himself.[83] Notably, this group also included two Copts, one Anglican and a number of women, presumably as a means of demonstrating the group's commitment to the rights of non-Muslims and women. The former was a particularly controversial subject within the Ikhwan, not least because of Mustafa Mashour's comments in 1996 that Christians should not be permitted to join the armed forces and that they should pay a *jiziya* (tax), something that he later retracted.

In January 1996 this group bypassed the Ikhwan machine and submitted their proposal to set up the party, Hizb al-Wasat, to the Parties Committee for approval. Although they had decided to act alone, they did have the support of key figures on the international Islamist scene including Sheikh Yusuf al-Qaradawi. Moreover, in a concession to the leadership they did inform Mehdi Akef, less hawkish than many of the others, of their plans. According to them, Akef supported them although he was not informed about the details of the new party. Akef, however, asserts that the whole al-Wasat project was his idea and said: 'I am the one who came with the idea of Hizb al-Wasat. We came with it in order to embarrass the government. Some of the Ikhwan set this party up and since 1996 the government has refused to accept it.'[84]

Regardless of Akef's role, the al-Wasat affair was clearly a shocking challenge to the Brotherhood leadership. It certainly met with the wrath of the leadership, who could not believe that such disobedience and rebelliousness that went so against the whole spirit of the Brotherhood had come from within its own ranks. In reality, the al-Wasat platform was not essentially very different from much of the thinking within the Ikhwan at that time and there was nothing especially controversial in their party programme. Rather, the young brothers had crossed the line of acting without permission. According to Abu Ala Madhi, al-Hodeibi and Mashour led a major campaign against the al-Wasat group. Al-Hodeibi summoned Issam Sultan to his house and their meeting was 'violent and crushing'.[85] As a result those involved in the al-Wasat affair resigned from the Ikhwan although there was an equal push from the leadership to get them out, as 'when Mashour discovered a new mentality that did not listen and obey in the traditional sense, he took a rigid decision against them and expelled them'.[86]

Needless to say, their application to become a political party was turned down by the Parties Committee and many of those involved, including Abu Ala Madhi, were arrested, prompting the vast majority who had signed the al-Wasat application to back down and rejoin the Brotherhood. Yet this al-Wasat group were to pay an even greater price for having dared to disobey the party line. When they went to appeal against the decision, the Ikhwan's leadership attended the court session and demanded that their appeal be turned down. Ironically, the al-Wasat group's bid to take political engagement to a new level was sufficient to make the Ikhwan's leadership close ranks with the regime against them.

What was notable about the affair was that other figures within the reformist current, who clearly supported a more open approach, did not join the initiative. This included Aboul Fotouh and al-Ariyan, who decided to remain within the ranks of the Brotherhood despite their closeness to Abu Ala Madhi. According to Sultan, whilst many of this group were ideologically with the al-Wasat current, they did not take the step of actually joining them because of 'practical and administrative considerations that made them stay within the Brotherhood'.[87] Aboul Fotouh described his differences with the al-Wasat current as being organisational in nature and as a split between those who wanted to see reform inside the *jama'a* rather than outside it. Yet the refusal of these individuals to join the al-Wasat group led some to assert that the true reformists within the Ikhwan left the movement at this time.[88]

However, it could be argued that the likes of Aboul Fotouh and al-Ariyan ultimately proved themselves to be shrewder: not only was the al-Wasat project rejected by the government; it was never going to gain any real public support. Such a project could never have any real populist appeal, given that in Egypt politics is still very much the domain of the urban elite and any party that is willing to work within the established system is likely to draw charges of having been co-opted by the regime. As Amr Shobaki has argued, Aboul Fotouh and al-Ariyan were all too well aware that their political ideas would have no real future outside the movement.[89] It is this very point that the old guard perhaps understood better than the reformist generation – to become a political party would bring charges of being compromised, leaving the Ikhwan as just one party among a number of others operating within the system.

Yet the al-Wasat affair did spark further internal debate within the Ikhwan. It caused figures such as Aboul Fotouh to begin questioning whether internal reform was possible whilst the Nizam al-Khass were in control. He allegedly began voicing his view that a *jama'a* that doesn't know democracy in its internal life is incapable of guaranteeing democracy outside of itself.[90] Over twenty years later, Aboul Fotouh, along with others of his generation such as Issam al-Ariyan, were still struggling with the same questions and challenges that the movement has been grappling with since the 1920s.

Post 9/11

The years after the al-Wasat affair saw a continuation of the reform debate within the Ikhwan and of the seemingly endless questions about how best to engage in the political process without selling out on the movement's core Islamic principles. This debate came into sharper relief following the 9/11 attacks on the US. Suddenly the world began to focus its attentions on the various Islamist movements, and what had until then been considered as domestic opposition groups now came to be viewed by some as part of a global Islamist network that threatened the whole of Western civilisation. Regimes were quick to pick up on this sea change of sentiment and sought to use the 9/11 attacks as evidence that they had been right to clamp down so hard on their Islamist opponents. The Egyptian regime was no exception. For the Brotherhood, with its somewhat questionable past, its role in the Afghanistan conflict of the 1970s and its aspiration to create a society ruled by Sharia, the imperative to demonstrate its commitment to moderation and to playing by the political rules was all too obvious. The fear of being labelled as a terrorist organisation prompted a greater urgency to be seen as willing to work within the political framework of the state.

In spite of the Ikhwan's deep reservations about the War on Terror and the role of the West in the Islamic world, it seems that the reformist current within the Egyptian Ikhwan somehow received a boost from this new international climate. It was as if now the world was watching they could come into their own and find a truly appreciative audience. The reformists, many of whom speak English, took advantage of renewed interest by scholars and journalists and were keen to engage in interviews and debates as a means of demonstrating their commitment to reform. In line with the globalised age they also began promoting themselves through the Internet, setting up their own English language website. In doing so these figures started to become personalities beyond the confines of their own environment and were able to project a new image of the Brotherhood that contradicted the picture of them as secretive, autocratic and aggressive that was doing the rounds in some Western circles. The group was given a further boost in 2004 when after the death of Maimoun al-Hodeibi, Mehdi Akef was appointed to the post of Murshid. Although Akef was a member of the Nizam al-Khass and part of the older generation of leaders, he had a reputation for being more tolerant and sympathetic to the reformist wing. As such he was widely considered to be a compromise figure who could bridge the gap between the old guard and the reformists. He was certainly a more acceptable choice for figures such as Aboul Fotouh who had huge personal antagonism with Akef's hardline predecessor.

Under Akef's leadership, the Ikhwan produced a series of reform platforms such as that of 2004 which was titled 'Muslim Brotherhood Initiative: On the General Principles of Reform in Egypt'. It laid out the movement's stance on a range of issues from political and legal reform to education and foreign policy. Although this rather thin document was in essence simply a reissuing of its 2000 election programme, it was touted as a new expression of the Ikhwan's commitment to progressive liberal ideas. This and other similar documents that the Ikhwan has produced in recent years stress the movement's belief in the civic nature of political authority and respect for the basic values of and instruments of democracy; the transfer of power through clean and free elections; and the acceptance of citizenship as the basis for rights and responsibilities for Muslims and non-Muslims.[91] Yet while this initiative represents a more progressive and open approach by the Ikhwan, it still comes across as somewhat of a muddle and contains a series of contradictions.

Although it expresses support for the peaceful transferral of power based upon elections and the freedom to establish political parties, the first section of the initiative states: 'We, the Muslim Brotherhood, have a defined mission which we present as a basic concept for reform ...

This mission is represented collectively in working to establish Allah's Sharia as we believe it to be the real effective way out of all sufferings and problems, both on the internal front – and the external one.'[92] The document goes on to assert that the starting point for any reform must be in reforming the Egyptian individual, who has become clouded by 'negligence and selfishness' and 'immediate desires and materialistic values', so that he can be purified on 'a base of faith, straightforwardness and good manners'. Therefore the initiative promotes democratic principles on the one hand, yet restricts individual freedoms on the other. It also promotes the rights of non-Muslims yet stresses the Islamic nature of the Egyptian state; it accepts the principle of free and fair elections and the civic nature of political authority yet asserts that the Ikhwan will strive to change the laws and purify them to be in conformity with the principles of Islamic Sharia.

The ambiguities in this document are hardly surprising. They simply reflect the Ikhwan's age-old problem of having to accommodate both tendencies present within the movement. As Shobaki has argued, the absence of detail is a deliberate means of protecting the Brotherhood from factionalism, as being clear and explicit will only exacerbate differences within the movement.[93] Yet this desire to conceal division is only part of the story of why the Ikhwan remained so ambiguous over concepts such as democracy or Sharia. The vagueness over these issues was also related to the fact that the Ikhwan has always had to play to several different constituencies simultaneously. For all its activity in the political arena, the Brotherhood has relied on a wide social base that supports the movement not because of politics, but because it is considered by many to represent Islam itself.[94] In stark contrast to successive regimes, the Brotherhood is seen by many Egyptians as pure and uncorrupted, standing for untainted Islamic concepts including Sharia law rather than the rather messy business of politics. As influential Kuwaiti scholar, Sheikh Abdullah Nafisi, has argued, 'People don't consider there to be any difference between their religion and the *tanzeem* [organisation]. They take a mixture of its religion, its orders, its instructions and its prohibitions.'[95] This is very well understood even by reformists. As Issam al-Ariyan acknowledged, the *tanzeem* is a central concept to the Brotherhood and is still considered the main source of its power.[96]

As such, there were many within the Ikhwan who feared delving too deeply into the mainstream political arena, believing that straying too far from the movement's core principles over issues such as Sharia, or women's status, would risk alienating its grass roots support base. This was one of the reasons why there was considerable hostility among some parts of the movement to trying to establish a political party. Although some of this hostility was linked to the knowledge that the regime would not permit it to do so, there was also a strong concern that going down the party route (as opposed to trying to influence the political process by standing as independents) would be a step too far from the movement's core ideology. As Abu Ala Madhi asserts, 'There is a mistaken idea in the Ikhwan that the government is the only obstacle to becoming a political party. There are powerful leaders in the al-Jama'a that object to the idea of a political party in spite of the fact that they say they want one. They prefer to keep al-Jama'a illegal.'[97] Thus, the push for the reform current was hampered as much by the challenges of maintaining the movement's social base as it was by the old guard.

This basic contradiction within the Ikhwan was demonstrated again in 2007 when it put forward a draft platform that was widely interpreted as an attempt to demonstrate what a Brotherhood manifesto would look like should it ever decide to apply to become a political party. It was also in part a response to the growing calls by commentators – including those from abroad – for the Ikhwan to be more explicit in articulating its policies. But as ever, the Ikhwan failed to spell out some of the more difficult elements and the draft was notable for avoiding any discussion of the future relationship between the political party they asserted that they hoped to build and the broader movement.[98] More importantly, although the platform's overall tone was in line with earlier reform initiatives that stressed a commitment to civic democracy and the rotation of power, in among this reformist language were two highly controversial and reactionary bombshells.

The first of these controversial elements was a call for the creation of a council of clerics that would be elected by religious scholars to advise the legislative and executive in matters of Sharia. The draft implied that the council's decisions would be binding in matters where Sharia was at stake. Secondly, whilst the platform acknowledged the rights of women and Copts as full citizens within the Egyptian state, it specified that neither could take the post of President. These proposals effectively killed all the progress that the Ikhwan had made in convincing the world that it had really changed, was committed to democracy and deserved a turn in power. Whilst likely to have pleased much of the Ikhwan's core support base, as far as the outside world was concerned these suggestions were a major step backwards and tantamount to the Brotherhood shooting itself in the foot.

Yet the platform was in part a means for the conservative old guard to reassert their control and take back some momentum from the reformist wing. According to some Ikhwani, those of a more reformist bent had agreed to a draft platform. However, those of a more traditional stance acted unilaterally and inserted these more controversial elements into the agreed document at the last moment, something that sparked fierce internal wrangling within the Ikhwan.[99] Clearly, in spite of all the talk of *shura*, just as in the days of al-Banna the leadership still considered it to be within their rights to act as they saw fit, regardless of the views of other key players in the movement.

The draft also did further damage to the Ikhwan's bid to present a united face to the world: the divisions over the platform came to be played out in the public domain. The conservative current accused the liberal camp of 'violating clear Sharia-based principles in the quest for momentary political advantage'.[100] Indeed, former Deputy to Murshid Mohamed Habib, along with General Secretary Mahmoud Izzat, defended the controversial elements in the draft platform. Allegedly, Izzat claimed that those who had objected to these controversial elements did not have any support in Sharia law.[101] The reformist camp, led by Aboul Fotouh, meanwhile told the press that the proposal about the court of clerics was simply 'bad editing', something that was completely at odds with Mohamed Habib's take on the document.[102] The divisions became so acute that they spilled over into the wider movement and a number of young Ikhwani activists complained on blogs and websites that the platform did not express their views and had been drafted in an undemocratic manner.[103]

As with many other key Brotherhood initiatives, this platform was by no means a truly consultative process that involved the movement's own grass roots. Yet interestingly the Ikhwan decided to present the draft to leading Islamists around the world. It held a major meeting in London, to which some parts of the Arab media were invited. If it had been hoping for acclaim at having advanced in its thinking, it was very much mistaken. The draft drew intense and very public criticism from the London audience that included many influential figures from within the Islamist milieu. The two controversial elements in the platform were criticised heavily, leaving the Egyptians looking as though they were somehow still in the dark ages. Yet it was perhaps easier for Islamists in Europe to be critical of such reactionary stances and to present a more progressive outlook, as unlike the Egyptian Ikhwan they did not have any real constituencies to play to. Therefore this draft should not be considered as a retraction or regression on the part of the Egyptian Ikhwan. Rather it is another reflection of the fact that the Brotherhood has always comprised a diverse array of opinions and tendencies and whilst the reformist current may have had a high public profile in the last years of the Mubarak regime, its power within the movement was always ring fenced by those of a higher standing within its leadership structures.

In fact, by 2010, the reformists found themselves more sidelined than ever after a crisis erupted among the upper echelons of the movement. The calamity was prompted when Mehdi Akef decided to bring Issam al-Ariyan into the Guidance Office to replace Mohamed Helal who died in September 2009. However, the Murshid met with stiff resistance from the Guidance Office, which rejected his attempt to bring new blood into the leadership body on the grounds that according to the movement's bylaws, it was necessary to hold an election before a new member could be admitted. Akef was so furious at the refusal to comply with his request that he stormed out of the Guidance Office meeting and announced his resignation, telling the press, 'I insisted on this issue [promotion of al-Ariyan] for two reasons. First, the interpretation and point of view of the general guide should be respected. Secondly, it is within my prerogative. However, they rejected it, and it is over.'[104] Although Akef subsequently withdrew his resignation, he insisted on keeping to an earlier pledge to leave office when his term expired in January 2010.

Akef's decision not to stay on sent the movement into somewhat of a disarray. It was the first time in the Brotherhood's history that a Murshid had voluntarily stepped down rather than hung on until death. Furthermore, there was no obvious successor to Akef, who, for all that he may have faced criticism for his leadership style, had some degree of charisma and presence and was able somehow to act as a bridge between the competing factions within the movement. Akef was also almost the last of the historical generation, one of the Brotherhood 'originals', who had joined the movement when it was under the leadership of al-Banna.

Yet as the movement deliberated over who should take over, Mohamed Habib, seemed to believe that being the Deputy to the Supreme Guide meant that he would naturally step in to fill the top post, especially after he took over many of Akef's duties following the Murshid's resignation announcement. However, Habib queered his pitch early on, as other members took umbrage at his rush to behave as if he were the next Supreme Guide before the succession had actually been agreed upon. [105] Habib also made himself hugely unpopular by speaking candidly to the media about the movement's internal wranglings, airing its dirty washing in public in an unprecedented way. Despite being warned not to talk to the press, Habib was particularly up front in some of his interviews about Akef's failure to bring al-Ariyan into the Guidance Office, disclosing, for example, that not one member of the office had voted in favour of al-Ariyan's being made a member. Habib also revealed that friction between the Murshid and the Guidance Office was a common occurrence.

In this way, Habib set himself on a collision course not only with Akef – who was already angry at his deputy's voting against his wishes over al-Ariyan – but also with other senior members of the Brotherhood. One such member was the powerful Mahmoud Izzat, a conservative hardliner who as General Secretary of the Brotherhood's Secretariat had been steadily increasing his grip on the movement and who disagreed with Habib's slightly more open and pragmatic approach.[106] Faced with such hostility there was no way that Habib was going to stand a chance of being the next Murshid. In any case, he was widely considered not to have the necessary gravitas or charisma to be able to lead not only the Egyptian Ikhwan, but to serve as spiritual reference to the entire Muslim Brotherhood movement.

Partly as a result of his rash actions, Habib not only lost out on the post of Murshid in January 2010, he also found himself excluded from the Brotherhood's senior body when he failed to uphold his position in the Guidance Office in the elections held at the end of December 2009. Yet it wasn't just Habib who lost out in the Guidance Office elections. Abdul Moneim Aboul Fotouh, the most prominent of all the movement's reformist figures, also failed to be re-elected for another term. Given Aboul Fotouh's high public profile, his removal came as a major shock. Yet for all that Aboul Fotouh's pronouncements about democracy and transformation might have been welcomed by parts of the international community, as well as some of the younger cadres of the Brotherhood, they were not going down so well with the more traditional elements of the movement. They certainly weren't appreciated by Mahmoud Izzat and other senior traditionalists, who believed that Aboul Fotouh was promoting ideas that were contrary to the ideology and values of the movement.[107] Perhaps more importantly, Aboul Fotouh was becoming too much of a personality in his own right and arguably the movement was finding it increasingly difficult to contain him within its tight organisational structures. In fact, according to some sources, Aboul Fotouh's departure had been planned up to a year before the Guidance Office election.[108]

Yet Aboul Fotouh's exit was a significant and symbolic blow for those Ikhwani with reformist aspirations. So too was the fact that the Guidance Office elections brought in a host of conservative figures, including Mahmoud Izzat, but also Mahmoud Ghozlan, Saad al-Husseini and Mohammed Badie, who dominated the leadership body. These traditionalists were of the opinion that the movement was best served by retracting somewhat from engagement in politics and focusing instead on its traditional activities such as proselyting and carrying out educational and social work. As such, these Guidance Office elections marked a watershed moment for the Brotherhood in so far as they consolidated the control of the conservative trend within the movement. Although somewhat ironically Issam al-Ariyan was elected to the leadership body, those of a reformist bent were largely wiped out of the picture.

The election of the new Murshid in January 2010 represented another triumph for the conservative trend. Three names from the Guidance Office were put into the hat for the poll: Mohammed Badie, Rashad al-Bayoumi and Giuma Amin. All three were conservatives and as one analyst has aptly remarked, they were carbon copies of each other.[109] However, Badie emerged triumphant, winning 66 out of 100 votes from the Shura Council, and took over as Murshid. Badie, who trained as a veterinary doctor and who, after working his way up the Brotherhood's ranks was appointed to the Guidance Office in 1993, had been imprisoned in the 1960s alongside Sayyid Qutb. He is described by some as a Qutbist.[110] Whether Badie would describe himself as such is doubtful. However, there is little doubting the new incumbent's uncompromising views. In November 2009, for example, during an interview with *Al-Youm Al-Sabi'e*, Badie allegedly commented, 'If the people choose something against the Sharia, it is not proper to implement it. If there is a conflict with the Sharia, it must not be put into force.'[111]

Thus, by the start of 2010 the conservatives within the Brotherhood had moved to reassert their dominance, clipping the reformists' wings and shifting the focus of the movement back more to its traditional core values and principles. This did not prevent the Brotherhood from competing (as independents) in the first round of the 2010 parliamentary elections, despite calls from within its ranks to boycott the polls. In fact, in a bid to avoid such boycotts and to ensure its members turned out to support it, the Ikhwan issued a fatwa proclaiming that participation in the elections was a religious duty and that boycotting them was sinful. This fatwa was an unusual move on the part of the Brotherhood and reflected its growing unease at its own support base given the fact that it had been significantly damaged by the large numbers of arrests and increased repression it had suffered since its achievements in the 2005 elections.

The Brotherhood needn't have bothered. As it turned out, the Mubarak regime was in no mood to compromise and was determined to send a clear message to the movement: its time in mainstream political life was at an end. The Brotherhood had an inkling that this was the case and had braced itself for a worse showing in the elections than it had achieved in 2005 (when it won 88 seats).[112] However, its members were stunned when all of its seats were completely wiped out in the first round. As a result, the Brotherhood, along with the other opposition force, the al-Wafd party, boycotted the second round of elections. If there was ever a reason for the conservative trend within the movement to stress that the Brotherhood should shift its attentions away from the political arena, this was surely it.

Yet the Brotherhood was soon to be overtaken by events. As popular protests broke out across the Arab world, the Brotherhood, much like the region as a whole, was shaken out of its inertia and forced to look beyond its internal crises and to decide upon what role it would play in the Arab Spring and in the new Egypt.

2

From Diplomacy to Arms
and Back to Diplomacy

The Evolution of the Syrian Ikhwan

Of all the Brotherhood's branches, the Syrian Ikhwan has perhaps the most controversial of histories. It is a history of extremes that has been characterised by violence and brutal oppression at the hands of the Syrian state and that has seen the movement go from being the most important Ikhwani branch after the Egyptians to little more than the shell of a leadership in exile. Plagued by internal division and bitter recriminations that have split the movement in two, the history of the Syrian Ikhwan is often written as the story of two competing wings – the Damascus wing known for its moderate outlook and the more militant action-oriented Aleppo wing. Whilst in reality the distinction between these two wings was never as clear-cut as is often made out, the factionalism and rivalry engendered by this division were enough to bring the movement almost to its knees. With so many challenges it is remarkable that the Syrian Ikhwan has been able to survive at all.

The most controversial element of the Syrian Ikhwan has been its involvement in the bloody events of the early 1980s, culminating in the Hamah massacre of 1982 in which the security forces razed the city to the ground, killing thousands of residents. Although the Ikhwan's leadership insist that they were not directly involved in or responsible for the violent uprising that prompted the massacre, the conflicting reports and testimonies of the leadership of this era indicate that they played a much more significant role than the official record would suggest. Whilst it is true that the leadership tried to distance themselves from the more extreme tactics used by some of the groups that operated around their margins, the moment it looked as though they were on the brink of a popular revolution, the Syrian brothers proved themselves to be just as impatient as all the other groups seeking to bring down the Ba'athist regime at the time. Interestingly this proved as true for the more moderate Damascus wing as it did for the Aleppo wing. For all the Brotherhood's protestations that they have never sought to rule but only to instigate gradual change by educating society from below, it seems that once the temptation of power was in their reach they grasped at the chance with both hands.

Of course this willingness to take up arms did not come out of nowhere. Rather it was the manifestation of a growing radicalisation that developed inside the Syrian Ikhwan during the 1960s and 1970s. This was in part a response to the enormous political and economic upheavals that were taking place within the country at the time, overturning existing social structures and threatening traditional values. Certainly such changes were not unique to Syria during this period, but what differentiated the Syrian case was the fact that the ruling Ba'athist regime that took over in 1963 came to be dominated by the Alawites whilst the majority of the population were Sunni, thereby adding a sectarian dimension to the struggle between ruler and ruled. It is no coincidence that the works of the Syrian medieval jurist Ibn Taymiyyah, whose uncompromising stance against the Alawites, had a particular resonance among the Syrian Ikhwan. Moreover, by the early 1980s the mood of the country was one of revolt with strikes and protests breaking out across the country. Therefore, the Syrian

Ikhwan's increasingly forthright bid to confront the regime was in line with the growing radicalisation of the wider political scene.

The radicalisation of the Syrian Ikhwan was also in keeping with the emergence of more militant currents in other branches of the Brotherhood at the time, also inspired by the ideology of Sayyid Qutb and his ilk. The Egyptian Ikhwan also underwent a perceptible radicalisation during this period, with groups such as Organisation 65 coming on to the scene. Yet whilst the Egyptians succeeded in shedding many of their more extreme elements, who moved out of the Brotherhood to form their own organisations, the Syrians were never able to cut off ties with their own militants in the same way or to prevent a more wholesale radicalisation of the movement.

This failing was primarily due to the weakness of the Syrian Ikhwan's own leadership. From the mid-1960s the leadership had become so embroiled in their own internal battles and power struggles that whilst they busied themselves with these matters, the body of the movement took on a life of its own. The situation was further aggravated by the fact that for much of this period many of the movement's leaders were absent from the country either by force or by choice. Although the leadership made some efforts to urge moderation and condemn the actions of the more extreme groups that were operating around the Ikhwan's edges, they were ultimately unable to prevent this slide into militancy. By the time of the Hamah uprising events seem to have completely overtaken the leadership; once they realised what was happening, they could do nothing other than to join in the revolt for fear they would be left behind should the regime actually be brought down.

This recklessness was to prove disastrous. The Ba'athist regime responded to the challenge by doing its utmost to crush the movement and ended up finishing it off inside the country. Those brothers who managed to escape death or arrest fled the country, leaving the Ikhwan to become nothing more than a movement in exile. Humbled by their experience, with no grass roots support base inside the country, over the past twenty years the Syrian brothers have focused their energies on trying to negotiate their return home. As part of this effort they have sought to reinvent themselves and to turn themselves back into the progressive and open movement that was originally established by their founder Mustafa al-Sibai. In many ways they have achieved this metamorphosis: the reformist platforms that they have put forward in recent years mark them out as perhaps the most progressive of all Ikhwani branches. Yet the Syrian Ikhwan is so tainted by its own past that it has struggled to be taken seriously. It has had to work harder than any other branch to try to prove both to the Syrians and to the rest of the world that it is once again a truly progressive and trustworthy organisation.

The Early Years: al-Sibai and al-Attar

Like many other Ikhwani branches, the Syrian Brotherhood emerged out of the ties between Syrian Islamists and members of the Egyptian Ikhwan. Mustafa al-Sibai, the first Syrian General Guide, came from a traditional religious family that had long supplied preachers to the Grand Mosque of Homs and was sent to Al-Azhar in Cairo aged eighteen to study Islamic law. Whilst in Cairo, he came into contact with Hassan al-Banna and became heavily involved with the Brotherhood. He returned to Syria in 1941 and set about trying to draw together the various Islamist groups that had sprung up there under the general banner of the Shabab Mohamed to replicate its counterpart in Egypt. These groups were composed mostly of intellectuals and students and focused their activities primarily on cultural, social and sporting events. Under al-Sibai's stewardship these groups came together; after a meeting in Aleppo in 1944 they formally adopted the name of the Muslim Brotherhood, appointing al-Sibai as their General Guide. Despite the fact that this new group was the product of an existing indigenous Islamic activism, al-Sibai was more than willing to submit to the authority of Cairo and give *baya* to his great friend Hassan al-Banna.[1]

Al-Sibai soon gained a reputation for his level-headed and enlightened approach, as well as for his openness to others. What he shared in particular with al-Banna was his strong sense of pragmatism. Although he was personally less interested in working in the political sphere, believing that the primary duty of the movement was *dawa* rather than politics, he was willing for the Ikhwan to contest the 1947 parliamentary elections, in which it won three seats to the parliament. More shockingly for some among the Ikhwan's ranks, after al-Sibai failed in his efforts to make Islam the official religion of the state in 1949 he was willing to compromise and accept the secular constitution that had been agreed in parliament.

As with the Ikhwan in Egypt, much of the movement's appeal lay in its simple message, which held that Islam was a comprehensive ideology that permeated every aspect of life, and also in the fact that its members were viewed as the guardians of tradition in a changing world. Al-Sibai further developed a specifically Syrian agenda that called for an 'end to dependence upon foreign powers, to feudalism and to the domination of the upper class elite'.[2] As such the Ikhwan tapped directly into the struggle being played out between the new middle and lower middle classes against the semi-feudal upper class, which had extensive control over trade and was closely allied with the interests of the colonial powers.[3] As a result, the movement in Syria drew much of its support base from the Sunni urban trading and artisan classes, who were generally religiously oriented, although it also attracted middle-class professionals. These groups found in the Ikhwan a way to express their dissatisfaction with the status quo and a means of challenging the authority of the established elites.

Yet at no point did al-Sibai advocate taking up arms against the Syrian state; rather he sought change through social reform. However, his bid to bring about change was cut short in 1957 when a debilitating stroke left him largely incapacitated. He handed leadership of the Ikhwan to Issam al-Attar, who for the few short years of his stewardship of the movement represented perhaps the last voice of the old-style Syrian Ikhwan before it evolved into a more militant organisation.

Al-Attar, who is from Damascus, started his Islamic activism at the age of eleven when he was first introduced to the Shabab Mohamed. He came from what he describes as 'one of the oldest religious scientific families'[4] and his father was a civil and Sharia judge. When the Shabab Mohamed changed its name to the Muslim Brotherhood al-Attar continued to work with them, although he admits that his contact with them at that time was not especially strong because he was 'open to all currents of thought in order to discover the true path'.[5] However, in 1946 he became a member of the Ikhwan and soon gained a reputation for being extremely well read and intellectually gifted. He was clearly of a similar mould to al-Sibai and sought to take the movement down the same moderate path as its founder.

However, al-Attar took over the Ikhwan at a time of change; the tolerance that the state had displayed towards the Brotherhood until that time was about to come to an end. In 1958 Syria and Egypt joined forces to form the United Arab Republic. As with the Ikhwan in Egypt, the Syrians initially welcomed Nasser, viewing him as a hero of Arab nationalism and anti-colonialism. Although al-Attar was personally troubled by Nasser's secular stance, at the beginning of the union most of the Ikhwani leaders in Syria were pro-Nasser.[6] However, it wasn't long before the Syrian Ikhwan was facing the same uncompromising repression that Nasser had imposed upon the Egyptian Ikhwan. The Brotherhood was obliged to dissolve itself and the Syrian regime set up special militias tasked with rooting out members of the movement.[7] By the time the ill-fated union dissolved in 1961 the Brotherhood had been greatly weakened.

Surprisingly, the brutal oppression that the Ikhwan experienced at the hand of the state during the Egyptian-Syrian union did not herald a new radicalism within the movement. Instead, once the union was disbanded, the Brotherhood immediately sought to re-establish itself as a player on the country's political stage and continued in its path of moderation. The Ikhwan contested the 1961 parliamentary elections, winning ten seats, one of which was taken by al-Attar himself. The Ikhwan was also given four ministries at this time. Therefore, the Syrian Ikhwan's oft-repeated assertion that militancy within the movement has always been a response to repression – something it uses to explain the bloody events of the 1970s and 1980s – would appear to be somewhat misplaced. As this period demonstrates, there were clearly other factors at play that contributed to the later shift into armed violence.

Leadership Crisis

The coming to power of the Ba'athist regime in 1963 heralded the start of an even more difficult period for the Syrian Ikhwan and for Issam al-Attar in particular. Questions began to be asked of the leadership by members of the Ikhwan about how a movement as small and unknown as the Ba'athists had been able to attain power, whilst they were as far away from ruling as ever. As the late Mohamed Hasnawi, who until his death in 2007 had a leading role in the Syrian Ikhwan, explained, at this time 'self-criticism started spreading as to how the Ba'athists had managed to take power whilst we the stronger group couldn't manage it. All that criticism was channelled towards Issam al-Attar because he was the guide.'[8] Al-Attar came under intense scrutiny and pressure from within the ranks of his organisation.

However, the situation was to get even worse for both the Ikhwan and its leader. In 1964 al-Attar, who had gone on a trip to Saudi Arabia for the Haj and to attend a conference of the Arab Ikhwan, was prevented from returning to Syria by the authorities. The reason was that one part of the Ikhwan in Hamah, led by Marwan Hadid, had clashed with the authorities in a violent struggle that ended in the siege of the Sultan mosque (see below). As al-Attar said, 'Marwan was considered to be Ikhwani by the regime at that time and because I was the leader of the Ikhwan they put my name on the list at every entry point.'[9]

Al-Attar, who claims that he had no knowledge of Hadid's actions and only learned about them through the media, found himself stuck in Lebanon where he spent two months in prison before being deported. Unwilling to compromise his independence, he was confused about where to go. 'I didn't want to be used by Saudi Arabia or the Gulf states. King Faisal was willing to welcome me but I didn't want my current to be in the service of anyone else.'[10] After a brief stay in Kuwait and several spells in Jordan, in 1967 al-Attar went to Geneva and then to Belgium, but was ultimately to settle in Aachen in Germany.

Al-Attar's absence at such a crucial time came as a real blow to the Ikhwani. Whilst they blamed the regime for not allowing him back into the country, they were also frustrated at al-Attar himself for going to Saudi Arabia in the first place. According to Hasnawi, there was much disappointment that al-Attar had travelled outside of Syria without seeking proper permission from the rest of the group and that he had left them without a leader who could guide them as they readjusted to the realities of the new regime. There was a strong feeling that he had left them in the lurch, something that was only compounded when he was prohibited from returning.

Al-Attar was all too well aware of the problem of trying to lead a movement from exile. 'When they stopped me from returning to Syria I suggested I should give up the role of Syrian Guide but I was forced to continue. The Syrians insisted that I stay as their General Guide. When I came to Europe I raised the issue of resignation again. The issue of my still being General Guide became so pressing when I came to Europe.'[11] Al-Attar's being forced into exile at such a critical moment in Syria's political history would have far-reaching implications.

His banishment marked the beginning of a long period of absentee leadership that would have disastrous consequences for the movement as a whole.

The immediate impact of al-Attar's banishment was to create a vacuum inside the movement that not only led to a leadership crisis but also enabled more militant elements within the group to flourish. As he explained, 'At that time in Syria there were new currents that had emerged. There were people with different views from me and I was far from the country and I was ill.'[12] Other figures inside the Ikhwan inevitably came to play a bigger role and in the absence of a strong leadership the divisions that were already present between the Aleppo and Damascus wings came to the fore.

Broadly speaking, the Damascus group that was led by al-Attar was quite small and consisted mostly of those from the capital and included figures such as Muwafaq Da'bul, Dr Mohamed al-Hawari (who now resides in Germany) and Dr Hassan al-Huwaidi. It also had some followers from outside of the city. The Aleppo wing on the other hand comprised not only those Ikhwani from the ancient city of Aleppo itself, but also those from other northern cities including Hamah and Homs. It was led by Sheikh Abdul Fattah Abu Ghuddah and also included Sheikh Said Hawa and Adnan Saad Eddine. The Aleppo wing was always bigger than al-Attar's Damascus group, largely because there were other Islamist groups active in the capital such as the Sufists and Salafists that competed with the Ikhwan there. Moreover, Aleppo was always a conservative city with a strong religious tradition, making its inhabitants more perceptible to the ideology of the Brotherhood.

However, this split was not just geographical, it was also ideological. The Aleppo wing, who had a reputation for being tougher and more inclined to action than their brothers in the capital, began to advocate the idea of fighting jihad against the Ba'athist regime. This was rejected by the Damascus wing, who opposed the use of violence on the grounds that it would only bring retribution and destroy the movement. Of course these distinctions were not as clear-cut as is often suggested. As Mohamed Hasnawi explained, 'Generally speaking the Aleppo wing was more into armed struggle but there was interaction and it was mixed too.'[13] Moreover, it is true that much of the rivalry between the two wings concerned administrative issues and turf battles as much as ideological principles. However, it is fair to say that it was out of the Aleppo wing that the push for violence first emerged.

As tensions with the Ba'athist regime grew, the Aleppo wing became increasingly frustrated at the more moderate and passive stance of the Damascus wing. By the end of the 1960s they were using al-Attar's exile as an excuse to demand a change of leadership and a change of strategy. At a meeting in 1969 the Aleppo wing, aware of its numerical superiority, demanded al-Attar's replacement. However, feelings were running so high on both sides that the two wings could not come to an agreement. In 1970 the Murshid in Cairo was forced to step in and set up a special committee to organise an election for a new *shura* council. Al-Attar's faction boycotted the elections, refusing to accept anyone other than al-Attar as the General Guide.[14] Although the question of who should be the next General Guide was not resolved until 1975 when Adnan Saad Eddine took over, the election marked the formal domination of the Aleppo wing, which had been accepted by the Guidance Office in Cairo. This was to mark the real demise of al-Attar and his Damascus wing that became increasingly marginalised. Al-Attar himself became so disillusioned that he turned his back on the Brotherhood, establishing his own organisation in Europe called al-Talia (the Vanguard). He engaged in this project after a fraught meeting in Lebanon with a delegation from the Egyptian Ikhwan led by Ahmed al-Malat, a known hardliner and member of the Nizam al-Khass.[15]

As such, the history of the Syrian Ikhwan from the late 1960s until the events of Hamah in the early 1980s was essentially that of the Aleppo wing. This wing's hold over the Ikhwan would radically alter the character of the movement that al-Sibai had established and it distinguished the Syrian Ikhwan as the only Brotherhood branch that dared to move from the *dawa* phase to the jihad phase in the struggle to create an Islamic state.

The Slide into Violence

Whilst the Aleppo wing was the driving force for the militarisation of the Ikhwan's struggle against the regime, it was not the starting point of violent activism. The push for a more militant approach came predominantly from those Ikhwani from Hamah who made up one component of the Aleppo wing. According to Hasnawi, the shift into support for a more violent approach came from the fact that 'the Hamah branch, which was known historically for force and rigidity and toughness, joined them [the Aleppo wing] and also because of the presence of Said Hawa and Adnan Saad Eddine. They were from Hamah but part of the Aleppo wing.'[15]

Hamah already had a tradition of conservatism and militant Islamist activism, which had first emerged in the early 1960s. Much of this activism was focused around the Sultan mosque that was the base of the famous Hamah scholar Sheikh Mohamed al-Hamid. Known for his rigidity and uncompromising stance, he had left the Ikhwan on account of Mustafa al-Sibai's moderate and flexible stance but remained close to the movement. As Syrian Ikhwan Said Hawa observed:

> He educated his brothers to love Hassan al-Banna, to love the Muslim Brothers, and to love all the Muslims ... He believed that in order to stop the apostasy the Muslims must join hands despite their many controversies. And although he was

a Hanafi Sufi, he had always declared his readiness to put his hand in the hand of the fiercest Salafi to stop this apostasy.[16]

Al-Hamid was an ardent anti-secularist and anti-nationalist and his ideas had a strong following among Hamah residents who had a reputation for being closed and introverted.

The citizens of Hamah were particularly agitated by the policies of the new Ba'athist regime. They reacted extremely negatively to the influx of newcomers from the countryside that flooded into urban centres during the 1960s. Furthermore, the fact that the new Ba'athist regime was Alawite created particular resentments. There had been a long-standing feud between a number of Alawite peasants who worked the land belonging to rich Hamah landowners who had been officers in the Ottoman army. The coming to power of the Alawites only served to exacerbate existing tensions in the area. Therefore it is not surprising that it was out of the Hamah branch of the Ikhwan that support for a more radical alternative emerged.

However, this more radical approach was not confined to Hamah. The 1960s and 1970s had seen a progressive radicalisation of the Syrian Ikhwan that was in line with the increased radicalism of other Ikhwani branches at the time, inspired by the Islamic revivalist current that was taking hold across the Arab world. It was also a reflection of the fact that some of the Ikhwani who had spent time in the Gulf came under the influence of a more inflexible interpretation of Islam that they then spread among their fellow Ikhwani upon their return to Syria.[17]

This radicalisation was also a response to the policies of the Ba'athist regime, which were upsetting traditional structures and patterns and threatening certain interest groups. Growing political and cultural disaffection within Syria during the 1960s and 1970s brought the Ikhwan increased popular support, as it sought to articulate the forces of conservative Islam and to represent those parts of society that were most affected by the regime's policies of nationalisation and centralisation. These included the professional classes and traders – the Ikhwan's natural constituency – who were adversely affected by the rise of agricultural co-operatives in rural areas and consumer co-operatives in urban areas.[18] The regime's large-scale land reform and wealth redistribution projects were considered a threat to the very way of life of this class. Urban traders, well known for their conservatism and religiosity, were also perturbed by the flow of migrants coming into the cities from rural areas and upsetting the traditional social balance. Slogans such as 'Aleppo for the Aleppans' began to appear in the cities, reflecting this malaise. The Ikhwan was quick to capitalise on this disaffection: as one commentator has described, by the 1960s the Brotherhood had become 'the most implacable opponents of the Ba'athis and the forward arm of the endangered urban traders'.[19] As such it became the staunch defender of the urban middle class against the encroaching rural population. It is perhaps no surprise that many Ikhwani who went on to take up arms against the regime came from traditional conservative urban families.

The Ikhwan also tapped into growing feelings of resentment related to the Alawite nature of the Ba'athist regime. For many Sunnis, the fact that the new regime was dominated by Alawites who represented a minority in a country with a Sunni majority was too much to take. Even the moderate al-Attar commented when the Ba'athists came to power: 'I saw the sectarian face of that movement'.[20] The Ikhwan was therefore able to play on the sectarian dimension of the country's political landscape to further discredit the regime and to justify taking a more militant stance against it.

Of course not all the Syrian Ikhwani subscribed to this more militant approach; those in the Damascus wing continued to advocate restraint. Yet their voices were increasingly ignored as the more radical current surged ahead and stamped its mark on the movement. As one Syrian Ikhwani noted, 'This radical *jihadiya* in the Ikhwan wanted to assassinate the approach of al-Sibai. We were studying "Milestones on the Road" at that time rather than "Preachers not Judges".[21] The desire to 'assassinate' al-Sibai's teachings was such that his book *Islamic Socialism* was banned within the movement in the 1960s as it was considered too liberal. At this time, young Ikhwani also began reading other radical thinkers including Abu Ala Maududi, Abu Hassan al-Nadwi and Ibn Taymiyyah. Clearly the movement had completely shifted in nature from the early days of al-Sibai to take on a new uncompromising rigidity. One indication of this is that whereas the Ikhwani scouts of the 1940s and 1950s used to play drums and sing songs, by the 1970s the brothers were writing books recommending that tambourines be banned for being un-Islamic.[22]

The Syrian Ikhwan also began to produce more militant scholars, the most important being Said Hawa, who was to become one of the most respected jihadist scholars of his generation. Hawa, who came from Hamah and joined the Brotherhood in the 1950s, came to advocate the idea that Muslims were once again in the time of *Riddah* (apostasy); they had abandoned Islam and this dangerous situation must be countered. His stance centred around the quest for purity in internal and public life and he taught his followers that they should distance themselves from the impure *kafir* (heathen) world and refrain from listening to the radio or watching television, going to the theatre, reading newspapers or magazines, or engaging in the study of any philosophy, literature or ethics.[23] He also advocated jihad against those he considered to be impure: Shi'ites and Sufists, not to mention communists, nationalists, Nasserists, leftists and liberals. Hawa's book *Soldiers of Allah: Culture and Manners*, which called for jihad against the regime, was distributed in its thousands in bookshops, street stalls and mosques and became a major point of discussion for all Syrian Ikhwanis.

Hawa was extremely frustrated by what he described as the reactionary stance of the Ikhwan's traditional leadership. After he returned from a stint in Saudi Arabia in the 1970s he called upon the Syrian Ikhwan to restructure itself so that it could move away from being a party of *dawa* to one of jihad. Hawa was a charismatic figure who, because of his scholarly achievements, had more influence than other leading figures within the Ikhwan. As such his call to turn the Brotherhood into a jihadist party that could lead a rebellion against the Ba'athist regime could not be ignored. His comments provoked a major internal debate within the Syrian Ikhwan and exacerbated the factionalism that was already present. Whilst the traditional leaders were calling on the Brotherhood to work behind the scenes and to focus their efforts on *dawa*, Hawa instigated his followers to prepare for military action. He allegedly involved his young followers in physical training including wrestling, boxing and street fighting, and he divided those who followed him into family units and fighting brigades.[24] By this point, the traditional Ikhwani ideas of the Damascus wing were clearly completely out of tune not only with the Ikhwan in Hamah but with the movement more widely.

The Fighting Vanguard

As this more radical mentality permeated the movement, some elements began to take matters into their own hands and to carry out targeted attacks and assassinations. The 1970s saw an escalation of violent incidents against the regime, which the authorities blamed on the Ikhwan. The most important group that became engaged in violent jihad at the time had its roots in the Ikhwan. This was the al-Tali'a al-Muqatila (Fighting Vanguard), established by the Hamah resident Marwan Hadid whose armed exploits against the regime dated back to the early 1960s. Hadid, who came from a relatively prosperous family of cotton farmers, had grown up in the circles of the Muslim Brotherhood, where he had come under the charge of Adnan Saad Eddine during his time at secondary school. As a young man, Hadid was awarded a small loan from the Brotherhood in Hamah to complete his studies in agricultural engineering in Egypt and whilst he was there he befriended Sayyid Qutb. Hadid was so smitten with Qutb's more militant approach that upon his return to Syria in the early 1960s he became one of the most prominent proponents of the Egyptian's radical rejectionist ideology. As Adnan Saad Eddine explained, 'When he looked at the Syrian regime he decided to divorce life and to go down the path of martyrdom and martyrs.'[25]

Hadid's more revolutionary ideas resonated with the younger generation in Hamah and he soon developed his own group of followers, many of whom were still in secondary school. In 1964 this group came into direct conflict with the new Ba'athist state during a stand-off with the security services that resulted in Hadid and his followers taking refuge in the Sultan mosque.[26] The new Ba'athist regime responded by attacking the mosque with tanks and artillery, bringing the sixty-foot minaret crashing to the ground and leaving 115 dead.[27] Hadid and those of his companions who survived the assault were arrested and sentenced to death. However, Hadid was later released after an intervention by Mohamed al-Hamid, who pleaded his case with President Amin al-Hafez.

This experience did not deter the young Hadid, who after his release took to walking the streets wearing only a white jelaba, as if trying to create an iconic image of himself as a humble and devout man. Hardened by his prison experience, Hadid's resolve to bring down the Ba'athist regime was stronger than ever. Yet where in earlier years he had appeared like a reckless hothead, his agenda was now in line with the increasingly radical mood of the time and he had no problem in drawing recruits. He set up the Fighting Vanguard, sending its members for military training in Palestinian Fateh camps in the Jordan Valley, and by the mid-1970s this underground group was carrying out targeted assassinations of figures within the Syrian regime. However, Hadid was tracked down and arrested in 1976 and died in prison following a hunger strike and sustained torture.

Although the Fighting Vanguard was clearly Hadid's personal creation, the exact nature of its relationship to the Ikhwan remains deeply contentious. The Ikhwani maintain that at the time they had no control over Hadid's actions and that they did not even know who was perpetrating the attacks. According to Adnan Saad Eddine in 1975:

> People started wondering who was committing these killings. We were surprised but we were also embarrassed by it. One day we had a meeting of the Hamah administration in the house of Brother R ... It was almost midnight when there was a knock at the door by a brother sent by another brother who said that an assassination attack had taken place in Damascus of a very important person.[28]

Similarly, Ali Saddredine al-Bayanouni, who had been arrested in 1973, noted, 'At that time whilst we were in prison, I had no idea who was behind these attacks. When I left prison in 1977 I found that no one knew who was behind them.'[29] As such the Ikhwan asserts that Hadid was not acting in its name but only in the name of his own group.

It certainly appears that the Ikhwan's leadership had endeavoured to contain Hadid and to dissuade him from such reckless action. According to Obeida Nahas, a Syrian brother based in the UK, in 1968 the Ikhwan leadership warned the grass roots that they should not follow Hadid.[30] Similarly, al-Bayanouni has stated:

> Yes Sheikh Marwan was from the Ikhwan. He was of the opinion that a regime that took over by force can only be removed by force. This was contrary to the approach of the Jama'a. Therefore the Jama'a didn't respond to his way of thinking and we resisted him through several dialogues. We had continuous dialogue with Sheikh Marwan in Hamah especially.[31]

Much of this bid to contain Hadid was driven by a fear that his actions, which had already resulted in Issam al-Attar being banned from the country, would bring further trouble for the movement. It seems that in typical Ikhwani style it wasn't so much the fact that Hadid was prepared to use violence that bothered the leadership, but rather that he was doing so in an unprepared and reckless manner.

Al-Bayanouni has also asserted that because they were unable to convince Hadid to change his stance, the leadership expelled him from the Brotherhood.[32] He has also stated that the leadership expelled other elements: 'Some groups affiliated to Marwan Hadid adopted that name [Fighting Vanguard], but when the Brotherhood found out about their association, it expelled them from the party and cancelled their membership.'[33] Yet in direct contradiction to these assertions, Adnan Saad Eddine, who was particularly close to Hadid and who was General Guide at the time, has explained the relationship somewhat differently. 'Marwan and his like set up an extreme wing of the Ikhwan. He stayed in the Ikhwan and he didn't leave it. We never kicked him out. But he had a wing that behaved the way it saw fit – it had nothing to do with the leadership.'[34] Furthermore, regardless of what they thought about his approach, the Ikhwan was willing to provide Hadid with financial support to enable him to continue his jihad. Adnan Saad Eddine explains:

> From his hideout he sent someone to me asking for support.
> I sent him two brothers ... They met with him and told him
> what I thought of him and that I believed his programme
> would not bear any fruit and that it would be harmful to him
> and others. However, they told him that if he wanted financial
> support to cover his expenses we would give it to him.[35]

Moreover, the Ikhwan maintained links to the Fighting Vanguard right up until the Hamah events through Riyath Jamour, who was the secret link between the two groups and whose confession under torture led the regime to engage in a number of arrests of the Brotherhood.

Some of this ambiguity may be attributed to the fact that the Syrian Ikhwani have always had a contradictory relationship to Hadid. They have rejected his reckless approach but he has also commanded great respect on account of the heroism of his struggle. Hadid went beyond the Brotherhood, capturing the imagination of many Syrians, and when his death was announced there were large demonstrations in several cities. As such, there is still a great reverence for him inside the Ikhwan. Hasnawi, for example, referred to him as the movement's 'first mujahid'.[36] In spite of the Syrian Ikhwan's revisionist approach to its own history, it is difficult for it to completely dismiss or disown a figure such as Hadid who was viewed as a martyr and who arguably had more popular support than any of the leadership could ever have commanded. However, the current desperation of the leadership to whitewash their past and to prove that they have moved on has prompted them to do their utmost to distance themselves from Hadid and to play down the ties that were clearly present between them and the Fighting Vanguard.

Crisis Point

Hadid's death was to have the opposite effect of that intended by the Ba'athist authorities, as it acted as a catalyst for further violence. The Fighting Vanguard was taken over by Dr Abdel Sattar al-Zaim, a dentist son of a tradesman who was 'even better than his Sheikh [Hadid]',[37] and the assassinations and attacks continued. The best known attack, led by Adnan Aqla, was the 1979 assault on the Aleppo Artillery School, which left eighty-three Alawite cadets dead and scores of others wounded. This attack escalated tensions between the Ikhwan and the regime as the authorities blamed the Brotherhood and embarked upon a widespread campaign to root out and arrest its members. It also precipitated the executions of a number of Ikhwani who were already being held in prison. The regime launched a propaganda campaign and began publishing articles glorifying 'unorthodox' movements in Islamic history that had fought against the Sunnis.[38] Such moves were felt deeply by the conservative religious Sunni population as a whole and not just the Brotherhood. Clearly the Ikhwan was at crisis point.

By now, however, the Syrian Ikhwan had become like a headless body; it had no leadership that could direct the movement, let alone rein it in. This was because by this point much of the leadership had travelled abroad leaving the rank and file without proper control or direction. As Adnan Saad Eddine explains, 'By then there was no member of the leadership there to guide the Jama'a. Some were in prison, some had left Syria, some had disappeared. We were in Paris attending an Islamic conference ... whilst we were there someone came and told us of the news of the arrests.'[39] As the jihadist current had taken root and the state intensified its clampdown on the movement, many key figures within the Syrian Ikhwan simply left the country. Syrian thinker Mohamed Jamal Barot has argued that after they had realised that they could not put the genie back into the bottle without breaking the bottle itself, the leadership fled before the adventure became too strong for them to stomach.[40]

This absence had a major impact on the Ikhwan's evolution: many of the younger more militant elements, left without any clear guidance, simply took events into their own hands and the whole movement started to unravel. Adnan Saad Eddine explained: 'We fragmented. The leadership left. Everyone started behaving the way they wanted.'[41] Similarly Hasnawi has remarked: 'The leadership of Aleppo left for Saudi Arabia and because of the persecution of the state, we the young people took the leadership position. That gave momentum to the violence.'[42] These younger cadres deeply resented the fact that their leaders had left them at a time of crisis and this prompted further recriminations. Adnan Saad Eddine observed: 'Dislike developed between the brothers in Syria and those in Arab or foreign countries. The brothers inside accused them of leaving their duty behind and of fleeing the al-dawa field. The brothers outside accused those inside of not thinking properly and of being a bit reckless.'[43] The already divided movement fractured further. Hasnawi also explained:

> Sheikh Abu Ghuddah was outside, even Hassan al-Huwaidi was outside, as were Abdel Kanan and Abdelrahman Qura Hamoud. All of these historical leaders were outside. We understand why they left but not fully. As a result there were differences in experience and age. We were in crisis ... Because the leadership wasn't there our secret work wasn't linked up. We were separate groups and not one *tanzeem* as such.[44]

Although Adnan Saad Eddine was clear that 'any unequal battle with the very hated regime'[45] would be disastrous for the Ikhwan, he was clearly in no position to do anything about the increasing violence from outside the country. He did engage in vain attempts to bring the more militant elements under his control but these were largely futile. He was often the last to know about what was going on inside his own movement. He claims that in the mid-1970s he was shocked to discover that some Ikhwani groups were stockpiling weapons and tried to dissuade them. He has also asserted that whilst he was abroad the Ikhwan's Shura Council took the decision to engage in weapons training, something he asserts was reversed after he found out about it and threatened to resign.[46] By this point the jihadist current had developed its own momentum and such moves were too little, too late. The Ikhwan's weak and fragmented leadership could do little but sit back and watch events unfold.

And unfold they did. By the early 1980s it appeared as though Syria was on the brink of a popular revolution. Spurred on in part by events in Iran the year before, in March 1980 there were massive demonstrations and protests against the regime after it dissolved the unions that called for an end to oppression and they were backed by the Brotherhood. A general strike was also called in Aleppo, and it soon spread to Hamah, Idlib and other major towns. Posters began appearing in cities such as Aleppo demanding a commitment to Sharia law in all legislation and an end to the state of emergency in Syria.[47] In June 1980 there was an assassination attempt on President al-Assad and in retaliation the authorities carried out a massacre in the Tadmur prison, where many Ikhwani were being held, killing between 600 and 1,100 prisoners in their cells. The authorities also introduced Law No. 49 which made membership of the Brotherhood punishable by death.

It was at this time, when the whole country was like a powder keg waiting to go up, that the Ikhwan's leadership finally decided to act. Once it looked as though the regime was about to be toppled and a popular revolution might be a reality, the ever-opportunist Ikhwan did its utmost to capitalise on the situation and to ensure that it would be there to reap the spoils should such an outcome ensue. The Ikhwani jumped to take control of the Islamist current and in August 1980 the leadership issued a letter calling upon all Syrian mujahideen to close ranks with the Brotherhood under the auspices of a broader, non-partisan leadership.[48] They also established the Islamic Front in Syria, a gathering of Islamist groups of differing persuasions led by the Ikhwan. The most prominent figures in the front included al-Bayanouni, his brother Abu Naser al-Bayanouni and Said Hawa.

In October the front issued a proclamation that read like a political manifesto, laying out its position on a range of political, social and economic issues. The first proclamation, written by Adnan Saad Eddine, was reportedly endorsed by all the branches of the Brotherhood outside of Syria. Its programme was liberal and spoke directly to the interests of the urban Sunni civil trading and manufacturing class, who still felt that their status and wealth were being squeezed by the socialist policies of the state. It also sought to touch a chord by playing on the sectarian divide, positing the Ikhwani as the main representatives and defenders of the Sunni population against their Alawite rulers. 'Nine or ten percent of the population cannot dominate the majority in Syria ... The Alawi minority has forgotten itself and is ignoring the facts of history.'[49]

At this time the Syrian Ikhwani united even further. After years of acrimony, the various factions of the movement came together in a show of unity not seen since the 1960s. A new leadership was elected that was represented on the Damascus side by Hassan al-Huwaidi, who was elected as the new General Guide, Muhammad al-Huwari, Abu Nizar and Osama Dandelle and on the Aleppo side by Said Hawa, Adnan Saad Eddine, Ali Saddredine al-Bayanouni and Mohamed Said. Also involved were the Fighting Vanguard who were represented by Adnan Aqla, Adel Fares and two others.[50] As Obeida Nahas has explained, 'At that time all the Ikhwani were in the same shoes and they joined forces with the Fighting Vanguard.'[51] He also asserted that at the height of the violence, 'It came to a point where one couldn't draw a line between the two factions.'[52] Although Adnan Aqla would split again from the Ikhwan just a few months later, the willingness of the other currents to strike such a union at this time suggests that they were more than prepared to accept the more radical ideology in order to see their dream of establishing an Islamic state come true. The same year the Ikhwan also held a meeting in Amman and decided that it would join the armed struggle. Hasnawi has said: 'because of people's demands and pressure and all the arrests we decided we had no choice other than to declare resistance'.[53]

The willingness of the Damascus wing to join with the Vanguard was particularly surprising given their more moderate stance and their earlier refusal to adopt the jihadist path. Yet once it looked as though revolution was possible, even they were quick to take part. Mohamed Hasnawi explained:

When the events of Hamah took place the Aleppo group were more engaged in the events but the battle brought all the Islamists together including the Damascenes. They took part in it and they have martyrs and people who were arrested. At the peak of the conflict the two wings unified and we became one group and the General Guide was Hassan al-Huwaidi who was from the Damascus wing.[54]

According to some sources even Issam al-Attar came back into the fold temporarily from his exile in Germany.[55] However, he had withdrawn again by March 1982.

The readiness of the Damascus group to come on board can be explained by the fact that although they were perceptibly more moderate than their Aleppan counterparts, they had never been opposed to the principle of violence. In traditional Ikhwani fashion, they simply believed that violence should only be used when the time was right. As Barot has explained, 'They didn't refuse the principle of violent jihad strategically, but they sought to put the brakes on it tactically and temporarily. It was the growth of the jihadist currents among the young of al-Jama'a and their initiative to act that took the old al-Jama'a [the Damascus wing] ... into the suicidal jihadist venture.'[56] Therefore once it appeared that the more militant elements were gaining ground, the Damascus wing proved just as anxious to be part of the action as the more militant elements.

However, this new show of unity was to prove short lived, as once again events overtook the Ikhwan. By February 1982 things had become so tense that a populist uprising broke out in the city of Hamah. This uprising became a large popular insurrection. Many Ba'athists were attacked in their homes and killed and people began looting and burning, giving vent to their frustrations. The governor of Hamah, Mohamed Khalid Harbah, claimed afterwards that he had been woken up by the 'sounds of the mosques' loudspeakers instigating people to fight'.[57] The regime responded harshly, sending around 12,000 troops to the city, sealing it off and then pummelling it with heavy artillery, tanks and helicopter gunships. The whole city was razed to the ground. According to Amnesty International the number of citizens killed in this assault ranged between 10,000 to 25,000.[58]

Clearly the uprising in Hamah went far beyond the Muslim Brotherhood and represented a much wider general dissatisfaction with the ruling regime. However, it is obvious that when the time came the Ikhwani were willing to support the use of violence in order to achieve change. The Hamah events also demonstrated how far the Ikhwan had misjudged the situation. Carried away with their own sense of importance, the brothers clearly believed that they had the power to take the street with them and that the population would rise up behind them.

Yet with the passing of time, the Syrian Ikhwan has sought to rewrite its own history in relation to the Hamah crisis and has done its utmost to distance itself from the bloody events. Ali Saddredine al-Bayanouni has categorically stated that the Ikhwan was not responsible for the violence of that era:

> I was the deputy leader at that time and I can tell you that the Syrian Muslim Brotherhood had no involvement in violent events whatsoever. Two influential people in particular reacted to Ba'athist repression in a violent manner; Adnan Aqla, who was dismissed from the Muslim Brotherhood five years before the outbreak of full-scale violence, and Ibrahim el-Youssef, who was an officer in the Syrian army and a Ba'athist with no relations to the Muslim Brotherhood whatsoever.[59]

Al-Bayanouni's reference to Aqla is rather confusing given that he himself stated in an interview with Al-Jazeera that he had come together with Aqla and others from the Fighting Vanguard in the early 1980s.[60]

Moreover, it is clear that despite condemning the use of violence, the Ikhwan ultimately supported the uprising. As Hassan al-Huwaidi explained, 'Enthusiasm overshadowed reason and the reins of power had disappeared.'[61] Having unleashed the beast with their ill-sighted absences and weak leadership, the Ikhwan simply went with the flow when it seemed as though it had the chance to take power.

Blame Game

The events in Hamah would almost completely crush the Syrian Ikhwan. Those who managed to escape death or arrest fled the country and have remained in exile ever since. Some went to Iraq, where they sought protection from Saddam Hussein's Ba'athist regime. They still held the vain hope that they could continue the struggle from the neighbouring country, where they set up training camps. However, they soon realised the impossibility of such a task. As Adnan Saad Eddine, who fled to Iraq, explained: 'We formed groups to train and go to Syria ... We weren't able to achieve anything ... We had a camp but we realised we were wasting our time. Even the Iraqi regime wasn't really very keen.'[62] Others settled in Jordan, which became the main centre of the Syrian Ikhwan abroad.

From its imposed exile, the Syrian Ikhwan had little to do other than reflect on the actions that had resulted in its own destruction. Unsurprisingly, the divisions soon resurfaced and there was much recrimination over who had been responsible for taking the Ikhwan down such a disastrous path. Adnan Saad Eddine describes it thus:

Hamah was like an earthquake for the Muslim Brotherhood. The differences among us surfaced and some of us started looking for scapegoats and a lot of people published memoirs about what happened. We thought that we should evaluate what went wrong. We all supported that idea. The brothers in the leadership agreed to nominate some people but when someone was appointed to head the committee, others protested. This evaluation continued for twelve years.[63]

The attempt to engage in an internal assessment of what had happened proved to be as contentious as other parts of the Ikhwan's history. They did succeed in producing an evaluation report. Yet this document remains a closely guarded secret and attempts to procure a copy are met with the answer that it is an internal document that is not for public consumption.[64] According to some accounts, only forty brothers were permitted to see a copy and it was completely withheld from the organisation's grass roots.[65]

Although not in the public domain, it appears that the thrust of this evaluation was to lay the blame for the Hamah events on certain individuals. The main casualty of this process was Adnan Saad Eddine – who himself struggled to get his hands on a copy of the report. As General Guide during the second half of the 1970s, he was blamed for the slide into violence despite the fact that by 1980 his role had been taken over by Hassan al-Huwaidi. Indeed, Adnan Saad Eddine appears to have become a convenient scapegoat for the whole of the movement's going astray.

In response to these accusations Adnan Saad Eddine wrote a book outlining his own version of events and refuting some of the accusations made in the evaluation report. *Mesirat Jama'at al-Ikhwan al-Muslimeen fi Suria* (*The Journey of the Syrian Muslim Brotherhood*) offers a number of insights into this highly secretive part of the Ikhwan's history. According to the book, the evaluation report first blamed the shift to armed action on the 'emotional mobilisation' that had developed inside the Ikhwan because of its reliance on the ideology of Sayyid Qutb and the works of Said Hawa.[66] The report then accused Adnan Saad Eddine of having created in 1977 a special committee consisting of Ali Saddredinne al-Bayanouni, Abdullah Tantawi, Riyath Jamour, Adeeb Jaj and Mohamed Hasnawi to secretly co-ordinate with the Fighting Vanguard.[67] It also detailed how Abdel Sattar al-Zaim, who was leading the Fighting Vanguard at the time, had promised to develop his group within the Ikhwan's structures while the Ikhwan agreed to nominate its best jihadist elements to support his group and expand armed activity in order to establish active groups in all the country's governates. Adnan Saad Eddine fiercely refutes these allegations and insists that its only support to Abdel Sattar Zaim was to provide him with financial assistance. However, he asserts that the stance of the leadership was 'to support everyone without any distinction between members of the Vanguard and members of the Jama'a because the authorities were after all of us'.[68]

These allegations were extremely damning to Adnan Saad Eddine, not least because the Ikhwan expelled him from the movement on account of them. As such he has remained the main scapegoat for this period in the Syrian Ikhwan's history. Other figures who were clearly deeply involved at the time and who are still in key leadership positions within the Ikhwan, such as al-Bayanouni, still refuse to acknowledge that they played any part in the tragedy. It seems that the Ikhwan has dealt with Hamah by blaming a handful of individuals and explaining events as a response to state repression, as if this were sufficient to exonerate it of all responsibility.

A New Phase: Reform and the National Salvation Front

At the end of the 1990s the Syrian Ikhwan began another period of evolution that saw it come back full circle. In a bid to leave their past behind them the Syrian brothers once again took to advocating a more moderate approach that was far more in line with the spirit of Mustafa al-Sibai than Said Hawa. In many ways this more liberal stance represented a maturing of the Ikhwani leadership, most notably of al-Bayanouni, who took over as General Guide in 1996 and who had been residing in the UK since 2000 when he was forced out of Jordan under pressure from the Syrian regime. A lawyer by profession, al-Bayanouni's time in Europe seems to have mellowed him and he was the key driving force in this return to more moderate and progressive values.

Like their Egyptian counterparts, the Syrian Brotherhood began producing a number of reform platforms. In May 2001 they issued the National Honour Charter, a precursor to the Political Project of 2004 that outlined their future vision for Syria and which reads very much like a political manifesto. Crucially, this document is explicit in its condemnation of violence as a means to induce change. Of course, it asserts the importance of fighting jihad when Muslim lands are under occupation, yet it clearly rejects the idea of taking up arms against one's own government. There is a special section in the document dedicated to explaining away their own past. In line with their revisionist approach, the document states that after coming under pressure from the increasingly brutal policies of the state, 'our Group found itself caught up in a cycle of violence which it had no hand in creating or initiating'.[69]

As well as condemning violence, the document is littered with liberal notions such as tolerance, mutual co-existence, human rights and pluralism. It promotes the concept of the civil rather than the Islamic state, something that the Egyptian Ikhwan has also been keen to endorse in recent years. Of course, like the Egyptians they assert that this civil state will work within the framework of the Sharia. The opening lines read: 'Our future vision for our Arab homeland of Syria stems from its belonging to the Arab and Islamic dimensions and from our firm belief in Islam as a code whose texts and scriptures interact with the realities and emerging challenges of life, all within the general framework of the main objectives of Sharia.'[70] The document also lauds the ballot box as 'one of the practical means through which the objectives of Sharia and its general rules within the political system can be attained'.[71] It further states: 'We want Syria to be a country where all who live upon its lands enjoy life under the shade of the legislation of Allah Almighty, through the free and fair choosing of its people.'[72] However, the Syrian project is as ambiguous as the Egyptian one over exactly how this interaction between Sharia and democracy will pan out. Moreover, in spite of its promotion of civil democracy it also stipulates that the group would seek to 'Islamise the laws in a gradual manner, due to our belief that Sharia revealed by Allah is a source of mercy for all mankind and that it consists of the most humane, wise and prudent measures that are in the best interest of all people'.[73]

The document is also contradictory in its approach to minorities. On the one hand it is clear that it considers all citizens as equals and will not discriminate against non-Muslims. (Al-Bayanouni has been particularly keen to push this last point and at the meeting held in London in 2007 to discuss the Egyptian Ikhwan's reformist programme, the Syrian leader was highly critical of its stipulation that the President could not be a woman or a Copt. He also censured the Egyptian proposal for an elected council of clerics who would determine whether or not legal rulings conform to Sharia.) Yet at the same time it states unequivocally that Islam should be the basis of the state and of Syrian identity. Furthermore, it views Syria as a specifically Arab state, ignoring not only the country's Kurdish population but also other non-Arab minorities such as the Assyrians. Ironically, their talk of the *umma* notwithstanding, the Syrian Ikhwani have been unable it seems to free themselves from the Arab nationalism that was one of the driving ideologies behind the Ba'athist state. In addition, although it promotes freedom, the document displays the traditional Ikhwani concern with public morality and makes clear its desire to legislate for the private lives of its citizens. It bemoans the moral decline in Syrian society and determines to fight alcohol, drugs, gambling and prostitution. It also aspires to ensure that the media supports and publishes 'innocent entertainment'.[74]

Given the Brotherhood's role as a fundamentalist Islamist movement these principles can hardly be compromised on. But these issues aside, the document marks a major shift in the Syrian Ikhwan's ideology and is a complete departure from the ideas that held currency in the 1970s and early 1980s. Demonstrating just how far the Syrian Ikhwan shifted in its thinking, the document specifies a willingness to initiate a dialogue with European governments and with the government of the United States, as well as with the people of both regions. Even the arch reformers within the Egyptian Ikhwan were not willing to go this far. Undoubtedly, some of these proposals were written with a specifically Western audience in mind. Given the changed international climate since September 2001, the Syrian Ikhwan became more anxious than most to demonstrate to the outside world that there was no justification for labelling it as a terrorist organisation and that it could stand as a credible alternative to the Ba'athist regime.

Part of the reason that the Syrians were able to make such bold statements and play to a Western audience is that unlike the Egyptians, they did not have to think about their grass roots support base in the same way. Because the movement was more or less eliminated inside Syria following the events in Hamah, the Syrians had a much greater flexibility in their approach. Indeed, until the events of the Arab Spring, the Syrians did not have to trouble themselves too much about the need to play to a populist base that was counting on them to act as the defenders of Islam as was the case in Egypt. That is not to say that they weren't trying to reach out to the Syrian population, but they were well aware that as 'outsiders', exiled for so many years, their relevance inside the country was limited.

It is for this reason that the Syrian Ikhwan's main preoccupation since the late 1990s was how to negotiate a way to return home. Its whole attempt to reinvent itself as a moderate progressive organisation that had turned its back on the more questionable elements of its past, should be viewed within this context. The Ikhwan's hopes in this respect were heightened in 2000 when Bashar al-Assad succeeded his father as President. The young Bashar had been hailed as a reformer and the Brotherhood believed that he might consider opening up to the Brotherhood and other opposition currents. However, these hopes were soon dashed; in spite of an optimistic start, it was not long before Bashar proved himself to be almost as inflexible as his father. As al-Bayanouni himself noted, the Bashar regime 'cannot be reformed. We waited more than five years after this regime was established and said that if the President wished to carry out reform or has a reform programme, he would have started it. But after five years we have found that the state of affairs remained as it is and the situation was even deteriorating.'[75]

In the face of this disappointment, the Ikhwan continued to make desperate attempts to reach out to the regime. In the run-up to the war in Iraq, when the Ba'athist regime was coming under increasing international pressure, the brothers declared that they would defend the regime in the face of external aggression. This was clearly a tactical move aimed both at playing the populist card and at convincing the regime that it should allow them space inside the country because they were true nationalists at heart. Then in 2004 senior Syrian officials, including the President himself, met with leaders who had ties to the Brotherhood, which prompted Syrian parliamentarian Mohamed Habash to comment, 'The commonalities between the Islamic movements and [the] national movement are stronger than at any time before.'[76] Therefore despite its call for freedom and justice, the Brotherhood displayed a willingness to negotiate with the very authoritarian regime that had slaughtered thousands of its own supporters in order to get closer to achieving its objectives. The promotion of democracy clearly came second to securing a place at the table.

Ultimately, these attempts at negotiation failed, leaving the Ikhwan as isolated and as far away from the country as ever. So much so that in 2006 the leadership made an even more desperate and expedient move in its attempt to manoeuvre its way back into having some sort of relevance in the Syrian political context. In March 2006 the Brotherhood officially teamed up with former Syrian Vice President Abdul Halim Khaddam, who had defected from the regime in 2005, and the two formed a joint opposition platform called the National Salvation Front. The front was a collection of different opposition groups, including Kurdish and liberal groups, but it was driven by Khaddam and al-Bayanouni. This curious union provoked widespread surprise, given that Khaddam was considered to have been one of Hafez al-Assad's right-hand men throughout the period in which the Ikhwani suffered their most brutal oppression at the hands of the Syrian state. Questions were asked as to how the Ikhwan could stomach working alongside such a notorious figure, but Khaddam's offer proved an opportunity that was too good to miss.

Contact between these two unlikely partners was initiated by Khaddam after his defection. Al-Bayanouni was apparently unsure in the beginning as to how to respond to Khaddam's overtures. He told the *Financial Times* in January 2006 that the Ikhwan was willing to work for political transition in Syria with former regime officials who were prepared to commit themselves to democratic change.[77] However, two days later, during an interview with Al-Jazeera, he is alleged to have referred to Khaddam as 'a partner to the four-decade regime of corruption and despotism in Syria'.[78] There were also reports that al-Bayanouni had demanded that Khaddam apologise for the crimes committed by the Syrian regime against the Syrian people. Khaddam denies that any such request for an apology was made by the Brotherhood and asserts that in any case he has nothing at all to apologise for.[79] However, Obeida Nahas has confirmed that the Ikhwan did ask the former official to clarify some issues in relation to his past and that Khaddam explained that he was never involved in any torture or killing but accepted responsibility for being part of the Ba'athist regime.[80]

Such obstacles were clearly overcome and al-Bayanouni even seemed to be making excuses on behalf of Khaddam, declaring, 'Today his stance is one of regret, and he is very serious about democracy in Syria ... There is a death sentence against him. He is being chased now like they chased us. He does have some responsibility for what has happened in the past, but it is clear he has changed.'[81] Al-Bayanouni also stated: 'Mr Khaddam himself has relatives from among the Muslim Brotherhood whom he couldn't rescue from the grip of the Syrian regime.'[82] Other members of the Ikhwan were less forgiving. Mohamed Farouq Tayfour, for example, who in spite of being al-Bayanouni's Deputy at the time was a strong opponent of the 2004 reform initiative, declared that Khaddam was 'the last to talk about reform in Syria'.[83] Nonetheless, his name appeared on the list of the founding members of the National Salvation Front, as did Adnan Saad Eddine's.[84]

Predictably, the alliance was to prove relatively short lived: in April 2009 the Ikhwan pulled out of the front. The Ikhwan asserted that its withdrawal was due to a difference of opinion within the front over the offensive that Israel launched on the Gaza Strip in December 2008. The Syrian brothers had made a controversial declaration on 7 January 2009 in which they announced their decision 'to suspend activities against the Syrian regime to devote all efforts to the main battle' in Gaza.[85] This announcement taps into what was one of the Syrian Ikhwan's core problems prior to the Arab Spring, not only in its relations with the rest of the Brotherhood but also with its public image more widely – the very regime it was fighting against was hailed as heroic across the Islamic world for its unfailing support of Hamas. This means that the Syrian Ikhwan was never able to compete with the Ba'athist regime in Damascus over the issue of Palestine, an issue that has been the bread and butter of many other Ikhwani groups. The Syrians came under enormous pressure from other parts of the Ikhwan over this issue, which is dealt with in greater detail in Chapter Three, because of the fact that they opposed the al-Assad regime when others considered it to be the only true defender of the Palestinians and of Hamas throughout the region.[86] Their comments about supporting the efforts in Gaza were therefore a desperate attempt to try to demonstrate that they, too, were forthright defenders of the Palestinian cause.

Khaddam, meanwhile, who referred to the Ikhwan as a 'burden' on the front, suggested that the real reason why the Ikhwan left was because it had opened another dialogue with the Syrian regime.[87] Although such a dialogue has not been confirmed, al-Bayanouni told the Arab media, 'The issue is in the Syrian regime's court. The regime may use this overture to open channels of dialogue.'[88]

It would appear that, seeing a chance to move closer to the regime, the Ikhwani seized the opportunity to capitalise on the situation and had no qualms about walking away when it suited them. In any case, the alliance with Khaddam was always tactical, more a reflection of the weakness of both parties than any real shared ideological conviction. The front was set up at a time when the Syrian regime was under intense pressure from the Bush government and the Ikhwan was keen to demonstrate to the outside world that it was capable of working with other currents in the promotion of democracy.

More importantly, Khaddam failed to deliver what the Ikhwan was hoping for. Al-Bayanouni observed at the time of the front's establishment: 'It is important to form a coalition with Abdul Halim Khaddam because he has got powers inside the regime. These insider powers are ready to work and participate in the process of moving towards democracy in Syria.'[89] However, Khaddam's bid to win over other important parts of the Syrian regime, thus weakening the Ba'athist state, proved completely untenable. He was also unable to bring the support of Saudi Arabia, which would have given the front some real weight. Given all these issues, not to mention the usual in-fighting that goes with being an opposition in exile, the Ikhwan simply dropped its new allies when they were no longer useful.

Such political expediency inevitably raises questions about the Ikhwan's commitment to democracy. So much of the Syrian Ikhwan's history has been reactive rather than proactive that one is left wondering whether its reformist platforms are just another opportunistic move born out of the experience of exile rather than a genuine change of heart. Indeed, the Syrian Brotherhood has often appeared to be engaged in a politics of desperation that has seen it seize any opportunity that presents itself and that has caused it to oscillate from armed insurrection to appearing as the most progressive of Ikhwani branches.

These questions are all the more pertinent given the recent unfolding of events in Syria. The popular uprisings that erupted in March 2011 and the subsequent descent into civil war have opened up the possibility of a real future for the Ikhwan inside Syria. The movement has been quick to take advantage of the opportunity. Although, like its Egyptian counterpart, the Syrian Brotherhood was initially hesitant to give its support to the protests, once it became apparent that the demonstrations were going to endure, the Brotherhood gave them backing. Indeed, like the Egyptian Ikhwan, once they saw which way the wind was blowing, the Syrian brothers determined they had to join in if they wanted to secure a place for themselves in the country's future. Thus at the end of April 2011, the Syrian Brotherhood issued an official statement in support of the uprisings and went to on to play a major role in the Syrian National Council (SNC), an umbrella opposition front. Also in line with the Egyptian Brotherhood, in July 2012, the Syrian Ikhwan announced that it intended to establish a political party.

Given its history, the Syrian Brotherhood has been at particular pains since the start of its involvement in the opposition to demonstrate its moderate credentials. The movement has repeatedly stressed that it is not seeking to dominate the post-Assad political arena and that it is seeking an inclusive solution for Syria. As Mohamed Farouk

Tayfour, the Deputy of the movement declared, 'The Brotherhood will not monopolize power in the political arena and in managing the coming period ... They will be a part of the overall Syrian framework of rebuilding our country and healing the wounds of Assad family rule.'[90]

Such remonstrations are clearly reminiscent of the pledges made by the Egyptian Brotherhood when they entered the fray of the Egyptian revolution. However, once again, the Syrians went further than the Egyptians. In March 2012, the Syrian Brotherhood published a ten-point Pledge and Charter outlining its vision for the future. This document is overtly progressive in its outlook. Not only does it pledge that the movement will aspire to a modern civil state that is democratic and pluralistic and that operates on the principle of transition of power, it also advocates a state based upon, 'citizenship and equality, in which all citizens are equal regardless of their ethnicity, faith, school of thought, or [political] orientation.'[91] It aspires, too, to a state that upholds, 'freedom of thought and expression, freedom of religion and worship, freedom of the media, political partnership, equal opportunities, social justice, and the provision of basic needs for a dignified life. A citizen shall not be discriminated against due to his faith or [religious] practices, and shall not be restricted in his private or public life.'[92]

What is particularly notable about this document, however, is that unlike previous reform documents produced by the movement, it does not emphasise Syria's Islamic identity. Indeed, the references to Islam are limited to the preamble, which simply states that the charter is based upon the tenets of Islam. Even more surprising was that shortly after the charter was published, the Brotherhood's leader, Mohammed Riad al-Shaqfa, who succeeded Al-Bayanouni as General Guide in 2010, went as far as to declare in an interview with Dubai TV that the movement would have no objections to a Christian or a woman becoming President, so long as they were the people's choice.[93] Although Shaqfa can clearly make such pronouncements safe in the knowledge that neither a woman nor a Christian would have any chance of being voted to the post, his willingness to go that far clearly separates the Syrian Brotherhood from its Egyptian counterpart.

However, the Brotherhood's declarations of moderation have not convinced everyone, including some members of the SNC. Some elements within the 310 seat council, a quarter of which is dominated by the Brotherhood, criticised the movement for its excessive influence over decision making within the body. This includes the Kurds, who have deep reservations about the Brotherhood, not least because of its resistance to Kurdish demands for federalism or for Kurdish autonomy within Syria. Accusations were levelled at the Brotherhood to the effect that it was trying to control the SNC through its influence over independent Islamist members of the council and that it was channelling funds to favoured groups inside Syria in a bid to build its presence in the country.[94] This lingering suspicion of the movement and its real intentions prompted some more secular elements to object to the SNC's being absorbed into the Syrian National Coalition, a body established in November 2012 to try to unify the opposition. For all its efforts to present a more moderate face to the world, therefore, the Syrian brothers clearly still have a long way to go to convince everyone.

It is still too early to ascertain what will unfold in Syria. What is certain, however, is that when the al-Assad regime finally goes, the Brotherhood will make sure it is there to play a part in whatever comes next. It goes without saying that doing so will not be easy. The movement's long absence from the country means that it will be competing with a host of other Islamist forces and currents, many of which are likely to have a stronger local following. Whether in the face of such competition the Brotherhood will stick to its more moderate stance or whether it will feel compelled to retract down a more conservative line of thinking has yet to be seen. However, given the mood of the region, all the indications would suggest that the Brotherhood will once again become a force to be reckoned with in the Syrian context.

3

The International *Tanzeem*

Myth or Reality?

One of the most contentious issues that has haunted the Muslim Brotherhood in recent decades has been its so-called *Tanzeem al-Dawli* (international organisation). Much of the controversy has arisen on account of the secrecy that has surrounded this organisation since its inception in the 1970s. There even seems to be confusion within the Brotherhood itself as to what exactly the international *tanzeem* is and what role it plays. Whilst some Ikhwani talk about it as if it were an active component of the Brotherhood, part of its transnational identity that is actively directed from Cairo, others dismiss it as little more than a co-ordinating body, with no significant function. Egyptian brother Dr Kamal Helbawy, for example, has described the international *tanzeem* as no more than 'international co-ordination'.[1] Similarly, the Syrian brother, the late Dr Hassan al-Huwaidi, who was a Deputy to the Supreme Guide in the international organisation until his death in March 2009, referred to it as 'an advisory body that has no executive power'.[2]

Some Ikhwani are so sensitive about the subject that questions about it sometimes engender irritation. In 2006 the Guide of the

Jordanian Ikhwan, Abd al-Majid al-Dhunaybat, asserted: 'The so-called international organisation is a wrong name and a term used by adversaries to refer to the brothers in various countries and who try to standardise the understanding, ideology and positions of the groups regarding world events.'[3] Guidance Office member Abdul Moneim Aboul Fotouh claimed that the international *tanzeem* was something that existed primarily in the minds of those in the West, angrily complaining, 'You find that a lot with the westerners!'[4] Egyptian Ikhwani Youssef Nada, who ran the Al Taqwa Bank, explicitly stated, 'As far as I know this so-called international *tanzeem* never existed.'[5]

There is also a strong divergence of opinion among commentators. According to some detractors, the international *tanzeem*, along with the various plans and documents that have been ascribed to it, is an elaborate network set up by the Brotherhood to infiltrate Europe with its dangerous and fundamentalist ideology.[6] The Egyptian state also sought to portray the organisation as a sinister entity, poised to topple regimes throughout the world. Former Egyptian Interior Minister Hassan al-Alfi described it as 'the base from the cloaks of which have emerged all these [extremist] organisations which betray their religion and their countries'.[7] For others, however, the international *tanzeem* is nothing more than a 'loose and feeble coalition scarcely able to convene its own members'.[8] Some commentators have gone even further, suggesting that the organisation is completely irrelevant and incompetent. Abu Ala Madhi, who broke away from the Brotherhood in 1996 to form the Al-Wasat party in Egypt, has described the international movement as a fantasy, a failure that is incapable of carrying out any objective.[9]

To add to the confusion, whilst some have suggested that the Ikhwani are deliberately evasive when talking about the international *tanzeem* in order to make themselves appear more powerful than they actually are, others have accused them of downplaying the organisation so as to detract attention from it. It is true that after

9/11 the Brotherhood was especially concerned about being branded as an international terrorist organisation and there appeared to be a concerted effort to refute the suggestion that the mother branch in Egypt might be directing the policies of Ikhwani groups elsewhere. Rather they were keen to promote the idea that the local branches are independent and are not obliged by decisions made in Cairo. As Mohamed Habib, the former Deputy of the Brotherhood in Egypt, explained:

> There is an international organisation, but the groups within it operate in a decentralised way, giving it flexibility ... what is more important is that the aims of the international tanzeem are one and it has one methodology so all the branches aim for the same things but within the framework of the legislation of their own countries.[10]

Given the tense security situation that existed in Egypt prior to the Arab Spring and the pressures that the Egyptian Brotherhood was under, this decentralised scenario would certainly seem to be the most likely way in which the transnational movement operated in the years leading up to the 2011 revolution. It would seem far-fetched to imagine that the leadership in Cairo could have been in any position to run a fully functioning international organisation. Yet at the same time it was difficult to ignore the *Tanzeem al-Dawli* completely, not least because it continued to have an international Guidance Office headquartered in Cairo. Furthermore, for all that it might have been organisationally weak, the international *tanzeem* represented an important feature in the Brotherhood's history and has played a key role in the movement's evolution. Its fortunes have ebbed and flowed according to the personalities who have been at the helm of the movement and it has been as wrought with internal division as each of the individual branches themselves. On occasion, such as in 1990–1 during the Gulf war crisis, these divisions threatened to rupture the entire Brotherhood. The story of the international *tanzeem* therefore highlights the Ikhwan's never-ending difficulties in reconciling being both a local organisation with national branches and priorities and an international body and school of thought.

Origins

The fact that the Brotherhood set up an international organisation is hardly surprising. The movement's internationalist outlook was established from its very inception, thanks to the vision of its founder Hassan al-Banna. The Ikhwan was formed largely in response to the fall of the last caliphate, the Ottoman Empire, and the movement stressed the universal nature of Islam and the *umma* (one Muslim nation). Moreover, although al-Banna's main focus was on local issues, he also sought to spread his ideology and his movement beyond the confines of Egypt. To this end, he sent members of the Brotherhood abroad to spread *dawa* and to expand the movement in other Arab states.

However, for al-Banna, Egypt was always the centre and he considered it to be the true heart and soul of the movement. The fact that the Brotherhood was founded in Egypt, al-Banna's birthplace, has always given Cairo a certain moral authority, so much so that the Murshid of the Egyptian branch has always been the supreme leader and spiritual reference of the entire movement. As Syrian Ikhwani Adnan Saad Eddine said, 'The Murshid has [overall] moral responsibility.'[11]

The importance of Egypt notwithstanding, the Brotherhood has not been averse to trying to create alternative centres of power whenever Cairo has found itself under extreme pressure. In 1954, for example, after the Nasser regime clamped down particularly hard on the Ikhwan, arresting most of its leadership, the then Murshid Hassan al-Hodeibi held meetings with Ikhwani leaders in Syria, Iraq, Jordan and Lebanon to develop plans to set up an executive office for the Arab world.[12] According to Issam al-Attar, after al-Hodeibi returned to Egypt he became busy with local issues once again and the idea of the regional office slipped down the agenda.

The idea was resurrected in the early 1960s and during the Haj of 1963 a number of Ikhwani from Arab states held a conference, during which they elected al-Attar as the head of an Arab executive bureau to be known as the *Maktab al-Amm* (General Office). The main function of this office, aside from acting as a focal point for the Ikhwan outside Egypt, was to collect funds and donations for the Brotherhood and to promote *dawa*.[13] There was no direct obligation to Cairo within this set-up; according to Sudanese Ikhwani Dr Hassan al-Turabi, it worked on the basis of voluntary co-ordination.[14] Yet due to the ongoing restrictions on the Egyptians, this office remained largely the domain of the Syrians, who were experiencing a more flexible domestic situation at that time. It was never able to really develop, not least because al-Attar himself was forced into exile in 1964 but also because once the Egyptians had no immediate need or interest for it, it was left to wither away.

As the Ikhwan continued to develop internationally, with branches springing up across the Islamic world, Cairo came to act as a natural arbiter and leader and it intervened to resolve issues in local branches where it saw fit. For example, in the late 1960s the Guidance Office in Egypt stepped in to sort out the conflict that had built up between the Aleppo and Damascus wings of the Syrian Ikhwan. Cairo organised an election for a new Shura Council for the Syrian branch. Therefore, although it had no formal role in this respect, there was a general assumption that the Guidance Office in Egypt had a natural responsibility to solve problems that occurred in other parts of the movement. However, as the Sudanese Ikhwani leader has described, the relationships between Cairo and other branches at this time were largely spontaneous and done without any real organisational formality.[15]

Whilst Cairo had always had this informal moral authority over other branches, it was in the early 1970s that a hawkish group of Egyptian Ikhwani sought to amplify Cairo's role and to use the movement's international dimensions to their advantage. This group, which included Mustafa Mashour, Ahmed al-Malat and Kamel Sananiri, were all members of the Nizam al-Khass and were released from prison shortly after President Sadat came to power in 1970. As explained in Chapter One, immediately after their release this group sought to wrest control of the Egyptian Ikhwan away from the Murshid and to reinvigorate the movement, which had dwindled significantly since the heady days of the early 1950s. Yet their ambitions for the Ikhwan went beyond Egypt, and they were to become the real driving force behind the international *tanzeem*.

The group's bid to make use of the movement's international aspect was partly driven by the fact that once they left prison they discovered that other Ikhwani branches around the world had flourished whilst their own had withered. The brothers in Jordan had gained much popularity and had a good connection to the monarchy, which like the Gulf states viewed the Ikhwan as a useful bulwark against nationalist or leftist forces. The realisation that other branches had become stronger than the mother group provoked a 'big organisational crisis' within the Egyptian Ikhwan.[16] They could see that whilst they were being stifled by the Egyptian regime, the international environment offered distinct opportunities that they could use not only to strengthen their influence within the movement as a whole, but also to increase the authority of their own particular clique within the Egyptian branch. As such they took steps to begin bringing the other branches under their control.

Whilst the other Ikhwani branches had always given their loyalty to the Murshid as a matter of tradition, this group placed a new insistence on the obedience that other parts of the Ikhwan should display towards the Murshid. Following Hassan al-Hodeibi's death in 1973 the group, who had by then appointed themselves as members of the Guidance Office, decided to select a new Murshid whom they could control from behind the scenes. However, this Murshid, who had agreed to take on the position very reluctantly, did not want his identity to be disclosed and became known as the Secret Murshid. Once they had appointed him, the group then demanded that the leaders of the various national Ikhwani branches come to Cairo to swear *baya* to the new guide, even though his identity was a secret.[17] Adnan Saad Eddine has described how after he had been elected as the new General Guide of the Syrian Ikhwan in 1975 he was obliged to go through this process: 'Omar al-Tilimsani called on me to go to Cairo to give *bayá* to the Murshid in the name of the Syrian *tanzeem* ... I went to Cairo to Dr Ahmed al-Malat who took me to a Cairo suburb to visit al-Murshid and I performed *baya* after I promised that I would not reveal or mention his name.'[18]

Some Ikhwani rejected the idea of giving allegiance to a Murshid they did not know, forcing the Egyptian group to come to a compromise. In 1977 they brought in Omar al-Tilimsani as the new Supreme Guide. However, the incident reflects the sense among this group of Egyptians that they were at the top of the Ikhwan's international hierarchy. As Issam al-Attar has explained, 'They imagined themselves as the real leaders of all the Ikhwan in the Arab world because Egypt for them was the real leadership of the movement as a whole. They wanted to make the Murshid everything in the movement.'[19]

As well as strengthening their control over existing branches in the Arab world, the group also sought to harness opportunities on offer in other parts of the world where the Ikhwan had a presence. Many of these openings were in Europe. The seeds of the Brotherhood had been planted in Europe in the 1950s by a number of Ikhwani who had sought refuge on the continent, such as Said Ramadan, the son-in-law of Hassan al-Banna. Ramadan, who had always had international ambitions, arrived in Europe in 1958. There, according to his son, Tariq, he was generally considered to be in charge of the Ikhwan abroad.[20] He settled in Geneva, where he began publishing Islamist literature and set up the Islamic Centre of Geneva. Keen to expand his influence further, Ramadan also opened a centre in Munich and another in London in 1964.

Although Ramadan had left the Ikhwan by the end of the 1970s, his presence in Europe and the opening of his Islamic centres were to lay the Ikhwan's foundations on the continent. These centres became key hubs for other influential Ikhwani who had settled in Europe, including Issam al-Attar, Youssef Nada, and later the Lebanese scholar Sheikh Faisal al-Mawlawi. These individuals, along with Ramadan, found an environment where they could operate with a relative degree of freedom and where they could take advantage of the media opportunities that were on offer to promote their cause. As one commentator explained, 'Leaders of the Ikhwan organisations were surprised by the Western openness to Islam and the facilities that were given to fugitive Islamic leaders.'[21] Indeed, this group of highly ambitious and hawkish Ikhwani saw possibilities in Europe that they could not even dream of inside Egypt.

Much of the spread of this Ikhwani activism in Europe was thanks to the large sums of money that the Saudis had been prepared to direct into the continent to support their activities. As such, Saudi Arabia offered another opportunity for this group of Egyptians. The Saudis had built strong relations with the Brotherhood in the 1950s and 1960s, when the Kingdom had become the most important place of refuge for the Egyptian Ikhwani facing persecution at the hands of the Nasser regime. The Saudi monarchy welcomed the Ikhwan, partly as a means to shore itself up against the nationalist regimes that were spreading in the region, but also as an opportunity for the Saudis to use the Brotherhood to fill the gaps in their own society and institutions.

The Saudis offered the Ikhwani, who were generally members of the educated intelligentsia, posts within the administration and government, enabling the Ikhwan to penetrate the Saudi establishment to the highest level.[22] At the same time the Saudis gave the Ikhwani key posts in many of their charitable organisations including those in Europe. As the former Murshid Mehdi Akef, who himself worked as a consultant for the World Assembly of Muslim Youth (WAMY) in Riyadh in the 1970s and also spent several years at the Islamic centre in Munich, commented, 'The Muslim Brotherhood is like a beauty spot on the face of Saudi Arabia because of what it provided the country.'[23]

However, the Ikhwan's links into the Gulf did not rest solely with Saudi Arabia. They also developed a presence in other Gulf countries including Kuwait, Qatar and Bahrain, and the richness of these branches was an appealing prospect for the struggling Egyptian Ikhwan, whose finances had been strangled by the state. The new leaders in Cairo realised that there were established networks operating outside Egypt unburdened by the kinds of restrictions they were facing at home and with a ready supply of petrodollars. They therefore set about trying to develop a way to bring all of this activism, not to mention the supply of resources, under their control.

The Internal System

Much of this push to harness these opportunities was driven by Mustafa Mashour, who seems to have taken on establishing the international *tanzeem* as his personal project. The highly ambitious Mashour, who one Sudanese brother described as a 'very centralised man',[24] seems to have had an almost romantic vision about what such an organisation could achieve and he invested a huge amount of time and effort in trying to turn his vision into a reality. During the 1970s he began making regular visits to Europe, consulting with different figures within the Ikhwan and trying to persuade them of the benefits of restructuring the movement in a way that would bring it under a single united leadership. He even courted figures who had moved away from the Ikhwan, including Issam al-Attar. Al-Attar recounted that Mashour, accompanied by Ahmed al-Malat, visited him in his home in Aachen, where they tried unsuccessfully to persuade him to return to the Ikhwan.[25] However, Mashour was more successful with other parts of the Ikhwan. The Jordanian Ikhwan, for example, was quick to support Mashour, which accounts for the important role that the Jordanian General Guide Mohamed Abdelrahman Khalifa came to play within the Brotherhood's international structures.

By the early 1980s the pressure to activate some kind of international body had become even greater. Whilst there had been some room for manoeuvre during most of the 1970s, in 1981 President Sadat decided that it was time to clamp down on growing Islamist activism and embarked upon a major sweep of arrests that included large numbers of Ikhwani. Mustafa Mashour discovered that he was about to be detained and fled to Kuwait just four days before the arrests began. From Kuwait he moved between Germany and the Gulf, doing his utmost to push this new international system, something that was even more urgent now that the Ikhwan had such limited room to manoeuvre inside Egypt. After Sadat was killed in October 1981, his successor, Mubarak, continued with this repressive policy, preventing the Ikhwan from having any real space to develop inside the country.

However, the freedom that Mashour had found abroad was to consolidate his power and influence within the movement. Dr Kamal Helbawy has observed of this period that 'Mustafa Mashour was busy supervising and running activities whilst the Murshid in Egypt was unable to move a lot.'[26] Just as had occurred in earlier years, the Egyptians once again focused their efforts on alternative centres that could sustain them whilst they weathered a particularly difficult period in Egypt. This time, however, the efforts were much more sustained and developed.

In July 1982 the Ikhwan produced a document titled *La Iha al-Dakhiliya* (*The Internal Statute*). This was the culmination of the meetings that Mashour had been holding across Europe and elsewhere. This document, which is widely considered to mark the official establishment of the international *tanzeem*, reads very much like a constitution and lays out the new internal structure for the Ikhwan that had been approved by the Murshid in 1978. The document essentially formalised the existing relationships between Cairo and the Ikhwan's other branches into one official system. As such, it was a way for the Egyptian Ikhwan to bring an unwieldy movement of disparate parts spread far and wide across the globe into one formalised body.

The document made provision for new international leadership structures comprising a General Guidance Office and a General Shura Council. The General Guidance Office was to consist of thirteen members, eight of whom must be from 'the region in which the Supreme Guide resides', with another five being chosen 'in accordance with regional representation'. Under the Guidance Office was the General Shura Council, comprising at least thirty members who represented Brotherhood organisations in different countries and further including three 'specialised and experienced members who are nominated by the Guidance Office'. At the top of this new hierarchy, heading both the General Guidance Office and the General Shura Council, was of course the Murshid. He was formally tasked not only with representing the movement, but also with supervising all departments and summoning the general guides of different countries to meetings when necessary. Somewhat surprisingly, the document did not specify that the Murshid should be Egyptian. Instead he was to be nominated by the General Guidance Office from among the most popular candidates in the various national branches and elected by the General Shura Council, where he had to receive at least three quarters of the votes. Hence in theory a Murshid could be chosen from any of the national branches.

In many ways therefore this was a compromise document, allowing other branches to take part in the leadership structures and in theory enabling non-Egyptians to have a shot at taking on the role of Murshid. However, the weighting of the new bodies, and of the General Guidance Office in particular, clearly enabled the Egyptians to dominate. Moreover, in spite of the elaborate structure put in place to choose the new Murshid, the rules were not followed in subsequent years. As former Egyptian Ikhwan Abu Ala Madhi has described, 'The first test for the new system was in 1986 when Omar al-Tilimsani died. However, the Ikhwan chose Mohamed Hamed Abu Nasser without going through the stages.'[27] Nor was the new system followed when Mohamed Abu Nasser died in 1996 and Maimoun al-Hodeibi appointed Mustafa Mashour as the next Murshid in the famous graveside pledge described in Chapter One. Clearly this document was something that the Egyptians believed they could pick and choose from, using its rules and regulations only when expedient.

As well as consolidating the Egyptian presence in the new leadership structure, the document also put in place a system whereby the national branches were formally bound by decisions made by the centre. The leaders of national branches were obliged to 'commit to the decisions of the general leadership represented by the Supreme Guide, the Guidance Office and the General Shura Council'; to adhere to the 'policies and positions of the Muslim Brotherhood towards public issues as determined by the General Guidance Office and the General Shura Council'; and to commit to 'obtaining the approval of the Guidance Bureau before making any important political decisions'.

The leaders of national branches were also required to consult and receive the approval of the Murshid or the Guidance Office before they adopted resolutions, and to inform the Guidance Office of their political stances towards local issues. In addition, they were expected to set their own local statutes, which must be approved by the General Guidance Office before they could become effective. Each local branch had to pay an annual subscription for *dawa* work. The document also ruled that Ikhwani residing outside of their own countries should 'comply with the leadership of the movement in the country in which they reside'.

As such, the new system was very much a way of controlling the activities of the various national branches, which had until then been able to operate as largely independent bodies with informal ties to the mother branch. Egyptian intellectual and well-known critic of the Brotherhood Dr Rifat Said explained this new relationship between the mother branch and the other national branches: 'Every national branch has the right to do what he wants under the banner of the Ikhwan but it should be linked to the centre by money and by following instructions such as "You should change your attitude towards this or that."'[28] Although this comment is somewhat of a harsh oversimplification, it certainly captures the essence of what this group envisaged the international *tanzeem* to be. Former Ikhwani and highly respected Kuwaiti scholar Sheikh Abdullah Nafisi was heavily critical of this internal restructuring, observing that all the articles related to membership 'emphasise the member's duty, from the giving of *baya* to membership payments and even to punishment procedures that the *tanzeem* should adopt against those members who are not fulfilling their duties. Yet we can't find any article that gives the members the right to complain.'[29] He added that this system 'opened the door for the leadership to expel, make exempt or freeze members who differ with them in one thing or another regarding the group's affairs'.[30] Similarly one Egyptian Islamist complained: 'Despite the fact that a great number of those who have talent and intellectual expertise are outside Egypt, we find a tendency in the general system and more importantly in practice towards confirming the Egyptian leadership and orientation.'[31]

Abdullah Nafisi did not restrict his criticisms to the centre's attempt to consolidate power; he also complained that the Gulf countries were given a far greater weighting in this new system than that afforded to those Ikhwani in 'more important' Arab countries such as Syria and

Algeria. He asserted that this unfair weighting enabled the Ikhwan from the Gulf to 'manipulate the political and social path of al-jama'a and to shape its 'social and political stances according to their own way of thinking'. Nafisi put the reason for this over representation of those from the Gulf down to the international *tanzeem*'s need for money. It is true that the financial opportunities provided by the Gulf states were always a driving factor in Mashour's bid to develop an international organisation. As Ibrahim Ghuraiyba has commented, 'The Egyptians were the most interested party in the international *tanzeem* in order to get donations.'[32] As such Nafisi's argument would appear to hold water.

What appeared on paper to be a relatively equitable way to bring the Ikhwan's different branches into one unified system was, in fact, a means to create a highly centralised system that gave an ambitious group access to control and to finances that would feed both their local and international ambitions.

Whilst some elements within the Brotherhood, such as those in the Gulf and in Jordan, were broadly happy with this new system, others were less than enamoured with the new set-up. This included Sudanese Brotherhood leader, Hassan al-Turabi, who resented Mashour's mission to bring everything under his control. Turabi, himself an ambitious internationalist, who had become somewhat of an Islamic personality in his own right, refused to be put under such a tight yoke and refused to give his *baya* (allegiance) to Mashour. Unable to accept such disobedience, the Guidance Office in Cairo took to wooing those Sudanese Ikhwan who were uncomfortable with Turabi's stance. This included Sheikh Sadeq Abdelmajid, who had been educated in Egypt and whose 'heart was with the Egyptians'.[33] According to Sudanese brother, Dr Alamin Osman, Mustafa Mashour 'fought harshly against Dr Hassan al-Turabi and encouraged Sheikh Sadeq to break away'.[34] Consequently in 1985 a number of Sudanese brothers led by Sadeq split from Turabi and joined the Ikhwan's international structure, thereby splitting the movement inside Sudan.

Turabi's refusal to submit to Cairo's authority came as a major blow to the Egyptians and shook their confidence at a time when they believed that the world was their oyster. As part of the Nizam al-Khass, they prized obedience as a core principle of the Brotherhood and they clearly could not countenance any challenge to their belief that as Egyptians, they were the natural leaders of the entire Ikhwan movement. Yet the inflexibility of this group at this time highlights one of the Ikhwan's more systemic problems. Their rigidity and unwillingness to accept anyone with a different political or intellectual approach has meant that they have never allowed any space for personalities to develop inside the movement. This has resulted in figures such as Hassan al-Turabi, Yusuf al-Qaradawi and the Tunisian scholar Rashid al-Ghannouchi moving out of the Brotherhood and its tight hierarchy in order to progress their thinking. Indeed, Cairo's insistence on running the show and keeping the role of Murshid an exclusively Egyptian post has lost the Ikhwan some key thinkers who might have moved the movement forward in a more creative way.

Golden Age

The Turabi crisis aside, the Ikhwan continued to develop its international structures and to expand its reach. As Hossam Tamam has correctly observed, 'The 1980s were the golden age for the Ikhwan. They established themselves everywhere.'[35] Indeed, the brothers made the most of the Islamic revivalism that flourished at this time to build up their networks of mosques and activities in Europe, which became a key propaganda centre. They also made use of their global networks to support their activities in Afghanistan and Pakistan. The international *tanzeem* used its close relationship with Saudi Arabia to facilitate money flows and propaganda efforts aimed at bolstering the mujahideen in the Afghan struggle.

It was also in the 1980s that the Ikhwan made use of important personalities like Egyptian businessman Youssef Nada to extend their international reach. Nada, who was dubbed the King of Cement, having made his fortune in the Egyptian cement business and supplied cement to Saudi Arabia during the boom building time of the early 1970s, had fled Egypt in 1960 and eventually settled in Campione, an Italian municipality in Switzerland. Although a member of the Brotherhood, Nada was an important figure in his own right and his immense wealth, important connections and shrewd intellect made him a valued resource that the Ikhwan was keen to make use of. As a result Nada who held no official position with the Guidance Office or other organisational structures became a sort of roving ambassador for the Ikhwan and was responsible for managing the movement's important international relationships.[36] He guided the Ikhwan's relationship with the new regime in Tehran following the Iranian revolution of 1979 and arranged for a number of Ikhwani delegations to go to Iran to pay their respects to the new leadership. Nada used his finances to fund some of these visits, allegedly paying $30,000 in one instance to charter a special aeroplane to take one Ikhwani delegation from Islamabad to Iran.[37] He also mediated on behalf of the Ikhwan in relations between Saudi Arabia and Iran, Saudi Arabia and Yemen, and between the Algerian Front Islamique du Salut (FIS) leaders in prison and the Algerian government during the 1990s. He was clearly a linchpin in the Brotherhood's international structures.

However, Nada is perhaps most famous for setting up the Al-Taqwa bank in 1988 along with Syrian Ikhwani Ghaleb Himmat and Ahmed Idris Nasreddin. After the 9/11 attacks, the US treasury accused the bank of financing terrorism and funding al-Qa'ida and in 2001 the US pressurised the Bahamas to revoke the bank's licence. Nada himself was also put under investigation by Swiss prosecutors, who raided his villa and that of Himmat in 2001. Although the case was eventually dropped through lack of evidence, the controversy did little to assist the Ikhwan in its bid to be the moderate face of political Islam. Al-Taqwa is often referred to as the 'Ikhwan's bank'. Furthermore, many of the bank's shareholders were members of the Ikhwan and other figures with close links to the Ikhwan also held shares. Sheikh Yusuf al-Qaradawi, for example, is reported to have held 5,285 shares in the bank as at April 2000.[38] But to present Al-Taqwa as a financial arm of the Ikhwan is to misrepresent it somewhat: as Nada himself explained, 'The Ikhwani do not have money in the bank as a group, but as individuals.'[39] However, whilst Al-Taqwa was not a Brotherhood institution as such, it was a useful conduit for financial flows that enhanced the Ikhwan's international position at the time.

Just as Nada brought the Ikhwan unwanted controversy so too did a document that was found in the house of his colleague Ghaleb Himmat during a police raid on his villa. Dubbed 'The Project', some commentators have portrayed this document as evidence of the Brotherhood's sinister project to take over the Western world.[40] The document dated 1 December 1982 laid out the Ikhwan's goals in its bid to create an international Islamic strategy. These goals were divided into twelve key points, and include the following pledges:

To know the terrain and adopt a scientific methodology for its planning and execution.

To reconcile international engagement with flexibility at a local level.

To work loyally with Islamic groups and institutions in multiple areas to agree on common ground.

To accept the principle of temporary co-operation between Islamic movements and nationalist movements in the broad sphere and on common ground such as the struggle against colonialism, preaching and the Jewish state, without however having to form alliances.

To construct a permanent force of the Islamic *dawa* and support movements engaged in jihad across the Muslim world

To use diverse and varied surveillance systems, in several places, to gather information and adopt a single effective warning system serving the worldwide Islamic movement.[41]

In spite of the allegations, this document is a fairly mundane wish list and would appear to be largely an expression of intent that reflects the ambition and optimism of the time. The document was produced at the beginnings of the international *tanzeem* and seems to be a broad set of objectives that were typical of the ideas that were doing the rounds then. Helbawy noted that there was much consultation and many such documents being produced in the early 1980s. Nada also asserts that he has no idea what the document is.[42] Therefore, whilst much has been made of this text, it would simply seem to reflect the dream of internationalisation that was taking place within the movement at the time.

The Kuwait Crisis

By the end of the 1980s, however, this dream was looking increasingly distant as a far more serious crisis was to unfold. It would kill the dream of the international *tanzeem* and flag up serious doubts about how far 'international brotherhood' could really extend. This crisis was Saddam Hussein's invasion of Kuwait, which plunged the Ikhwan into complete disarray and that challenged its administrative and ideological unity. Whilst some branches were more sympathetic to the Kuwaiti predicament, others felt that their loyalties lay with Saddam. According to Bassam al-Amoush, a former Jordanian brother, 'The Ikhwan's stance during the second Gulf crisis was terrifying. There was a big division in the movement and no clear Ikhwani vision as to which stance to take.'[43] Just when the Ikhwan needed to take a clear stance and to direct the movement's response, the international *tanzeem* proved unable to step up to the mark.

On the day that Saddam's tanks rolled into Kuwait the Guidance Office in Cairo issued a statement signed by Murshid Mohamed Hamid Abu Naser. Although the statement expressed the Brotherhood's surprise and disappointment at the Iraqi regime's actions, it came across as a rather lukewarm and unconvincing denouncement of the invasion that simply called upon Iraqi leaders to 'reconsider what they had done' and expressed the Ikhwan's hope that these leaders would 'go back on their steps'.[44] Whilst the statement asserted that the Islamic world and the *umma* had condemned Iraq's actions, there was no explicit condemnation of Iraq by the Muslim Brotherhood itself. As the former General Guide of the Syrian brotherhood Ali Saddredine al-Bayanouni admitted in retrospect, 'The first statement we issued, we condemned the occupation of Kuwait by Iraq. We condemned the occupation in a way that might be considered to have been mild.'[45]

The statement was so tepid that just nine days later the Guidance Office issued another in which it tried to clarify its stance. This was slightly more forceful in its criticism of the invasion although still not particularly strong and simply stated that the Brotherhood 'opposes any military intervention by an Arab or Muslim state against another Arab or Muslim state.'[46] But by this point the international situation had changed. The first US forces had arrived in Saudi Arabia in preparation for action against the Iraqi regime. Furthermore, the Arab League had also voted to send Egyptian, Syrian and Moroccan forces to join the Western troops in their bid to force Saddam Hussein out of Kuwait. The Brotherhood therefore came forward in this second statement to express their total rejection of the presence of American forces in the region, declaring:

> The Muslim Brotherhood condemns and fiercely opposes the American military intervention in the Gulf crisis whatever justification the US is using for their presence ... Their presence is rejected on every level and by every means because it will result in a return to the era of the protectorate and to occupation of the region.[47]

The statement was also unequivocal in its objection to Arab troops working alongside those from Western countries.

The contrast between the Ikhwan's lukewarm criticism of Iraq and its outright condemnation of the US in this statement is striking. It was as if America's entering the conflict had provided the Ikhwan with a much-needed get-out clause. It gave the brothers a rallying point that they could focus on, as it was far easier to retreat into the safety and comfort of anti-Westernism than it was to take sides between Iraq and Kuwait. Opposing the 'Western enemy' not only had a broad populist appeal; it was also something that the various national branches of the Brotherhood could be guaranteed to agree on. As Tunisian leader Sheikh Rashid al-Ghannouchi summarised, 'We are not worshiping personalities, but anyone who confronts the enemies of Islam is my friend and anyone who puts himself in the service of the enemies of Islam is my enemy.'[48]

However, some branches were so forthright in their condemnation of foreign intervention that to some Kuwaiti eyes they appeared to be supporting Saddam Hussein. As Dr Kamal Helbawy tactfully explained:

> The official stance was that we were against the invasion of Kuwait and we were against seeking assistance from the

Americans. But individually yes maybe some people were ...
the Palestinians and the Jordanians were closer to Saddam
Hussein and some other countries and personalities were
with the Kuwaitis, you could say. But I am sure everyone
was against the presence of the American troops in the area
... Some of the Syrians who had lived with Saddam Hussein
maybe supported him beyond the reasonable limit. But it
was a time full of crisis and that is why the Ikhwan advised
Saddam to pull out.[49]

Whilst figures such as Mustafa Mashour had close ties with the
Kuwaitis, who had been willing to provide the movement with much
needed financial assistance, others had a much stronger personal loyalty
to Saddam Hussein. Some of the Syrian Ikhwani had particularly close
ties with the former Iraqi leader, who had offered them support when
they were being persecuted by the Ba'athists in their country. Dr Hassan
al-Huwaidi, Ali Saddredine al-Bayanouni and Adnan Saad Eddine all
spent time in Baghdad under Saddam's protection even though he had
persecuted Iraqi Ikhwani; as Adnan Saad Eddine explained, 'I knew
Saddam very closely and knew all the [Iraqi] leaders.'[50]

Those who felt most honour-bound to stand with Saddam, however,
were the Jordanians, who were particularly vocal in their objections to
the presence of American troops in the region. According to Kuwaiti
brother Mubarak al-Dwaila, 'The Muslim Brotherhood in Jordan were
the most aggressive and differed a lot from the Muslim Brotherhood
in Egypt whose stance was good.'[51] These loyalties derived largely from
the fact that Saddam Hussein was widely considered at that time to
be the champion of the Palestinian cause; given the large numbers
of Palestinian refugees in Jordan, including within the Jordanian
Ikhwan, the brothers there felt duty-bound to defend Saddam.
They issued a number of statements following the invasion such as
that of 5 August, which made no criticism of the Iraqi invasion but

declared: 'We condemn the stance of the American crusaders that are leading the forces of arrogance. America is the state that is leading all the forces that are hostile to Islam and Muslims.'[52] Jordanian brothers also voiced their anger in other arenas and some joined pro-Saddam demonstrations in the streets. One Ikhwani Deputy to the Jordanian parliament, Yousef al-Athaum, declared, 'Iraqi feet on Kuwaiti territory are better than American feet.'[53] Feelings were running so high in Jordan that the Jordanian Ikhwan was eventually forced to issue a statement reminding the Jordanian population that whatever the politics involved, the Kuwaitis should be treated with respect, not least because the 'Muslim Kuwaiti people gave a lot to our *umma* and were the most interested in the Palestinian cause. They gave a lot of their money to help their brothers everywhere.'[54]

Whilst the Jordanian Ikhwan maintains that its protests were aimed solely at preventing external military intervention in the region, the Kuwaiti Ikhwan interpreted them as overt support for Saddam Hussein. This was a very bitter pill to swallow. Mubarak al-Dwaila has commented, 'The stance of the Muslim Brotherhood in Jordan was shameful.'[55] The Kuwaitis became even more angered when the Brotherhood began mediating directly in the conflict. Following a meeting of Ikhwani leaders and Islamic personalities including Dr Hassan al-Turabi, Rashid al-Ghannouchi and Turkish Islamist Necmettin Erbakan in Amman on 12 September 1990, the Brotherhood sent a delegation to Saudi Arabia, Iraq and Iran. This delegation – which was headed by the Jordanian Ikhwani leader Mohamed Abdelrahman Khalifa because the Murshid was prevented from travelling by the Egyptian authorities – went to Baghdad to meet with Saddam Hussein. After the meeting they issued a statement in which they declared that they had had a 'frank and friendly discussion' with the Iraqi leader, whom they praised for his 'steadfastness'.[56] After concluding that the whole crisis had come about as a result of the 'absence of Islam', the statement, like those before it, strongly condemned the presence of foreign forces that sought to 'destroy the Iraqi military forces in order to serve the Zionist scheme and to enable Israel to absorb citizens from the Soviet Union so it can strike against the intifadah'.[57] Once again, the issue of Saddam's invasion of Kuwait was relegated to generalities related to finding an Arab and Islamic solution to the crisis. This time, however, the statement went as far as to declare, 'We have to pay attention to Iraq's demands and look at its legal demands in line with Islamic rulings.'[58]

It is therefore easy to see why the Kuwaiti Ikhwan felt so betrayed by the Brotherhood. Even those Ikhwani who had traditionally been close to the Kuwaitis proved unwilling to openly condemn Saddam Hussein and his invasion. This was hardly surprising given that the public mood in the Arab world at the time had come to view Saddam Hussein as a hero who was standing up to the imperial forces of the West. Mustafa Mashour made some attempts to redress the balance when he gave a statement at a conference in Saudi Arabia on 19 November 1990 in which he declared: 'Some people believed that our explanation of what was occurring meant that we were biased towards Iraq. This is a misunderstanding. We didn't only issue condemnatory statements but we set up an Islamic delegation from several Islamic movements and countries to bring about a peaceful solution for the *umma*'.[59] But even in this statement his focus on fighting the Western presence in the region was still far stronger than his condemnation of Iraq. Even Mustafa Mashour, who had particularly strong ties with the Kuwaitis and Saudis, was so bound by the sentiment of the street that he could do no other than focus on the issue of foreign intervention as the primary crisis of the region. As such, just like the other Ikhwani branches, Mashour and the Guidance Office were ultimately considered by the Kuwaitis to have taken the side of secular Ba'athist Iraq over the conservative religious monarchy of Kuwait.

The Kuwaiti Ikhwani were so angered by the stance of their fellow brethren that they froze their membership of the international movement. Prominent Kuwaiti brother Ismail Shati explained:

> I stayed in Kuwait working with those of the Kuwaiti Brothers who stayed ... The start of the dispute was the arrival of US troops. Prominent Brotherhood branches visited Baghdad and issued statements condemning the US presence in Kuwait in language that seemed to support Saddam. So we froze our membership of the Brotherhood.[60]

However, whilst the Kuwaiti Ikhwani condemned the rest of the movement for their stance, some of their protestations appear to have emerged somewhat later in the day. Some have interpreted their position during the early stages of the invasion as ambiguous. According to Kuwaiti researcher Falah Limdaris, 'the official line of the Kuwaiti Ikhwan was oscillating in the beginning [of the crisis]'.[61] The reason for this indecision appears to have been that the Kuwaiti Ikhwan was open to the possibility of an international Islamist force moving into Kuwait to resolve the crisis. This idea had been mooted at a meeting of the Kuwaiti Students' Association in November 1990. Dr Kamal Helbawy, who had been in Pakistan during the Afghanistan conflict, proposed pulling together the mujahideen who were still in Afghanistan to create a force that could be directed against US troops in Kuwait and that would ensure Iraq's withdrawal from Kuwait.[62]

Although the Kuwaiti government rejected this proposal it was supported by some Kuwaiti brothers, who despite their horror of the Iraqi invasion preferred an Islamic solution to one that involved Western forces. Saud al-Nasser, the Kuwaiti ambassador to Washington at that time, claims that he was visited by a delegation of Kuwaiti brothers that included Ismail Shati, Tariq al-Suwaidan and Abdullah Utaiki, who asked him to give them $50 million for their project to fight against the US presence in the region.[63] Although the Ikhwan rejects his allegations, al-Nasser recounts, 'I can't forget this incident. I asked them what the suitable alternative would be to foreign forces. They said we have to replace them by Islamic forces. I smiled at this nonsense.'[64] Al-Nasser also recalls how he found members of the Kuwaiti Students Association – an organisation heavily dominated by the Ikhwan – harassing delegates at a meeting in a Virginia hotel for those who wanted to sign up as Arabic interpreters for US forces in the Gulf. Al-Nasser claims that the group of Islamists were creating chaos and telling those present not to work for 'Christians and Jews'.[65]

However, in typical Ikhwani expediency, as soon as it became clear that the proposal was a hugely unrealistic option, the Kuwaiti Ikhwan split from the international *tanzeem*. On 31 March 1991 the Kuwaiti Ikhwan formed its own movement, which it named the Islamic Constitutional Movement (ICM) and that was independent of Cairo.

This split came as a major blow to the international *tanzeem* so painstakingly put in place just a decade before. It also had financial implications; Kuwait had been an important source of funds. More importantly, this episode demonstrated the difficulties of being an international movement. Whilst the Ikhwan could broadly agree on theological issues, politics was a different matter; in spite of the dream of the *umma*, nationalistic priorities and interests ultimately continued to dominate. Indeed, transnational Islamism proved to be just as flimsy a concept as Arab nationalism before it.

Moreover, the Kuwait crisis reflects a wider conundrum that the Ikhwan has always struggled with. In their quest for survival, individual Ikhwani or branches have tended to display an incredible pragmatism and adaptability. As we have seen, this has resulted in some instances in a willingness to deal with authoritarian regimes abroad even if these same regimes are persecuting their own Ikhwan. The readiness of the Syrian Ikhwan to defend Saddam Hussein during the Gulf crisis was a direct result of the protection and support he had offered them when they were being persecuted by the Ba'athist regime in Damascus, even though he was repressing his own Iraqi Ikhwan at the time.

This opportunistic pattern has repeated itself over and over in the Ikhwan's history. When asked, many Ikhwani put such behaviour down to the politics of the day or the need for brothers to find refuge wherever they can. However, whilst such a flexible approach has certainly helped individual branches to survive, it has also sowed division and discord within the movement as a whole.

Decline

The Kuwait crisis was to mark the end of the heyday of the international *tanzeem*, which limped along through the 1990s encountering further crises along the way as different branches pulled away from the centre. By this point, it seems, Cairo had come to acknowledge the limits of its power. This became evident when the General Guide of the Algerian brotherhood, Mahfoud Nahnah, decided to stand in the Algerian presidential elections of 1995.

Nahnah and his group had become part of the formal structure of the international *tanzeem* in the early 1980s after Nahnah's Deputy Sheikh Busuleimani attended a conference in Tunis at which Sheikh Rashid al-Ghannouchi invited the Algerians to join the *tanzeem al-dawli*.[66] His bid to stand in the presidential elections was not appreciated by Cairo. It also angered other Islamist groups inside Algeria, including the Front Islamique du Salut (FIS), whose ideology was not far removed from that of the Brotherhood and who had issued a call to boycott the elections. Under the rules of the internal system, Nahnah had to put forward his proposal to the Guidance Office for approval. Jordanian brother Bassam al-Amoush recalls:

I remember Mahfoud Nahnah came and in one of the sessions he talked about nominating himself for the presidential election in Algeria. He was advised by some of those present not to take part but this advice was not obligatory and came in the form of advice. He nominated himself and he didn't win. The *tanzeem al-dawli* is not a supreme committee that issues decisions and rulings as some of the countries and governments think.[67]

It would appear that this willingness by the Guidance Office not to try to oppose Nahnah's decision was a reflection of the growing realisation that the centre could no longer hold in the way that Mashour and his colleagues had first envisaged. The international *tanzeem* had suffered so many knocks since its inception that it had been weakened considerably and Cairo no longer had the energy to keep such a tight grip on the actions of the various branches. Moreover, the appointment of Mustafa Mashour as Murshid in 1996 had an impact, as the architect of the international organisation came to focus his attentions much more on the situation inside Egypt. In addition his Deputy, Maimoun al-Hodeibi, who was becoming an extremely powerful figure within the movement, strongly disapproved of the international *tanzeem*, believing it to have weighed heavy on the shoulders of the Ikhwan.

Al-Hodeibi's disapproval was so great that in the mid-1990s he is believed to have cancelled Kamal Helbawy's post as international spokesperson for the Brotherhood. Helbawy had taken on this role after he arrived in London from Pakistan and had set up a Muslim Brotherhood media office in London that began issuing statements and publications in the name of the Ikhwan. However, there was some confusion over exactly what role he had been given. According to Azzam Tamimi, 'None of us were clear whether this spokesman was able to speak for the Brotherhood outside of Egypt, nor did we know his connection to the International Organisation ... no one told us anything.'[68] Helbawy maintains that he resigned from the post, explaining, 'I was caught in the crossfire of the Wasat affair during which I tried to advise both sides. But the situation was difficult and people used fiery language. So I resigned and asked the Murshid to find someone else.'[69] However, Mustafa Mashour told *Le Monde Diplomatique*, 'The Brotherhood in the United Kingdom appointed him and I don't know why they ended it.'[70] Helbawy has explained that al-Hodeibi was always uncomfortable with the amount of freedom he had in London and that some more conservative elements in Egypt did not appreciate the statements he was issuing. He even received telephone calls from some within the Brotherhood's hierarchy in Cairo, telling him not to make such statements.[71]

Whatever the truth of this episode, it is clear that al-Hodeibi and others in Cairo had a somewhat antagonistic relationship with some of those Ikhwan who were outside and became determined to limit their power and influence. Things became even worse for the international *tanzeem* when al-Hodeibi was appointed to the post of Murshid in 2002. However, by this point the events of 9/11 had given the Ikhwan further impetus to try to relegate the role of the international *tanzeem*. As the world reacted to the shock of the attacks and began talking about international jihadist networks with a global agenda, the Muslim Brotherhood became increasingly anxious that it might be labelled as an international terrorist organisation and find itself on the list of designated terrorist groups. Since then, the Ikhwan has done its utmost to give the impression that the international *tanzeem* is simply a co-ordinating body that meets as and when it gets the opportunity and that has no power over decisions made at the local level by the various national branches. Dr Helbawy offered this explanation in 2007:

> When we refer to an organisation, it is something similar
> to military factions that have a leadership and where its

members heed commands and obey, whereas what does exist is international co-ordination. It's almost like federal work; there are meetings, continuous consultations, exchange of experience, networking and joint efforts.[72]

Many Ikhwani are keen to stress that each branch is free to make its own decisions. Dr Hassan al-Huwaidi, for many years the Deputy to the Supreme Guide in the international *tanzeem*, described it as an 'advisory body' in which '95 per cent of issues are resolved locally. For those that cannot be resolved, they are taken to the international *tanzeem* for consultation. This has no executive power. It is just an advisory body.'[73] Ali Saddredine al-Bayanouni has echoed these sentiments: 'There is no structural relationship with the international *tanzeem*, rather there is consultation. Every country has its own conditions.'[74] He also claims that the international *tanzeem*'s meetings are 'nothing specific' and that each branch sends a representative but 'some don't attend'.[75] The former Deputy to the Supreme Guide, Mohamed Habib, also explained, 'We as the Guidance Office don't interfere in local entities, in their work or performance ... They know their circumstances better. We might have intervened in the past.'[76]

As such, by the 2000s, the international *tanzeem* appears to have been reduced to a body that promoted organisational co-ordination without obligation. That is not to say that Cairo did try to convince other Ikhwani branches of what to do or how to act in certain situations. Jordanian militant and former Ikhwani Bassam al-Amoush, who was a member of the international *tanzeem*, complained in 2007 that whilst it is 'nothing more than a co-ordinating body between the Ikhwani branches ... it suffers from the control of the Egyptian brothers'.[77] Similarly, according to one Iraqi brother, although Egypt has not exercised its power to prevent members from taking certain decisions and leaves it to local branches to decide, 'it sends members to ask what happened and why. If the movement goes astray ... the international Brotherhood decides which faction is the most faithful and says to the one that isn't "You don't represent the Ikhwan."'[78]

In fact, the Guidance Office has made its disapproval of the actions of some branches overtly clear in recent years. The leadership in Cairo found it extremely difficult to accept that the Syrian Ikhwan had formed an alliance with former Syrian Vice President Abdul Halim Khaddam. As explained in Chapter Two, the Syrians joined Khaddam to establish an opposition platform called the National Salvation Front. Akef states: 'I sent for them and I told them my view but they are free to make their own decision. I don't intervene as long as their decision is based upon their views and their Shura Council.'[79] He also says:

> I gave them space to move around because I am not under
> the same pressure that they are because hundreds of their
> families are suffering under bad laws ... So I gave them space
> to move around, but I am not with their view in this case ...
> If I were fighting with the Palestinians I would oblige them
> to follow my decision but because I am not fighting with
> them I give them the chance to take their own decisions.[80]

This reference to the Palestinians goes to the core of why the Guidance Office and many other Brotherhood groups were so opposed to the Syrian bid to strengthen the challenge to the al-Assad regime. Following the toppling of Saddam Hussein, the Syrian regime became known as the primary champion of the Palestinian cause within the Arab world. Its intransigence towards Israel and the West combined with its support for Hizbullah and more importantly Hamas brought it praise from groups such as the Brotherhood. Bashar al-Assad's willingness to host Hamas leader Khalid Meshaal was seen as almost heroic by many Ikhwani. Given the primacy of the Palestinian issue in the Arab world and within the Ikhwan's own platforms, the Guidance Office believed it should be quietly supporting the Syrian regime rather than an opposition platform, even if that platform was shared by the Syrian brothers. Although Cairo did not forbid the Syrian Ikhwan from joining Khaddam's platform, it certainly brought some serious pressure to bear on the movement over the issue.

The Guidance Office in Cairo was also deeply troubled by the Iraqi Islamic Party's willingness to take part in the political process in Iraq following the 2003 invasion. However, the Iraqis were not afforded the space given to the Syrian Ikhwani to forge their own path, because Iraq was a clear case of a foreign power occupying a Muslim land. The statements and pronouncements made by key Ikhwani leaders in relation to the situation in Iraq are completely at odds with the stance taken by their Iraqi brothers. According to the spokesman for the political arm of the Iraqi Muslim Brotherhood, the Iraqi Islamic Party, when the party decided to take part in the Iraqi elections 'the International *tanzeem* opposed it because they didn't understand it'.[81] He also complained that there had been particular problems with some Ikhwani 'of a more nationalistic outlook'.[82]

According to Akef a group of Iraqi Islamists including Tariq al-Hashemi, the head of the political arm of the Iraqi Muslim Brotherhood and the Iraqi Islamic Party, Harith al-Dari the head of the Iraqi Scholars Committee and Adnan Dulaimi, the head of the Sunni Al-Tawafaq Front, came to see him in Cairo. During the meeting al-Hashemi explained that his party believed that they should take part in the post-Saddam political process. Akef goes on:

> I told them literally, 'Are all of you agreed that resistance is a must?' They said yes. All of them. So I told them, 'Okay, you agreed on resistance so let's look at what methods we can use to achieve it, whether political or resistance.' They all answered, 'We agree on resistance and we will resist in the way we see fit.' I told them, 'You can agree on resisting through the media, writing, politics, but you mustn't take

part in ruling because the Iraqi rulers are traitors who were brought in by the occupiers and who are so keen on remaining there.'[83]

The Iraqi Islamic Party determined to take part in the political process in spite of the Murshid's objections. This angered Akef: 'As for the Iraqi Islamic Party, it doesn't represent the Muslim Brothers. They say they are Muslim Brothers but they are not. They are not Ikhwan and they don't represent the Ikhwan in Iraq. I told them that clearly to their faces. What is happening in Iraq is a very dangerous situation. It is run by occupiers.'[84] Akef also states that there was still a group of Muslim Brothers operating underground in Iraq who were not taking part in the ruling structures. In a scene reminiscent of the earlier days of the international *tanzeem*, the Guidance Office decided to back a group of Iraqi Ikhwani who were not taking part in the political process whilst marginalising those who disagreed with it. Cairo's need to voice the sentiment of the street and to be seen to be standing up to the occupying power once again overrode its commitment to the political wishes of individual branches.

That both the Syrians and the Iraqis chose to ignore Cairo's objections is testimony to the fact that after all these years the international *tanzeem* had been reduced to little more than a talking shop. As Mohamed Habib explained, 'As the international *tanzeem,* we discuss challenges facing Islam and nationalist causes.'[85] However, for all that it might have had limited importance in recent years, contrary to the assertions of some brothers, the international *tanzeem* is most definitely a reality rather than a myth. Yet, the international *tanzeem* appears to have been primarily the romantic and unattainable dream of a group of Ikhwan led by Mustafa Mashour. The project was very much personality driven and it is no coincidence that the decline of the international organisation corresponded to the demise of Mashour. For a movement made up of so many different currents all facing different challenges the idea of pulling them together into a cohesive ideological and administrative unit was clearly over-ambitious and doomed to failure. The core concept of the international *tanzeem* went against the very characteristic of the Ikhwan that has enabled it to endure for so many years, namely its flexibility.

Whether the Arab Spring will see a renewed push for this international body to be reinvigorated has yet to be seen. The Brotherhood's emerging on to the political mainstream not only in Egypt, but also in Libya, has certainly opened up new possibilities for greater co-operation on the international level. Indeed, such co-operation is inevitable. Some elements within the Egyptian Brotherhood, however, have already taken to calling for the reactivation of the international *tanzeem*.[86] Senior Egyptian Brotherhood member, Sofwat Hijazi, meanwhile, has called for the setting up of an alliance of 'Ikhwani *wilayas*' (governates). Hijazi has also spoken of his dream of establishing a new caliphate across the Islamic world.[87] Whilst such talk of a new caliphate is clearly exaggerated, and whilst national priorities continue to dominate, not least because of the precariousness of the post-revolutionary climate, particularly in Egypt, there may well be a growing momentum among some parts of the movement to try to extend the Brotherhood's international reach through the international *tanzeem* once again.

4

A School of Thought

The Ikhwan in Europe

Whilst the main focus of the Ikhwan's activity has been the Middle East and the Islamic world, Europe has also provided an arena for this transnational movement. The Ikhwan put down roots in the continent in the 1950s and 1960s, through students who had come to Europe to study and figures such as Egyptian Ikhwani Said Ramadan, who sought to spread *dawa*. The Ikhwan's numbers were bolstered too by those fleeing persecution from their own regimes who sought refuge in various European countries. Through the 1970s and 1980s, when the period of Islamic revivalism swept Islamic communities in Europe, just as it did the Arab world, the Ikhwan was able to capitalise on the renewed religious consciousness combined with increased politicisation. During the 1980s in particular, when the international *tanzeem* was at its peak, Europe became an important financial centre for the Ikhwan as well as a media centre that could assist in instrumentalising the struggle in the Middle East. The Brotherhood built up a network of mosques and Islamic centres, often with money from backers in the Gulf, and was able to spread its *dawa* among Islamic communities. By the end of the 1990s the Ikhwan had in many countries been able to establish itself as the primary Islamic organisation, quietly dominating religious institutions across the continent. As Dr Kamal Helbawy observed, 'Wherever Muslim Brothers go they establish institutions. They don't like to work individually.'[1]

Whilst the Ikhwan had its differences with those of a more militant bent who were also active in the continent, the distinction between moderates and radicals was not so clear-cut at this time. The nature of the community was such that these groups orbited around each other, disagreeing bitterly with each other's methods but ultimately feeling that they were part of the same Muslim minority. The events of 9/11 would change this situation: the Ikhwan suddenly found itself forced to take a very public stance on a range of issues from violence to terrorism to radicalisation.

The Brotherhood has responded to these new challenges with characteristic pragmatism, seeking to posit itself as the main interlocutor between Muslim communities and governments in a bid to extend its political and educational influence. This in turn has given them a greater control over their own communities. In this way, they have almost become pillars of the establishment, part of the status quo; something that has brought them the ridicule of more hardline elements, who accuse them of selling out. Their willingness to work with the establishment is partly a continuation of the Ikhwan's tradition of working within existing political frameworks, but it is also symptomatic of the limited appeal that they have among Muslim communities, leaving them desperately seeking a way to increase their own political leverage. Moreover, the Ikhwan has generally been considered as an elitist group within the Islamic milieu.

Analysing the evolution of the Ikwhan in Europe is particularly challenging because in many cases its members are reticent about their links to the Brotherhood. Their desire to avoid such linkages is understandable in that many Ikhwani brought the mentality of their own countries to Europe, fearing that their own security services would target them even whilst they were there or, worse, that their families back home would be harassed as a result of any open connections to the Ikwhan. Such concerns are not as far-fetched as they may appear. In 1981 Syrian Ikhwani Issam al-Attar was targeted by the Syrian security services in Germany in an attack that left his wife dead. The Libyan regime was also known for getting rid of troublesome opponents during the 1980s. However, the fear of being openly associated with the Ikhwan extends further. Many Ikhwani are wary of being associated with an organisation that has such a negative reputation in some Western circles and that – despite its pacific stance – has been involved in violence on occasion. Such concerns became all the more pressing after 9/11, when the Brotherhood feared that it might be proscribed as a terrorist organisation.

Another reason that some Ikhwani in Europe have sought to conceal their links to the Brotherhood is their desire to reach beyond their natural constituencies to attract a wider support base. They have played on the idea that the Brotherhood is a school of thought rather than a movement. In some senses this is true; the reformist conservative Islam that they are promoting is the ideology followed by many communities across the Islamic world. As such they have tried to present their organisations as following the same broad philosophy as the Ikhwan but with no institutional linkage to the movement. However, the vast majority of those running these Islamic organisations in Europe are fully fledged members of the Brotherhood, in many cases tightly enmeshed into the Ikhwan's international networks through family, marriage or personal ties.

The bid to distance themselves from the Ikhwan is further driven by the fact that such linkages are a potential source of problems and embarrassment. Living as part of a minority community in Europe means that these Islamist leaders need to be able to dissociate themselves from some of the proclamations of key Ikhwani leaders over issues such as suicide bombing, the war in Iraq and Palestine, as well as over women's rights and the treatment of religious minorities. Ironically, this sometimes puts the leaders at odds with their own constituencies; such proclamations may represent popular opinion, yet these organisations cannot afford to be seen to be supporting such ideas within the confines of their host countries. In addition, there has been a need since 9/11 to distance from Saudi Arabia and the financial flows from the Gulf that had so assisted them in the past.

However, Ikhwani unwillingness to come forward and be frank about their origins and their relationships only serves to increase suspicions about the movement and its true objectives within Europe. Some commentators have even suggested that the Ikhwan seeks to extend Sharia law throughout Europe and the US.[2] Such suggestions smack somewhat of scaremongering. In any case the Ikhwani are realistic enough to understand that this is far beyond their capabilities. They are more interested in furthering the rights of their own communities through the small steps that they can achieve. Moreover, due to the fact that many Ikhwan-oriented organisations are still dominated by first-generation immigrants, their preoccupations are in many cases still centred on the Arab world. Ikhwani organisations in Europe have remained mostly the domain of Arab communities; despite their desire to represent European Muslims, they are still unable to reach out beyond their own ethnic groups.

Whilst it is incorrect to read the evolution of the various Ikhwani-oriented organisations in Europe as the evolution of the Ikhwan *per se*, the links between these groups and the Brotherhood are too strong to be ignored. Ikhwani in the Middle East, in Cairo especially, refer to these organisations as 'our brothers in France' or 'our brothers in the UK'. Similarly, others within the Islamic community in Europe refer to them as the Ikhwani and are frustrated at their unwillingness to admit to their relationship to the movement. However, the Ikhwan's main strategy in Europe appears to have been to find a way to make itself more acceptable to Western governments as a means of bolstering its political influence.

France and the UOIF

The main Islamic organisation in France is the *Union des Organisations Islamiques de France* (UOIF), widely regarded as the French branch of the Muslim Brotherhood, although the union itself rejects this affiliation. It is perhaps the most important and established national Islamic organisation in Europe. Although it was formally established in 1983, the history of Ikhwani activity in France goes back to the 1960s at least and the UOIF has its roots in other Islamic groups that were active at the time. These include the *Association des Étudiants Islamiques en France* (AEIF), a student body that was set up in 1963 by Indian Professor Muhammad Hamidullah who was linked to the Muslim Brotherhood through his ties to Said Ramadan and to Syrian Ikhwani Issam al-Attar, who was to have a major influence over the AEIF's teachings and ideology. The AEIF was predominantly an elitist organisation composed mostly of activist students from the Arab world. It was small but managed to establish branches in the main French university cities. During the 1960s and 1970s it focused its efforts on encouraging the Islamic renaissance and fighting the left-wing currents of the day and became one of the most established Islamic organisations in France.

The other key group that would go on to form the core of the UOIF was the *Groupement Islamique de France* (GIF), which was founded in 1979 in Valenciennes in northeast France, not far from the city of Lille. It was set up by a group of Tunisian students, led by Ahmed Jaballah, who were linked to the Tunisian opposition, *Mouvement de la Tendance Islamique* (MTI), which would later become An-Nahda. The MTI, led by Rashid al-Ghannouchi, was generally considered to be the Tunisian branch of the Muslim Brotherhood. However, whilst al-Ghannouchi was heavily influenced by the Ikhwan and by key Ikhwani scholars, by the early 1980s the MTI had begun to move away from the rigidity of the Brotherhood's approach. The GIF was intended to act as the French branch of this Tunisian opposition movement and as such much of its early activities were focused on the situation in Tunisia.[3] Unlike the AEIF, the GIF sought to appeal more to workers and to the grass roots rather than just to the intellectual elite, so began giving Friday sermons at the hostels for foreign workers that housed many North African immigrants with the aim of re-Islamicising those who had deviated from the straight path. They also engaged in typical Ikhwani community work: running summer camps, organising pilgrimages, visiting hospitals and prisons, holding conferences and organising demonstrations about issues related to the Islamic world.[4]

Although the GIF was the domain of the Tunisians, the driving force behind the organisation was actually Lebanese scholar Faisal al-Mawlawi, who the group chose as its spiritual guide. (Al-Mawlawi was a committed brother who was close to the Guidance Office in Cairo and who lived in France from 1980 to 1985.) This prompted a rather curious situation whereby whilst the vast majority of the Muslim population in France came from or had their origins in North Africa, it was left to the Lebanese al-Mawlawi and the Syrian al-Attar to lead and act as spiritual guides for these communities.

By August 1983 these Islamist groups decided to pool their efforts and come together under a new umbrella group called the *Union des Organisations Islamiques de France* (UOIF). A number of issues had prompted the establishment of this new union in particular. Firstly, the election of the socialist Mitterand government in 1981 liberalised legislation on the establishment of foreign associations in France. More importantly, the early 1980s were a time of immense optimism among Muslim communities all over the world. The Iranian revolution of 1979 had brought new hope that an Islamic alternative was possible, and the spirit of brotherly support incited by the project to liberate Afghanistan from communist rule had ushered in a new Islamic awareness and consciousness that these organisations were keen to capitalise on. It was also a time when the Ikhwan itself had renewed vigour and when Mustafa Mashour was trying to activate his international *tanzeem* in Europe in particular.

The main figures driving this new union in France were two students, the Tunisian Abdallah Ben Mansour and the Iraqi nuclear scientist Mahmoud Zouheir, who were both based in Meurthe-et-Moselle in northeast France. In spite of the Iraqi presence through Zouheir and the continued influence of al-Mawlawi, who remained the group's spiritual guide, the main group of activists in the new union were the Tunisians who had formed the core of the GIF. Their primary aim at this time was to forge an Islamic consciousness among Muslim communities in France. There was little real sense of the need to integrate into the host society at this point, and key figures within the Islamic movement were explicit in their aspirations to establish an Islamic state. In 1984 al-Mawlawi gave a lecture in a mosque on how to be a Muslim in France whilst at the same time pursuing one's own jihad in order to bring down impious powers and establish an Islamic state.[5]

There was also a distinct effort to encourage 'wayward' Muslims to turn away from the 'dangers' of corrupting French society and return to their faith. The association produced a magazine called *Al-Haqq* that carried articles and quizzes aimed at young Muslims in France. One such quiz, dated 2 April 1985, carried the question, 'Define a *kafir* [heathen].' The answer, which appeared in a later edition, was as follows: 'There are three sorts of *kafirs*. 1. Those who are Christian, Jewish, Atheist, Buddhist. 2. Those who are part of an organisation other than Islam. 3. Those who do not accept Mohamed our Prophet as God's messenger.'[6] Clearly these Islamists were deeply anxious about their own communities being 'corrupted' by the hedonistic attractions of French life and they were content to promote a divisive message aimed at promoting separation from the host community.

However, in spite of all its efforts to bring Muslims back to the straight path, until the end of the 1980s the UOIF was relatively marginal in the field of French Islam and had a very limited public voice. In particular it struggled to compete with the official Paris mosque, which was linked to the Algerian state and that dominated all alliances with the French government. However, one affair was to catapult the UOIF into the French limelight and allow it to garner grass roots support while the Paris mosque came to look like the staid voice of the establishment. This was the hijab (veil) affair of 1989.

In October 1989 three schoolgirls were refused entry to their secondary school in Creil because they were wearing the hijab. The issue was soon settled when a local Tunisian association leader stepped in to mediate: it was agreed that the girls could wear the hijab in the corridors and during playtime but that they would have to remove their veils during lessons. Yet by this time the increasingly assertive UOIF had seen a golden opportunity to raise its profile and it waded into the debate. Abdallah Ben Mansour and Mokhtar Jaballah, a leader of the UOIF's Paris branch, made a very public visit to the school to explain that Islam stipulated that women should be veiled. After this visit the girls broke their previous agreement and continued wearing the hijab in school, which prompted them to be excluded again. The UOIF's intervention had essentially radicalised the whole affair; it was not long before demonstrations were taking place in the streets of Paris. In the eyes of many within the Muslim community, the UOIF with its public activism had outshone the mosque of Paris, which had deplored the demonstrations. On 21 November the temperature was raised even higher when the UOIF's President, Ahmed Jaballah, wrote an open letter to the Prime Minister challenging the state and declaring that the Qur'an was explicit that it was the duty of all women to wear the veil.[7]

The affair had allowed the UOIF to act as the defenders of the Muslim community on an issue that touched many immigrants and families of North African descent, who were struggling to come to terms with their identities as a minority community in an avowedly secular state. Indeed, the UOIF's siding with the girls meant that 'the organisation won both in terms of its social and media visibility. From this event the union experienced an exceptional growth.'[8]

The veil affair marked a new consciousness in the UOIF of the role that they could play in shaping Islam within the French context rather than focusing their energies on struggles in their home countries. This was partly driven by the failure of the Tunisian Islamist opposition, which by the end of the 1990s had been stamped out by the Tunisian regime. Those running the UOIF were coming to understand that their main constituency was the young second- and third-generation immigrants, who required a different approach from the first-generation migrants who were less rooted in French society.

At the annual UOIF congress in 1989 Sheikh Rashid al-Ghannouchi declared that France should no longer be considered as *Dar al-Ahd* (land of covenant) but instead as *Dar al-Islam* (land of Islam).[9] This was a clear recognition of the fact that France was home to Muslims who were fully settled on French soil. These ideas had already been mooted by Faisal al-Mawlawi, who told a UOIF conference in 1986 that Western territories should be considered as *Dar al-Dawa* (land of *dawa*) and that the divisions between *Dar al-Harb* (land of war) and *Dar al-Islam* had no canonical basis but were simply an interpretation by Islamic scholars.[10] However, al-Ghannouchi's comments encapsulated a new way of thinking that asserted that Muslims must 'overcome prejudices whilst maintaining the principles of Islam and trying to establish a sincere dialogue in order to achieve a sincere integration'.[11] Within this same vein, in 1990 the UOIF changed its name to better reflect this reality, becoming the Union of Islamic Organisations *of* France rather than the Union of Islamic Organisations *in* France. In the same year they focused their annual Le Bourget gathering on 'Muslims and Integration'.

The UOIF began to focus its attentions on the student population and on the elite who could raise the banner of Islam inside France. This bid to appeal to the middle classes was typical of the Brotherhood, which had always drawn most of its support from this sector of society. Shortly afterwards the movement underwent another shift, as the more militant Tunisian leadership was edged out and a group of Moroccans took over stewardship of the organisation.

The new leaders were Lhaj Thami Breeze, who became the President, and Fouad Alaoui, who became Secretary General. Both men had studied at Bordeaux, Breeze reading political science and Alaoui neuropsychology, and neither had any theological training. These two men, who still run the organisation today, took the UOIF down a decidedly moderate path, giving it a softer, more accommodationist image.

According to some accounts, one of the reasons for this change in leadership was that at the time Tunisians involved in Islamist activism found it more difficult to obtain French nationality than their Moroccan counterparts.[12] Yet whilst this factor may have played into the change of leadership, the takeover by the Moroccan group was more likely to be a reflection of the nationalistic in-fighting that has traditionally characterised such organisations.

It is interesting to note that the UOIF has always been dominated by Tunisians and Moroccans despite the fact that the Algerians represent the most populous Muslim community in France. That is not to say that Algerians have not been involved in the UOIF or made up some of its grass roots organisations, but they have always had a limited impact on the organisation's leadership. It is not entirely clear why this is the case, but it would seem to be linked to the fact that the Algerians became increasingly tied into the unfolding civil war inside Algeria during the 1990s. As such the Algerians were attracted to organisations such as the Front Islamique du Salut (FIS) and the Fraternité Algérienne en France (FAF), which was essentially the French branch of the FIS who were fully engaged in events in the homeland. As UOIF representative in Marseille Mohsen N'Gazou explained, 'The Algerian community saw some kind of hope in the

FIS. We saw the opposite ... The Algerians tried to build up a good picture of the FIS in the Union.'[13] Indeed, as the 1990s developed and parts of the FIS became involved in violence against the Algerian state, there was a fear within the UOIF that it might be accused of supporting the FIS or of being linked to it in some way. However, in its bid to present itself as a broad-based movement the UOIF has had to make it look as though it is not purposefully excluding the Algerians. As a former French Interior Ministry official noted, 'It is important for the UOIF to say there are Algerians in the organisation. So they put some Algerians in the office.'[14]

The UOIF and the Ikhwan

Unsurprisingly, the issue of the connections between the Ikhwan and the UOIF is a highly controversial one that tends to irritate the UOIF immensely. It seems to see its connection to the Brotherhood as some sort of unshakeable albatross. The UOIF leadership has repeatedly denied any formal association with the Ikhwan. Sheikh Ahmed Jaballah has categorically stated, 'We have no formal relationship to the Ikhwan in Egypt.'[15] Fouad Alaoui says: 'We don't have any organic link with this organisation [MB] ... It is a movement among others. We respect it in the sense that it advocates a renewal and a modernist reading of Islam.'[16] He also stated: 'The UOIF has nothing to do with the Muslim Brotherhood.'[17] The UOIF has taken the line that it falls broadly within the same reformist school as the Ikhwan and relies upon texts of key Ikhwani figures as Islamic references but it has no institutional linkage to the movement.

This is not to say that the UOIF does not acknowledge its earlier links to the Brotherhood or the fact that it sought to model itself on the Egyptian branch. Breeze explained that at the time when the UOIF was set up: 'We were students and we looked to Egypt at that time including for our understanding of how to apply the Ikhwan project in Europe and how to apply concepts.'[18] French Islamic scholar Tareq Oubrou also explained that at that time 'the books of Mohamed Ghazali, Yusuf al-Qaradawi, and Sayyid Qutb were circulating on university campuses ... The reading that for us most reconciled modernity and tradition was that of the Muslim Brothers.'[19] Mohsen N'Gazou, meanwhile, has stated, 'We are ideologically Muslim Brothers.'[20]

Following the same ideological path as the Ikhwan does not of course equate to being formally linked to the Brotherhood. However, the informal ties are apparent and many figures who have played a key role within the UOIF have been closely connected to or members of the Ikhwan. This includes not only Faisal al-Mawlawi, but also Rashid al-Ghannouchi and Mahfoud Nahnah. According to Moulay Abderrahmane Ghoul, the President of the *Conseil Régional du Culte Musulman* in Marseille, 'Mahfoud Nahnah was very influential. He used to have a major influence and the UOIF had to consult with him.'[21] This was reiterated by the former Mufti of Marseille, Soheib Bensheikh, who observed: 'The UOIF has a connection with the Algerian Hamas. Sheikh Nahnah used to support the UOIF financially on very low levels.'[22] Nahnah was also a member of the orientation council of Château-Chinon. According to Ghoul, Sheikh Abu Jarrah Sultani, Nahnah's successor, also has close links to the UOIF: 'When they decide on who is in their councils, Sultani has the final say in the union and they have to consult with him.' Given that Ghoul is generally considered to be a representative of the Algerian state, this may be exaggerated. However, there are clearly very close links between the Algerian Ikhwani leaders and the UOIF. In addition, Ahmed Nachatt, one of the early leaders of the Union, was married to the daughter of Mustafa Mashour. Yusuf al-Qaradawi has also been closely linked to the UOIF. Although al-Qaradawi is not part of the Brotherhood, he is generally considered to be the most influential proponent of the Ikhwani way of thinking. All of these figures have been in regular attendance at the UOIF's annual Le Bourget gathering over many years.

As such, the UOIF is totally rooted in the Ikhwan tradition. However, figures such as Breeze have asserted that whilst the UOIF looked to the Brotherhood for inspiration in the early days, it soon came to realise that it needed a different kind of approach in order to survive in the French context. Breeze pinpoints this new understanding to the time when it renamed the UOIF, explaining, 'The Brotherhood and the community started looking at things differently. We realised that we couldn't just bring ideas and thoughts to Europe.'[23] He also stated that whilst the UOIF agreed with the Ikhwan's general approach, it disagreed with some of the Brotherhood's basic goals and objectives. 'We are not thinking of setting up an Islamic society, we are not thinking of an Islamic government ... We think as individuals, not as a collective. We cannot be an alternative to the state.'[24] As Breeze also described, 'The doctrine of the Muslim Brothers is certainly valuable in the field of Islam.'

He went on to explain that they didn't want to 'reproduce their objectives or their methods here without reflecting a different reality.'[25] Sheikh Ahmed Jaballah also supported this stance, noting, 'We don't want to be under the influence of Arab countries.'[26] However, he is famously alleged to have declared, 'The Qur'an is our constitution' during the UOIF's annual Le Bourget meeting of 2002.[27]

As such the UOIF represents perhaps the first evolution of the Ikhwan into an organisation that could sit relatively comfortably within Western society. However, the organisation faces the same problem as all Islamist organisations operating in the West, namely how to deal with being a minority community in a secular state. The UOIF is fully aware, for example, that it cannot maintain the same platform as its Middle Eastern counterparts if it is to play a political role in European countries. For this reason, the UOIF insisted that its members could not also be members of other political organisations at the same time. The UOIF reportedly told Tunisians from An-Nahda (formerly MTI), that they had to choose 'whether to focus on Tunisian politics or whether to move on'.[28] Likewise, the UOIF is alleged to have made it clear that if al-Mawlawi was to be their leader, he would need to cut his relations with the Ikhwan.[29]

However, others within the Islamic community in France remained less convinced by this separation. Former UOIF member Dhaou Meskine declared to the French media, 'The UOIF is a branch of the Muslim Brotherhood. Why are those in charge ashamed of saying so?'[30] He has also argued that in its quest for respectability the UOIF has masked its true identity. Similarly Sheikh Abdelhadi, a prominent Salafist imam at the Sunna mosque in Marseille, has roundly condemned the UOIF, stating, 'They are hypocrites. In front of the government they pretend they are not brothers but in the mosques they call upon the Ikhwan in their methods.'[31] He also asserts that they 'use these methods to gain power'.[32] Abdelhadi categorically states, 'Jaballah is a Muslim Brother. He goes to Saudi Arabia to get money.'[33] Clearly this is the view of someone who considers the Ikhwan as competition, yet there is much suspicion about the UOIF's links to the Brotherhood within the Islamist community at large. One former UOIF member also complained that having publicly linked the UOIF and the Brotherhood he paid a heavy price, suffering attacks in the media and having his financial flows cut.[34]

In some cases, the UOIF's policies have seemingly been very much influenced by Cairo. One former senior French Interior Ministry official recounted how the UOIF sought at one point to withdraw from the *Conseil Français du Culte Musulman* (CFCM), a consultation body set up in 2003 and tasked with defending the dignity and interests of the Muslim faith in France.[35] Alarmed at the UOIF's threat to pull out of the consultation process, the frustrated official allegedly complained to the then Murshid Maimoun al-Hodeibi. Al-Hodeibi reportedly told the official that the UOIF was free to do what it pleased, but mentioned that he would speak to Breeze. Shortly afterwards, the UOIF announced that it would be staying in the consultation process after all. This anecdote is clearly not sufficient basis upon which to claim that the UOIF is steered in some way by the Ikhwan in Cairo. However, it does reveal the importance of personal contacts and informal hierarchy in its relationship to the Brotherhood. Fouad Alaoui has admitted that he met regularly with the late Dr Hassan al-Huwaidi, the Deputy to the Murshid. Another UOIF member has also admitted, 'Once or twice a year we have meetings with the international *tanzeem* – with Islamists from Turkey, Pakistan, with Sufists in West Africa.'[36]

In spite of its initial threat to withdraw, the UOIF's membership of the CFCM became an important opportunity for it to make contacts with the French state and to act as stakeholders and representatives of the Muslim community in France. Yet this reconciliatory stance had the drawback of alienating the UOIF somewhat from its own constituencies. It was heavily criticised by other Islamic groups for selling out and forgetting the interests of Muslims. Perhaps no affair illustrated this more than the renewed saga of the hijab, which flared up again in 2004 when French MPs voted to ban all overt religious symbols, including the Islamic veil, from state schools. Unlike in 1989 when the UOIF jumped in and stoked up the situation, this time the leadership took a far more subtle approach, aware that its image was at stake and that its response would be heavily scrutinised in the post 9/11 Western obsession with 'moderate Islam'. As Breeze noted at the time, 'We do not want to provoke the French government so as not to lose the gains we made over the past few years.'[37]

Although the UOIF leadership initially encouraged street demonstrations, they made it clear that they did not want to create any trouble for the French state. They urged people not to engage in violence and made a series of accommodationist statements. Breeze said: 'We just do not want protestors to use slogans that are antagonistic to France, a country where Muslims also have the liberty to perform their prayers in mosques. The veil ban, after all, is only restricted to state schools and Muslim women are still free to wear it in public.'[38] He also explained, 'We are not telling Muslim girls to take off the hijab. We are saying they should go to school and not wear a veil which is a distinctive sign of their religion.'[39] Fouad Alaoui also made an appeal to young French women, declaring, 'They should make their schooling a priority.'[40] Yet in spite of all its efforts the UOIF had the rug pulled from under its feet by the French government. In 2003 whilst all the public debates were raging, the then Interior Minister Nicolas Sarkozy travelled to Cairo to meet with Sheikh Tantawi of Al-Azhar. He obtained a fatwa which ruled that Islamic headscarves were not obligatory if prohibited by a national law. Clearly this move left the UOIF and other Islamic organisations in France feeling as though they had been completely bypassed and snubbed by the same government that had courted them for membership of its CFCM.

For an issue that had provoked so much anger and frustration, not only in France but among Muslims the world over, the UOIF's approach was extraordinarily low key. Many believed that this should be its time to lead the way in fighting what was widely considered in Islamic circles to be an alarmist and Islamophobic gesture. Yamin Makri, the head of the more radical *Collectif des Musulmans de France*, criticised the UOIF for compromising and thereby losing legitimacy among young Muslims.[41] Makri also laid into the UOIF for betting its hopes on institutional acknowledgement and for becoming conservative and biased.[42] Yet the UOIF was clear that it did not want to lose the gains it had made in the French political sphere. As Breeze explained, 'We are willing to lose the battle of the hijab but not France.'[43]

As such, it would appear that the UOIF has prioritised politics over core religious values as a means of maintaining international respectability – arguably a risky strategy that has the potential to alienate key elements within its support base. This is an issue that many parts of the Brotherhood have struggled with over recent years, from the Syrians to the Egyptians to those in Europe. However, the Ikhwani in Europe are in a somewhat easier position than their counterparts in the Arab world in this respect. This is because their constituencies are very small and they are aware that they are in no position to become an alternative to the state. As such they have much less to lose.

Britain and the MAB

Britain has long had a reputation for being a hotbed of Islamist activism. This was especially true during the 1980s and 1990s, to the point where its capital city was dubbed Londonistan. By this point the country had become home to a wide array of Islamist groups from moderate to militant and was a veritable melting pot of ideologies and organisations. Among those groups who were active in the UK was of course the Ikhwan, who like the myriad of other Islamist currents there sought to promote its *dawa* and to bring people to its way of thinking. It is because of these competing ideologies and currents, as well as the presence of large South Asian migrant communities, that the Ikhwan in Britain has been far more difficult to pin down than its counterparts in France. In fact, Ikhwani activity in the UK has tended to revolve around a few key personalities and to be less institutionalised than across the Channel.

The Brotherhood's presence in Britain dates back to the 1950s, when Ikhwani students from the Arab world came to study in the UK. After 1954, they were joined by a number of key Egyptian brothers fleeing the clampdowns of President Nasser, who spent some time touring Britain to spread the word about the atrocities being committed by the nationalist regime, which was still being hailed as a great triumph by many Arab communities.[44] However, the first solid Muslim Brotherhood activity in Britain came in the form of two student groups. The first was the Muslim Students' Society (MSS), set up in 1961, and the second was the Federation of Student Islamic Societies (FOSIS), established the following year. Both societies were founded by Ikhwani who had strong links to the mother branch in Egypt. This included the Egyptian Sheikh Ahmed al-Ahsan, who was studying in the UK and who has been described as Sheikh Yuuf al-Qaradawi's twin because the two men went to school together and trained at Al-Azhar at the same time. Another key figure was the Indian scholar Mustafa Azami, who had been imprisoned in Egypt for his Ikhwani activities and had come to the UK to continue his PhD at Cambridge. With them were a number of Iraqi and Syrian Ikhwani students.

The main tasks of these organisations were to spread *dawa*, to organise demonstrations in front of Arab embassies and to support Muslim students in the UK by providing them with accommodation and 'helping them not to melt in this society'.[45] The main difference between the two groups was that the MSS was a purely Ikhwani organisation whose followers 'believed very strongly in the ideas of Hassan al-Banna and in the thoughts of Hassan al-Banna',[46] whilst FOSIS had a broader platform and sought to appeal to those beyond the Brotherhood. As such MSS was primarily an Arab organisation whereas members of the South Asian community became involved in FOSIS, bringing in the influence of Islamist groups from Pakistan. As Pakistani writer Ziauddin Sardar, who was the General Secretary of FOSIS in the early 1970s, explained, 'Like most members of FOSIS, I was strongly influenced by the Muslim Brotherhood of Egypt and Jama'at-e-Islami of Pakistan.'[47] Both groups were very active and were able to attract large numbers of Muslims to their events. For example, Egyptian Ikhwan Dr Kamal Helbawy gave a series of lectures in the UK in the mid-1970s on behalf of the MSS which he asserts were attended by between two and three thousand people.[48]

Among those Ikhwani who joined these organisations at the time were figures such as Ashur Shamis, Alamin Osman and the Iraqi

Osama Tikriti. It was also at this time that the Muslim Welfare House in Finsbury Park in North London was established. Inaugurated in 1970, this organisation aimed to provide support to Muslim students in the UK. It became another key Ikhwani hub in Britain and was part of the Brotherhood's network there. The centre continues to be a base for the Ikhwan; one of its imams explained that the Ikhwan still has its offices there.[49]

Said Ramadan also played a part in helping to establish the Ikhwan in Britain. In 1964 Ramadan set up his Islamic centre in London along with a group of fellow Islamists including the Iraqi Riad Al Droubie and the Sudanese Ja'far Sheikh Idris. The latter was a member of the Sudanese Ikhwan who had a reputation for being a purist; in the 1970s he broke away from Hassan al-Turabi, whom he later charged with apostasy. The Islamic centre became another key focal point for Ikhwani ideas. Ramadan himself maintained strong connections with FOSIS and was a regular visitor to their head office.

Although relatively small, these organisations were what Helbawy has described as the 'first institutional nucleus of the Ikhwan in Britain'.[50] However, as in many European centres, the relationship between these organisations and the Muslim Brotherhood was never clear. As Helbawy puts it:

> They never said 'we are Ikhwan' or established an Ikhwan centre publicly ... MSS and FOSIS and the Muslim Welfare House were the institutions ... They were not under the Muslim Brotherhood although they received the leaders from abroad, they helped them, they trusted them. The only [Brotherhood] public organisation or institution was when I started the Muslim Brotherhood media centre in 1994 or '95.[51]

These organisations may not have been directly under the control of the Ikhwan but its influence was unmistakable. Aside from the fact that the organisations had been established by members of the Brotherhood and were in many cases run by Ikhwani, they also hosted some of the most influential members of the Ikhwan at their events. The MSS has hosted numerous Ikhwani figures over the years including some of the most important individuals in the movement such as Hassan al-Banna's son Saif al-Islam, former Murshids Sheikh Hamid Abu Nasser and Mustafa Mashour, as well as Dr. Hassan al-Huwaidi and Hassan al-Turabi.[52]

Moreover, these groups were certainly promoting Ikhwani ideas and distributing key Brotherhood texts among Muslim students. As the climate in the Arab world and inside the Brotherhood radicalised during the 1960s and 1970s with the publication of texts by Sayyid Qutb, these ideas also came to gain currency in the West. Sardar says: 'The trials and tribulations of Sayyid Qutb resonated and had a very real meaning for us. Many older members of FOSIS had not only witnessed the events of Qutb's life but lived their own lives through them. We constantly read his commentaries on the Qur'an, *In the Shade of the Quran*, and chanted the slogans of the Brotherhood.'[53]

Qutb's famous text *Milestones* was also popular; Sardar explains how 'A truly appalling translation, complete with legions of typographical errors, was published in Kuwait and distributed free to members of FOSIS.'[54] This enthusiasm was hardly surprising: Muslims in Britain had also become swept up in the Islamic revivalism that was taking hold across the Islamic world and that seemed to offer such promise after the crushing disappointment of the Arab nationalist era.

In spite of its widening support base the Ikhwan in Britain did not evolve into one overarching public organisation until well into the 1990s and operated in a far less formalised way than its counterparts in France, for example. As Ashur Shamis explains, 'What existed in the UK were members from all over the Arab world affiliated to their [Ikhwani] groups back home, if such groups existed. These would work together as much as was practically possible. These people were not permanent residents here. It was a makeshift existence. There was no independent [British] group.'[55]

There were several reasons for this. Firstly, given the nature of migration patterns based upon the colonial experience, the most populous Muslim communities in Britain came from South Asia, leaving Arabs as a minority within a minority. Unlike in France, where the Muslim community was predominantly North African, the Ikhwani in Britain had to compete with a range of Islamic associations linked to Pakistan, Bangladesh and India. In spite of aspirations to the *umma*, even when there were close ideological connections between Arab and South Asian groups, these ethnic barriers could not be fully overcome. To take one example, although the Pakistani Jama'at-e-Islami essentially shared the Brotherhood's ideological platform and both organisations worked within FOSIS, these two groups were not prepared to merge into one organisation. As Dr Kamal Helbawy has noted, 'When we were in Pakistan, if anyone [Pakistani] came to me and said I would like to join the Ikhwan, I would say, go and join Jamaat-al-Islami.'[56] As such, there was less motivation and opportunity to come together under one large umbrella that would enable the Ikhwan to act as the primary representatives of the Muslim community in the UK.

The Ikhwan in Britain therefore relied heavily upon the presence of important Ikhwani figures who visited the country on a regular basis and made themselves available to the brothers there. This included some at the apex of the Brotherhood such as Omar al-Tilimsani, Mustafa Mashour, Hassan al-Turabi and Abdul Majid. They acted as informal guides to the other British-based brothers. 'In Britain there were senior brothers who were considered as a reference point. If someone needed anything, they rang him and said, "What do you advise us?" They were like institutions.'[57] That is not to say that there were not leaders of the Ikhwani in Britain at the time. At one point the Sudanese brother Alamin Osman was in charge of the brothers in the UK. However, this was a much more informal outfit that the UOIF in France.

Although the Ikhwan in the UK was still working through the MSS, FOSIS and the Muslim Welfare House, it was certainly part of an international Ikhwani consultation process. In view of its size, it was not awarded a place within the international *tanzeem*'s Guidance Office. Ikhwani groups in Europe were generally considered to be less important than those in the Arab world, not least because there was no chance of the Ikhwan in the West ever acting as an alternative to the state. As Helbawy explained, 'In Arab countries there were hopes to have an Islamic state. In Europe they are needed only for *dawa*. They are not expecting these people here to participate in the establishment of an Islamic state.'[58] But although these European groups were not able to participate directly in the formal institutions of the international *tanzeem*, they remained a key part of the consultation process by reporting to the leadership in Cairo on a regular basis. Every time an important Ikhwani figure came to the UK, the British brothers were expected to submit a written report detailing their activities, stance and any particular problems or issues that were affecting them. According to Helbawy:

> Britain was one of the countries where they had to give a report every time ... France came later but it was the same. We have people in Sweden, Denmark, Holland, Germany – whenever a responsible man from the Brotherhood comes for a visit everyone would like to see him and he would like to hear from everyone and carries this information back to the leadership ... This is the way the Muslim Brotherhood works.[59]

The lack of an official Ikhwani oriented organisation in the UK came to create problems within the wider Brotherhood movement. Some of these problems arose out of the fact that by the 1980s the UK had become a major centre of media activity. The brothers in Britain took full advantage of this fact and began publishing statements and giving interviews to the Arab media based in London. Their ability to use the media in this way came to be resented by some brothers in Egypt, who felt that those abroad were bolstering their own credentials at the expense of the local struggle in Egypt.[60] Moreover, on occasions the Ikhwan in London sent out contradictory messages to those being issued from Cairo. In 1981, for example, the Egyptian Ikhwan issued a statement about the Iran–Iraq war, denouncing the Iraqi regime and seemingly backing the Iranian side because of their Islamic revolution.[61] Shortly afterwards, a statement on the same topic was issued from the UK in the name of 'The World Muslim Brotherhood Organisation' and circulated by FOSIS. This statement took a different approach, seemingly treating Iran and Iraq as equals: 'The Muslim Brotherhood calls for putting an end to this war in order to direct the Muslim efforts towards the real battlefield with the international Judaism and confronting its dangers against Islam and Muslims all over the world.'[62]

However, Helbawy's arrival in London in the 1990s heralded a new phase in Ikhwani activity in the UK. In 1992 Helbawy decided to set up a media centre in London, breaking with tradition by publicly declaring it as a Muslim Brotherhood office. The main idea was to provide information about the situation in the Islamic world, especially in Egypt, Jordan and Syria. It issued an Eid message in February 1996 that read:

> This Eid has come at a time when the Muslim umma is in great pain and distress. A large part of Muslim umma is still suffering under persecution and oppression. Palestine is a bleeding sore in the heart of the Middle East. In Afghanistan, the Muslims continue to suffer; Kashmir is groaning under the weight of foreign occupation, Bosnia's wounds are painfully fresh, and Chechnya's courageous resistance to oppression has yet to witness the dawn of freedom from the 'evil empire'. Similarly, the Muslims in Algeria and Central Asia, and other places are embroiled in disastrous civil war and fighting. Muslim

minorities in different countries are still suffering from effects
of discrimination and prejudice against them.[63]

Helbawy, who was very active, was soon given the post of the
Brotherhood's spokesman in the West, which he took up in 1995.
However, as explained in Chapter Three, this did not work out due to
differences with Maimoun al-Hodeibi in Cairo.

Undeterred, Helbawy decided to continue with his Islamic
activities, although this time he opted to keep some distance from
the core of the Brotherhood in Cairo. In 1997 along with a number
of other brothers he launched a new umbrella organisation called the
Muslim Association of Britain (MAB). MAB was based in Kilburn,
a run-down suburb of northwest London. The new organisation was
to be a platform for the Ikhwan as well as being open to others who
were not necessarily members of the Brotherhood but who shared a
similar outlook and understanding of Islam. Again, the decision not
to link it directly to the Brotherhood was a strategic move that took
into account the very particular situation in which Muslims found
themselves in Europe. Helbawy explains:

> It was a British extension of Islamic dawa because saying that
> it is exactly like the Muslim Brotherhood would be difficult in
> the West ... Because if you go to the manhaj (methodology)
> of the Ikhwan you will find that in the East they are fighting
> for an Islamic state, for freedom, against dictatorship. We
> don't have anything like this here. So we were an extension, a
> tributary, to support just causes whether Islamic or not.[64]

However, to date there is little evidence to suggest that the MAB has
focused much if any attention on non-Islamic causes. A quick look
at the organisation's website news page reveals that the spotlight is
almost exclusively on Islamic issues, more often than not on Islamic

issues in the Arab world. The organisation remained a largely Arab affair; according to Hassan al-Khatib who chaired its Shura Council, 'We mainly come from Arabic communities and therefore Arabic will be MAB's first language and English the second language.'[65] In spite of the increased focus on integration into European society and its claim to 'represent British Muslims on all levels',[66] Arabic is still of vital importance. A job advertisement posted on its website in January 2008 for an Education and Sharia Consultant specified that the candidate should speak Arabic as well as English. This is an organisation that remains very much the domain of Arabs.

In traditional Ikhwani style the MAB has concentrated primarily on students and the middle classes. Shortly after the organisation was set up, Azzam Tamimi proudly declared that the founders 'are a brand of people who are the cream of society and come from diverse backgrounds and are highly qualified in respective fields.'[67] These accolades notwithstanding, the MAB has been unable to make any real inroads into the Muslim community in Britain. Its profile is far lower than that of the Muslim Council of Britain, often considered as its sister organisation, which is regarded as the main organisation for the UK's South Asian communities. The MAB appears still to be focused mainly around the key personalities who set it up, making little real outreach into the community.

Needless to say, the MAB became increasingly keen to distance itself from the Brotherhood in recent years. Its leader, the Somali Ikhwani Ahmed Sheikh, has categorically stated that the MAB is not part of the formal structure of the international Muslim Brotherhood.[68] He has also said 'our only link with the Egyptians is understanding. We co-ordinate over some activities.'[69] The official line of the MAB is as follows:

> The MAB enjoys good relations with every mainstream Islamic organisation in the UK and abroad. Among them is Muslim Brotherhood which is well respected not only by

> the common people on the street throughout the Arab and
> Muslim countries but also by politicians, intellectuals and
> opinion-makers in most Arab countries ... MAB reserves the
> right to be proud of the humane notions and principles of the
> Muslim Brotherhood, who has proven to be an inspiration
> to Muslims, Arab and otherwise for many decades. We
> also reserve the right to disagree with or divert from the
> opinion and line of the Muslim Brotherhood, or any other
> organisation, Muslim or otherwise on any issue at hand.[70]

Nonetheless, it is undeniable that most of the senior leadership of the
MAB are or were at one stage heavily involved in the Ikhwan. Aside
from Helbawy, Azzam Tamimi was active in Jordan within the Brotherhood and the Islamic Action Front.[71] Anas Tikriti, meanwhile, came
from a family associated with the Ikhwan, given that his father Osama
was head of the Iraqi branch of the Brotherhood.

The MAB may appear to be independent from the structures of
the Muslim Brotherhood but the informal linkages are undeniable.
Moreover, some figures within the MAB still consider themselves
part of the Brotherhood movement. One young member of the MAB,
Jamal el-Shayyal, who spoke on behalf of the organisation at the Stop
the War Coalition conference on 11 January 2003, stated that his
organisation was proud to be affiliated with the Brotherhood.[72]

He went on to explain during an interview with *The Weekly Worker*
magazine: 'As the Muslim Brotherhood, we have never seen a Muslim
state ... Officially, we emerged in the mid-1990s. Every single Muslim
organisation in Britain – apart from three – was set up under the
influence of the ideology of the Muslim Brotherhood. We have gone
from strength to strength.'[73] Such ambiguity does little to assuage
suspicions about the MAB and its links to the Brotherhood.

Like the UOIF, the MAB has been keen in recent years to promote a
more Europeanised version of Islam, one that fits with being a minority

community. Ahmed Sheikh supports the view that a new *fiqh* (school of Islamic jurisprudence) is required specifically for Muslims living in the West.[74] They have also sought to work as a lobby group engaging in local politics. The MAB channelled huge efforts into opposing the UK's role in the Iraqi invasion of 2003 and in 2004 it called on Muslims in Britain to vote only for candidates from parties that had steadfastly opposed the invasion of Iraq or any British military involvement there.[75] Yet it clearly advocated that Muslims participate in the electoral process. The MAB also threw its weight behind the former leftist London mayor Ken Livingstone, who controversially hosted Sheikh Yusuf al-Qaradawi in London. In addition it worked closely with non-Muslim organisations such as the left-wing Stop the War Coalition to organise anti-war demonstrations.

Yet whilst the Ikhwan in Britain may, through organisations such as the MAB, have found a stronger political voice in recent years, it remains a small group with very limited influence over Britain's Muslim communities. This is partly because many of the Ikhwani who came to Britain were students or refugees and the group was never able to spread beyond the elite. Nor has the Arab community in Britain been as settled as the South Asians who, like the North Africans in France, came *en masse* in response to demands for labour and settled into their own communities. For these reasons, organisations such as the MAB have not yet garnered any real grass roots support, leaving them largely irrelevant to the UK's vibrant Islamist scene.

Germany and the IGD

As in the UK, the first Ikhwani activity in Germany was begun in the 1950s by students from the Arab world. However, the first Ikhwani to establish a real base for the movement in Germany was Said Ramadan, who oversaw the building of a mosque and Islamic centre in Munich. The idea for the mosque did not come from Ramadan or the Brotherhood. The project was initiated by a group of Muslims who had fought with Germany against the Russians in the Second World War. They were led by Nurredine Nakibhodscha Namangani, an Uzbek who had been an imam for one of Hitler's SS divisions, and they also had German backing for their plan. Then a group of Ikhwani students in Munich heard about the project and called in Said Ramadan. One of these brothers, Mohamed Ali al-Mahgary, referred to Ramadan as 'a gifted orator', noting, 'we all respected him'.[76] Ramadan was quick to seize the opportunity to take over the mosque building commission in a bid to oust Namangani, whose traditionalist Turkic Islam was anathema to the purist Islam promoted by the Ikhwan. Ramadan was in a charmed position thanks to his generous supply of Saudi wealth; he was able to contribute an initial 1,000 marks to the mosque building commission, far outweighing the contributions of the other interested parties.[77]

As part of his strategy to dominate Islamist activism in Germany, in 1959 Ramadan also organised a European Muslim Congress in Munich. The following year he took over full control of the mosque construction committee, completely sidelining Namangani.

The mosque, which was given tax-exempt status by the West German government, was finally opened in 1973, reportedly with the help of generous contributions from Saudi Arabia. When the mosque opened, the building commission changed its name to the Islamic Community of Southern Germany, indicating its desire to extend its influence beyond the city of Munich. By this time, however, Ramadan had left Munich and the running of the mosque and organisation had been given to the Syrian Ikhwani Ghaleb Himmat. Himmat had come to Germany as a student and had little interest in what was going on inside the country.

Under Himmat's stewardship, the Munich mosque became a key centre for Ikhwani activity. This was not the only Brotherhood centre in Germany at this time. The town of Aachen, also known as

Aix-la-Chapelle, had also become an important Ikhwani hub on account of the fact that it was home to Issam al-Attar. Al-Attar had tried to lead the Syrian organisation from his exile, but the impracticality of such a venture, added to the fact that he was embroiled in a deep conflict over the leadership of the Syrian Ikhwan, resulted in his breaking away to form his own organisation, al-Talia, which was focused on activities in Europe. By the time he settled in Aachen, al-Attar had come to represent a new current of thinking that was similar to the Ikhwan's ideology but was largely independent from the Brotherhood. As such he only had the support of a minority of Syrian Ikhwani from the smaller and more moderate Damascus wing. Suggestions by some commentators that, 'while the Egyptian branch of the Muslim Brotherhood has chosen Munich as its base of operations in Germany, its Syrian branch is headquartered in Aachen, a German town near the Dutch border',[78] are therefore somewhat misplaced.

However, the Bilal mosque in Aachen developed as a magnet for Islamic activism and for other Syrian Ikhwani who had fled repression. West Germany was an important place of refuge and its hostility to the Soviet Union during the Cold War meant that it was ever ready to open its doors to refugees from Arab nationalist countries that had aligned themselves with the Soviet camp. Other Syrians who joined al-Attar in Aachen included Mohamed al-Hawari, who was also part of the sidelined Damascus group and who is now a member of the European Council for Fatwa and Research. The daughter of the late Dr Hassan al-Huwaidi also resides in Aachen with her family and so Aachen was al-Huwaidi's base during his many European visits.

However, the main centre of organised Ikhwani activity continued to be Munich. In 1981, still under Himmat's leadership, the Islamic Community of Southern Germany changed its name to the *Islamische Gemeinschaft Deutschland* (The Islamic Community of Germany, IGD), marking its territory over the whole country. The city drew many of the most important Ikhwani of the time. Mashour made several visits there after he fled Egypt in the early 1980s. The former Supreme Guide, Mehdi Akef, also spent time at the Munich centre. According to Egyptian intellectual Rifat Said, he was in Munich to mobilise the international *tanzeem* and control its financial flows.[79] The Egyptian leader, who had been part of the Nizam al-Khass, was based at the centre between 1984 and 1987.

> Being in Munich was a very pioneering experience and I used to deal with the German government in a very advanced way. There were some sensitive issues and I solved them with them because I felt they were well advanced in their thinking ... I used to have a conference every month in the mosque attended by thousands of Muslims from all parts of Germany. The mosque was at the entrance to the gate of an island and the inhabitants of that island complained. How did the government behave? They gave me a forest and cut down the trees and said this is yours.[80]

To give an indication of how important a base Munich was at that time, Akef has explained that whilst he was there statesmen from across the Muslim world visited the mosque to pay their respects to the world's most powerful Islamic organisation.[81] He also says that the Ikhwan sought to bring the various Muslim organisations under its banner: 'In Germany, when I lived there for a while, all our task was to unite the Muslims because there were different groups so we could be one representative to deal with the government.'[82]

Evidently, Germany was a key centre for the Ikhwan, although its importance rested not so much on its ability to attract the community, which after all was limited, but rather on the presence of important personnel, some of whom had access to money. Himmat was a successful businessman and the Deputy of the Al-Taqwa bank. The bank's head, Youssef Nada, was also on the council of the Munich mosque. The city became a kind of backroom powerhouse for the Ikhwan in the Arab world, where the Brothers could move around freely, use the Western media and presumably facilitate their financial operations.

The events of 9/11 would change this situation. Although the IGD allegedly came under greater scrutiny by the German intelligence services in the late 1990s, it was only really after the attacks on the US that the organisation was really put under the spotlight. Shortly after the attacks, an investigation was launched into the Al-Taqwa bank, which the US accused of indirectly providing financial investment services to al-Qa'ida. Himmat's assets were frozen, forcing him to step down from his position as head of the IGD in 2002.

Himmat's post was taken over by Ibrahim El-Zayat, who continues to run the IGD today. El-Zayat is a German national of Egyptian origin with an Egyptian father and a German mother. In spite of his relative youth, he has long been involved in Islamic work and comes from a religious family with a history of Islamic activism.

His father, Farouk El-Zayat, is the imam of the mosque in Marburg, near Cologne, and his brother Bilal, a doctor, and both his sisters are all involved in Islamic work. He is alleged to be the nephew of the famous Egyptian Islamist lawyer Muntassir el-Zayat, who was a member of al-Jama'at al-Islamiya.[83] He married within the Islamic community and his wife is Sabiha Erbakan, a niece of the Turkish Islamist leader Necmettin Erbakan. She is involved in the Centre for Islamic Women's Studies at the UOIF's Institute for Human Sciences in Paris.[84] El-Zayat's sister is married to one of Kamal Helbawy's sons. El-Zayat's background is therefore clearly deeply enmeshed in the reformist Islamist tradition.

El-Zayat's professional career is also a typical mix of Ikhwani-style Gulf-backed Islamic activism. He was head of the Muslim Students Association in Germany and co-founder of the Forum of European Muslim Youth and Student Organisations (FEMYSO), of which he was chairman from 1996 to 2002. In 1997 he became the head of the Islamic Centre in Cologne. He is on the board of Islamic Relief and a trustee of Islamic Relief in Birmingham.[85] In addition he was the European representative of the World Assembly of Muslim Youth (WAMY) and worked in the Islamic Council in Germany which is part of the Saudi Islamic World League. He is also linked into Ikhwani-oriented networks in France, being one of the trustees of the UOIF's school for imams at Château-Chinon.

While El-Zayat is personally very active, the IGD has never been able to attract large numbers of members either prior to or during his leadership. Although it is able to draw a sizeable congregation to its mosques, as El-Zayat notes himself, 'It is a body which has a very very limited membership.'[86] The very fact that the whole organisation shifted its headquarters from Munich to Cologne when El-Zayat took up the post is an indication of the group's limited influence. El-Zayat also acknowledges that when the IGD elects its Shura Council, the choice of who to elect is restricted because the number of qualified people is so small. This is partly because like most of the European Islamic organisations that follow the Ikhwani school of thought, the IGD is primarily an elitist group. It is also because, like the MSS and the MAB in Britain, the IGD has had to struggle against other Islamic currents. Given that the vast majority of Muslims living in Germany are Turkish, the Turkish organisations have always wielded the greatest influence and achieved stronger grass roots support. Where the IGD has only 600 recorded members and between thirty and forty Islamic cultural centres and places of worship, its Turkish counterpart, Millî Görüş, only one of a number of Turkish Islamic associations, has 26,500 members and between 400 and 600 cultural centres or places of worship.[87]

The IGD has close ties to Millî Görüş, so much so that the two organisations share the same premises in Cologne. Millî Görüş's General Secretary Oğuz Üçüncü has noted of the IGD, 'We consider us as brother/sister organisations. We work very closely together ... We co-ordinate our work and the executive bodies of the IGD and Millî Görüş meet twice a year.'[88] Such closeness is hardly surprising given that aside from the strong dose of nationalism that characterises the Turkish organisation, Millî Görüş broadly follows a similar ideology to that of the Brotherhood. But just as with the Jama'at-e-Islami and the MAB in Britain, the IGD and Millî Görüş have not sought to overcome their ethnic differences in order to join forces.

Ibrahim El-Zayat believes that the Turks need their own separate organisations because of the pervasive nationalism within the Turkish community and also because of language. 'Many Turks don't speak any language but Turkish – the first and second generation have no German. You will find very few who speak English. This limits the opportunities for mutual co-operation.'[89] On sheer numbers alone, the IGD is completely dwarfed by its Turkish counterpart.

As to the relationship between the IGD and the Ikhwan, like its counterparts in other European countries, the IGD has sought to distance itself from any such connection and has focused on its German identity. As El-Zayat emphasises, 'It is a German institution with German membership.' However, El-Zayat also openly admits connections with Said Ramadan and has said of the early days of the organisation: 'Naturally there were connections [with the Brotherhood]. It was an open body that was separate from what was called the movement body. At that time the Muslim Brotherhood was forced to work conspiratorially.'[90] Ghaleb Himmat has also acknowledged the influence that the Brotherhood had on the organisation whilst he was in charge. With typical Ikhwani ambiguity, Himmat declared that his mosque was open to everyone but the Ikhwani came to dominate because they were the most active. 'If the Muslim Brotherhood considers me one of them, it is an honour for me.'[91] Looking at those individuals who have been involved in the organisation over the years, not to mention the links with Saudi Arabia, the IGD has certainly grown out of the Brotherhood tradition and is typical of Ikhwani-oriented organisations in Europe.

The IGD acknowledges that it is part of the Ikhwan's reformist ideological tradition, but denies any organisational linkage to the movement today. Although El-Zayat accepts that the Guidance Office in Cairo is considered to be one of the IGD's spiritual references, he insists that no institutional ties exist between his organisation and Cairo or with the Brotherhood more broadly. His desire to be considered separate from the Ikhwan is so strong that he has stated categorically that he is not a member of the Brotherhood. In 2007 he published a statement on the Brotherhood's English language website after it had had referred to him as a Muslim Brother: 'Counterstatement: You wrote, "Eight Muslim Brotherhood members are scheduled to be tried in absentia in front of the military tribunal because five of them are living abroad" and then mentioned my name in a wrong spelling. I declare, that I am not a member of the Muslim Brotherhood.'[92]

In spite of the repeated visits of Mashour and Akef to Germany in the early 1980s when the international *tanzeem* was being established, El-Zayat insists that the IGD was never a member of the Ikhwan's international body. 'I think there was never a working international *tanzeem*. I think it was more of an idea to have something which is an international body, but from very early on Europe didn't understand itself as part of an organisation, but as a part of the thinking.'[93] This fits with Helbawy's explanation that the European branches had no formal role within the international Guidance Office, but reported to and consulted with the leadership indirectly. As El-Zayat also stated:

> It is not an organisational link or a clear affiliation because a clear affiliation won't work. If you bind a body that is working in Germany to a body in Egypt or Syria it won't work because in the end the variety of challenges that we have here are not connected to what is happening there. They cannot give instructions or say 'you have to do this or

> you have to do that'. It could be not a working relationship
> if we were dependent on a movement in Egypt or Syria.[94]

However, El-Zayat does acknowledge that there are 'personal relations' with the Brotherhood, but he adds: 'this is a completely different thing. There is no link and ... no directing of actions whatsoever by Egypt or by any other international body.'[95]

El-Zayat clearly wants to maintain the IGD's independence from any centre of power outside Germany. Touching on a very important point, he has also explained how Islamists in Europe are sometimes more progressive in their thinking than the Ikhwan in the Middle East:

> I think that maybe Europe has gone even beyond what the
> Muslim Brotherhood is thinking now as solutions. Take
> for example the issue of women in Islam. I am President
> of the IGD and my Vice President is a woman – she is in
> charge of many men. It is a point which you wouldn't find
> in the Muslim world at all. Even in Sudan. I don't know any
> Jama'at who would put any woman even as a Vice President.
> When I presented her I was very strict and keen on having
> a woman.[96]

This may be more the thinking of the second generation than of Muslims in Germany more widely. As El-Zayat himself says, some members of the IGD had difficulties accepting the fact that he had chosen to have a woman as his Deputy.[97]

El-Zayat has also raised concerns about the Ikhwani-oriented European Council for Fatwa and Research (ECFR), which was established in 1997 to provide fatwas specific to Muslims living in Europe as minority communities in secular societies. This council, headed by Sheikh Yusuf al-Qaradawi, is controversial: although it seeks to be relevant to the lives of Muslims in Europe, many council members reside in the Middle East and have never lived in the continent. Moreover, even though the council includes scholars from other ethnic groups such as the South Asian community in Britain and the Turkish community in Germany, it remains predominantly Arab, with an overwhelmingly Ikhwani flavour. (Prominent Ikhwani or Ikhwani-linked individuals on the council include its Deputy, al-Mawlawi; Sheikh Rashid al-Ghannouchi; Sheikh Abdul Rahman Al-Taweel in Spain; and Sheikh Mohamed al-Hawari in Germany.) It has also been contentious in so far as some of its fatwas do not sit comfortably with the concept of integrating into European society. Al-Hawari is reported to have written that adoption should be forbidden because a woman might be seen in a state of undress by a child other than her biological offspring.[98] In another fatwa, which responded to a question about whether it was permissible for a Muslim to eat with non-Muslim people who are drinking wine, the ruling was that, 'It is not permissible to sit with people who are drinking wine (alcohol), whether they are *kafirs* or Muslims.'[99] What is notable here is not the ruling itself, but rather the use of the highly derogatory term *kafirs* (heathens) to describe non-Muslims.

It is this very sort of attitude that El-Zayat has found difficult to deal with. He says that the council

> ... had an old fatwa on the issue of Palestine. This is a real difficulty that we have. We have two different positions on that. For me for example I am not a scholar but I follow the position that if we open up this door for suicide attacks then we cannot close it and there are no limitations afterwards ... The situation in Palestine for example is something where we should keep it clear what the Islamic framework is. But what people do afterwards may be different because I have never lived in one of the camps and ... if you hear some of the stories ... you understand why people are doing it but you also have to take a religious position on this.[100]

Al-Qaradawi has explicitly praised suicide operations in Palestine, which places those linked to the European Council or the European Islamist organisations that follow his Ikhwani school of thought in a somewhat difficult position. Although al-Qaradawi's ideas on this very sensitive topic are more reflective of the wider Islamist community, these organisations have to take their relationship with the European states in which they are based into consideration. Once again, they have been forced to put politics before religion, potentially alienating themselves from their core constituencies.

Yet like its counterparts in France and the UK, the IGD has had to focus on issues of integration. El-Zayat claims to envisage a situation in Germany where 'the Federal Chancellor in 2020 is a Muslim, born and raised in Germany, the Federal Supreme Court has a Muslim judge, and a Muslim representative will be on the Federal Radio/TV Council to secure Muslim citizens' constitutionally guaranteed rights'.[101] Such talk is clearly aimed at bolstering the IGD's position and convincing the German authorities that it is a tolerant organisation that supports multiculturalism. However, this tolerance seems to have its limits. In a telling incident in 2006 the German state held its first Islamic Conference in Berlin to discuss issues including the teaching of Islam in state schools and the qualifying of German imams, as well as how to encourage the reading of Friday sermons in German. According to the German media, both the IGD and Millî Görüş objected to this conference, outraged because the German government had invited some secular Muslims and critics of Islam to the conference.[102] Informed that a recent poll showed that a maximum of 15 per cent of Muslims participated in Islamic associations such as his and so the participation of secular elements in the conference was justified, El-Zayat retorted: 'We can't suppose that the current government doesn't represent all Germans because some of them didn't go to vote.'[103]

Some of this frustration may have been because the IGD has found it particularly difficult to act as an interlocutor between Muslim communities and the government on account of the suspicion that the German state has towards it. The Interior Ministry of Bavaria, for example, openly branded the IGD as a branch of the Muslim Brotherhood and an extremist organisation.[104] Moreover, the IGD has been plagued with scandal and investigations in recent years. The freezing of the assets of Ghaleb Himmat, who had been the face of the IGD for so many years, and the investigation into the Al-Taqwa Bank came as a major blow to the organisation's credibility. It was further alleged that Himmat had ties to the Saudi Arabian International Islamic Charity Organisation (IICO), which was accused of having links to terrorism and of financing Hamas.[105]

To make matters worse, in 2002 the federal police launched an investigation into El-Zayat himself, who, it alleged, had transferred more than $2 million on behalf of WAMY. It was claimed that some of the money had been sent to the Albanian charity Taibah, whose Bosnian branch has been designated a terrorist organisation by the US.[106] El-Zayat told the media that he had simply been acting as a member of the board of trustees of WAMY when he transferred the money.[107]

The IGD has also been investigated in relation to alleged financial irregularities. In 1999 it lost its non-profit status, reportedly as a result of sloppy bookkeeping.[108] According to officials, the organisation failed to inform state education bodies that it had lost its non-profit status and continued to receive funding for its private school illegally whilst allowing donors to write off their contributions.[109]

By 2003 the IGD had handed over the running of the school to another body, the German–Islamic Educational Enterprise, which was especially created for the purpose. However, in 2004 local officials denied the school a licence because they believed that the new organisation was simply a front for the IGD. Thomas Huber, a spokesman for the district government of Upper Bavaria, explained: 'We are afraid that the group running the school, which belongs to the Islamic Community of Germany, is using the school to spread Islamist ideology.'[110]

It is not clear whether these investigations were simply knee-jerk reactions on the part of the German state, but they have left the IGD more hemmed in than their counterparts in the UK or France, which are able to occupy a much greater political space. As such Germany has become a far less appealing centre for the Ikhwan in general. It would appear therefore that although Germany was an important Brotherhood centre during the 1970s and 1980s, today its importance has dwindled considerably. Even when the organisation was at its peak the Ikhwan was never able to command strong popular support and Germany was primarily a place to facilitate activities and act as a backstop to the Ikhwan in the Arab world.

The Grip of the First Generation

Whilst these three countries offer very different pictures of the Ikhwan's experience in Europe, what is common to them is that they were all born out of the Brotherhood but have sought to distance themselves from the movement. They have struggled hard to be seen as independent and primarily preoccupied with the role of Muslim communities in their respective European countries. However, their bid to represent these communities and to integrate fully into European society has been severely hampered by the fact that for the most part they are still essentially in the hands of the first generation of migrants or refugees. El-Zayat, as a member of the second generation, is the exception; the vast majority of the IGD's leadership are still from the first generation. As of 2006 only four out of the group's fifteen Shura Council members were from the second generation.[111] El-Zayat is aware of this problem: 'What I as a second-generation would want to achieve is support in the creation of a German Muslim identity ... bridging the gap and leaving [behind] the immigrants of an Arabic basis and to concentrate much more on the second-generation.'[112]

Other Islamist leaders in Europe have bemoaned the lack of second-generation migrants in their structures.

However, it is striking to note that in many cases the same few individuals have been in control of these organisations for years and appear unwilling to relinquish power. Figures such as Mahmoud Zuhair or Lhaj Thami Breeze have been in important leadership positions within the UOIF for decades despite the fact that the North African community in France is very well established. Dhaou Meskine has noted of Islamist organisations in general: 'A lot of organisations retained the backwardness of their own states back home. The leadership can't give up its position. It reflects the situation in the Third World where the leader can only be got rid of by death or a coup!'[113] Moreover, these organisations are like small cliques or in some instances almost a 'family business'. The same few individuals appear on the boards of each other's organisations and seem to have the Islamist circuit neatly divided up between themselves.

One of the problems engendered by this situation is that these leaders are so concerned about their own positions as foreign residents that they are unlikely to try to rock the boat too much, thereby decreasing their clout within their own constituencies. Meskine also noted: 'The mistake was setting up organisations with those from outside. If someone is linked to outside he says yes to everything they [the authorities] want him to do because he can't oppose anything or insist on anything. He fears for his papers and residency so he always says yes.'[114] In addition, despite their keenness to promote the idea of a European Islam, some of those first-generation leaders continue to feel that they are not truly part of European society. Some Muslim leaders of these Ikhwani-oriented organisations still frame their debates in terms of Muslims versus the West, or us and them, as if they are not themselves part of the Western world and Europe is an entirely different cultural entity.

In spite of having been in the UK since the 1970s, Ahmed al-Rawi, who established the Ikhwan's European network, the Federation of

Islamic Organisations in Europe (FIOE), talks about Europeans as if they are part of a separate world. In a 2006 interview he stated: 'Despite the hostility between us and them [the Europeans] and the negative image that they carry about Islam, they are in general very logical, so if they find someone who mixes with them and explains things to them, they would become convinced [about Islam].'[115] This approach is hardly surprising; the first generation may genuinely consider Europe as their home but they are struggling to find their own place in the continent and still consider themselves to be part of the Islamic world.

Being part of the first generation brings its own anxieties about preserving cultural and traditional values and these organisations repeatedly stress the need to refrain from being 'contaminated' by Western values. As a result these groups are keen to emphasise the merits of Islamic educational establishments and in some cases of Muslim communities being dealt with as separate entities. In one mosque in Manchester the Ikhwan-oriented imam was pushing in 2004 to be allowed to legislate for the local Muslim community under Sharia law. In a similar vein, a Libyan Ikhwani in the UK said that he was happy for his daughter to follow the UK's national curriculum but wanted her in a separate Muslim school so that she wouldn't be 'contaminated by the influences of the Western girls around her'.[116] Likewise Mohsen N'Gazou expressed his anxieties about the impact that mixing with French society would have on the next generation of Muslim children and lobbied to get the funds to set up a private Islamic school in the city.[117] Whilst this is understandable for the first generation, who are still grappling to come to terms with being a minority community, it risks emphasising and encouraging the differences between Muslims and non-Muslims and arguably makes life more challenging for the second and third generations.

Moreover, whilst the various Ikhwani-oriented Islamist organisations are stressing the need to focus on Europe, for many their primary references continue to be the Middle East and the Islamic world. Furthermore, although they may not be formally linked to the Brotherhood in Cairo, these organisations still consider Cairo to be a key spiritual reference. It is also notable that whilst these organisations stress their independence from the Brotherhood, many Ikhwani in the Middle East still tend to refer to them as extensions of the movement. The former Murshid has said:

> We are present in every country. Everywhere there are people who believe in the message of the Muslim Brothers. In France, the Union of Islamic Organizations of France (UOIF) does not belong to the organization of the Brothers. They follow their own laws and rules. There are many organizations that do not belong to the Muslim Brothers. For example, Shaykh al-Qaradawi. He is not a Muslim Brother, but he was formed according to the doctrine of the Brothers. The doctrine of the Brothers is a written doctrine that has been translated in all languages ... Everyone who believes in this doctrine can be considered as a Muslim Brother.[118]

He has also said of those institutions in Europe:

> These organisations and institutions are independent and autonomous. We don't control them. It is the brothers abroad who lead these organisations. The structures linked to Qaradawi are organisations of the Brotherhood directed by the brothers of different countries ... Those who co-operate with us are not all brothers ... but we tend not to make any distinction between them.[119]

In a parallel situation, Mohamed Habib has allegedly said of the Muslim American Society, 'I don't want to say MAS is an Ikhwan entity ... This causes some security inconveniences for them in a post-Sept.

11 world.'[120] Mohsen N'Gazou explains this mismatch thus: 'Those Ikhwan in the Middle East look at us as an extension of them because we are part of their school of thought. They are more extreme and think that we are lost.'[121]

Such contradictions do little to assist Ikhwani in Europe, whose main preoccupation seems to be carving out a niche for themselves within the European polity in order to have a greater degree of influence over their own communities in the continent. Their strategy appears to be to mould themselves as key interlocutors and reference points for European Muslim communities and since 9/11 in particular to demonstrate their willingness to move towards adopting more liberal values. There are of course still more rigid elements within their midst, but this approach is a clear response to the changing context within Europe and demonstrates classic Ikhwani pragmatism. However, by adopting such an approach these organisations will always have a limited appeal and will remain the realm of the few. Ironically, as a result of this narrow support base, other Ikhwani figures who reside in Europe but continue to be members of the Ikhwan in their home countries are much more powerful than those who are desperately trying to play a part in European societies. London-based Syrian Ikhwani leader Ali Saddredine al-Bayanouni was always far more influential than Ahmed Sheikh who leads the MAB or Ibrahim El-Zayat of the IGD. In many ways the power of the Ikhwan in Europe is still based upon its relationship to the Islamic world and the cause that it is supporting. The Palestinian cause will always hold more interest to the vast majority of the community than any discussion of creating a European *fiqh*. As such, the Ikhwan in Europe may be developing an increasingly sophisticated discourse and may dominate many of the continent's mosques and Islamist centres, but its ability to influence Muslims in the continent remains as limited as ever.

5

The Ikhwan and Violence

Perhaps the most controversial issue to haunt the Ikhwan since its inception has been its relationship to violence. In spite of its claim to be a pacific movement, it has been castigated in some circles as a violent organisation bent on imposing Islamic Sharia across the world. In 2006 *Front Page Magazine* carried an article that said:

> On October 28, 2005, President George W. Bush denounced IslamoFascist movements that call for a 'violent and political vision: the establishment, by terrorism, subversion and insurgency, of a totalitarian empire that denies all political and religious freedom'. The Muslim Brotherhood, also known as the Ikhwan, is a good example of what the President described and what he must protect us against.[1]

Others have observed that many of those who have gone on to advocate more militant interpretations of Islam had passed through the ranks of the Brotherhood, where they received their ideological grounding. Some analysts refer to the Ikhwan as a 'stepping stone': 'For someone who is interested in dedicating their lives to a radical Islamist cause, it can be a pathway up ... to a more serious dealing with Islam.'[2]

Many famous militants have passed through the Ikhwan's ranks, including al-Qa'ida ideologue Mustafa Setmariam, also known as Abu Musab al-Suri, who was a member of the Syrian Ikhwan before he moved on to join more radical groups. Similarly, the man known as the father of the Afghan mujahideen, Sheikh Abdullah Azzam, was a member of the Brotherhood before he became more engaged in violent jihad. Even 9/11 hijacker Mohamed Atta came from a family that was allegedly linked to the Brotherhood. As such the Ikhwan has been accused as acting as an incubator for more radical ideas and of spawning terrorist recruits.

It is not only in the West that such allegations are levelled at the Brotherhood. They have also been forthcoming in the Arab world. Intellectuals such as the Egyptian leader of the Ta'jamu political party, Rifat Said, have observed that whilst the Ikhwan's leaders deny that they have taken part in terrorist actions, they try to outdo each other by claiming, 'I killed more than the others.'[3] Perhaps the Brotherhood's greatest critics, however, were the nationalist regimes of the Middle East. The former Egyptian government repeatedly presented the Egyptian Ikhwan as the political face of a terrorist organisation.[4] There were also repeated assaults on and warnings about the Brotherhood in the state-controlled media. An article in *Al-Gomhuriya* in 2007 declared:

> The victory of Hamas and the Brotherhood at the ballot box does not mean that they are politicians and that they are capable of running the state ... All that Hamas is capable of doing is to be crack troops of suicide. Unfortunately, however, they are not committing suicide alone. They are forcing the entire people to commit suicide, and I fear that this is the same tactic and path that the Brotherhood in Egypt is taking.[5]

A few months earlier, following a martial arts demonstration by a group of young students linked to the Brotherhood, the editor of the same newspaper wrote:

> The fighting training, martial arts, and self-defence that the students demonstrated at Al-Azhar University revealed that the Muslim Brotherhood has a great measure of Fascism and extremism ... Like the Fascists and the Nazis, the Muslim Brotherhood is not interested in whether Egypt is destroyed or conquered ... These inciters strive for one thing only – to create a military, or militia, parallel to the Egyptian army ... the Muslim Brotherhood wants [Egypt's] sons to die in battles waged by the regional and neighbouring powers, in which we have no interest. Perhaps they are striving to brainwash the youth and to exploit them for other aims within the country that will lead the youth only to great danger.[6]

The Brotherhood fiercely denies such allegations, asserting that it is a moderate organisation that does not advocate taking up arms to gain power but rather prefers the slower approach of educating society from below in preparation for the eventual establishment of an Islamic order. When asked about the Ikhwan's desire to establish an Islamic state, Mustafa Mashour explained:

> ... we are not talking about seizing power in a coup d'état. Our method is peaceful; it is preaching and moulding public opinion to respond to our ideology. If we can succeed in establishing an Islamic state through elections, no one will be able to say that we overthrew the government, because we are using constitutional methods. We are not violent or bloody revolutionaries; we merely say that Islam is the solution.[7]

The Ikhwani have always stressed that they do not want to take power but rather wish that the ruler they are living under would apply Islamic laws correctly. This may in part be a reflection of the fact that the Ikhwan's leadership has tended to come from the professional classes and has therefore been less inclined to engage in violent behaviour than some of the more radical groups.

The Brotherhood has emphasised this pacific stance particularly forthrightly in recent years, especially since 9/11, and has done its utmost to distance itself from any connection with violence. Former Murshid, Mehdi Akef, has explained that the Ikhwan only co-operates with other Islamist movements if they have the same comprehensive understanding of Islam as the Brotherhood, if they use the principle of *shura* and if 'violence is not one of their methods'.[8]

Seizing on the radicalisation discourse that began doing the rounds in the West after 9/11, the brothers have even gone so far as to assert that they can teach people the 'correct' version of Islam, thereby decreasing support for more militant alternatives.

Yet whilst the Ikhwan is keen to present itself as a peaceful organisation and has proven itself to be largely pacific, it does have a history of getting involved in violence when the opportunity has presented itself. Right from the outset the concept of violence was enshrined in its famous motto, which remains the maxim today: 'Allah is our objective. The Prophet is our leader. Qur'an is our law. Jihad is our way. Dying in the way of Allah is our highest hope.' At its inception, the Ikhwan attached a far greater importance to the concept of jihad in both its violent and non-violent sense than was the tradition in the Islamic circles of the day. This differentiated it from other Islamic societies and organisations.[9] Moreover, the movement began engaging in violent acts during the very early days of its existence under Hassan al-Banna, through the infamous Nizam al-Khass. In the 1980s the Syrian Ikhwan had its own particular experience with violence, as explained in detail in Chapter Two.

In addition, the brothers also believe that fighting jihad against a foreign occupier is a religious duty and have openly supported the resistance in places like Palestine or Iraq.

Moreover, the Brotherhood has a complex ideological relationship to the use of violence. Whilst its members broadly reject the idea of fighting against their own regimes, they do not entirely disown scholars such as Sayyid Qutb, who was one of the early proponents of violent struggle against un-Islamic Muslim governments in the contemporary context and whose ideas radicalised a generation and more. They might refute some of Qutb's ideas but there is still a certain pride in him and they consider him as one of their most important martyrs. This gives the impression that there is still an ambiguity in their discourse on violence and that they do not come down on one side or the other.

Moreover, for all their refutations of al-Qa'ida and terrorism, there have been occasions when such assertions appear unconvincing. For example, in June 2006 a group of Jordanian Ikhwani Islamic Action Front (IAF) deputies caused controversy when they attended the funeral of the Jordanian al-Qa'ida in Iraq commander, Abu Musab Al-Zarqawi, and paid condolences to his family. Zaki Bani Irsheid, head of the IAF, claimed that this was simply 'part of our Muslim customs towards the family and it has no political dimensions';[10] nonetheless, the delegation's actions provoked outrage in Jordan and beyond. Whilst this stance clearly represents the exception rather than the rule and many Ikhwani would reject the brutality of Zarqawi's methods, the Brotherhood's flexible approach and willingness to accept those with a range of stances invite suspicion. Over the years, this flexibility has meant that the Brotherhood has inevitably accommodated and absorbed a number of more militant elements within its ranks. Whilst in the past such differences of approach were hardly noticed outside of their own communities or societies, in the post 9/11 world the Ikhwani have had to think twice about how such elements might affect the image of their movement as a whole.

Sayyid Qutb and the Ideology of Violence

Although the Brotherhood was accused of perpetrating a number of acts of political violence during the days of Hassan al-Banna, it was through the figure of Sayyid Qutb that the movement really became associated with the ideology of violence. As explained in Chapter One Qutb emerged as a scholar at a time when relations between the Ikhwan and the Nasserite state were fast deteriorating. Hopes that the new regime could find a way to accommodate the Brotherhood had disappeared; as the era of imprisonment, torture and execution was ushered in, Qutb responded with a major shift in ideology that was to have enormous impact not just on the Ikhwan, but on the evolution of radical Islamist movements across the board.

Qutb was born in 1906 in a small village in Asyut and migrated to Cairo in search of education and employment as a young man. There is a well-known story about Qutb visiting America and being disgusted and radicalised at seeing what he described as a couple making love in a church. Yet his moral anxiety and malaise were already deeply implanted in him before his visit. When he arrived in Cairo he was repulsed by the city, believing that below the surface trappings lay a sick, ugly and miserable face.[11] He joined the Ikhwan in 1953 and found himself arrested in the clampdown of 1954 and sentenced to fifteen years hard labour. Due to ill health, he spent much of this time in hospital. There he focused on his writing, which was smuggled out to those Ikhwani on the outside.[12]

Reflecting his frustration and the suffocating atmosphere of being imprisoned, Qutb's thinking became increasingly radical. Inspired by the works of Indian scholars Abu Ala Maududi and Abu Hasan al-Nadwi as well as earlier thinkers such as Ibn Taymiyyah, Qutb argued that Egypt was once again in a state of *jahiliya* (pre-Islamic ignorance). The only way to surpass this was to submit to *al-hakimiyya*, the total sovereignty of God. In bringing together the *al-hakimiyya* concept articulated by Maududi and the *jahiliya* idea espoused by al-Nadwi, Qutb believed he could create a new ideological structure for the Brotherhood.[13] As such his ideas constituted a rejection of the modern and a harking back to a morally 'clean' and innocent time that had not been sullied by materialism or un-Islamic practices. To achieve this state, one had to get rid of all the polluting non-Islamic influences and to take up the cause of jihad against those who got in the way. Qutb wrote that *al-hakimiyya* 'will not be achieved merely by teaching and preaching, for those who inflict the yoke on the necks of the people and who usurp the authority of God on earth will not concede their position through such explanation and sermonising'.[14] He was planting the seeds of *takfiri* (pronouncing others as heathen) thinking in his discourse and making it acceptable to struggle against Muslim leaders and governments, as well as wayward Muslim societies, in order to bring God's rule to earth.

Qutb's ideas represented a major shift from the traditional thinking of the Ikhwan and of Hassan al-Banna. While al-Banna viewed the imam or head of state as a civil ruler who takes his consensus from the *jama'a*, Qutb considered the imam to be a theocratic ruler who takes his authority directly from God. Moreover, whilst al-Banna was not opposed to the principle of the use of force and proved willing to engage in attacks against the colonising forces, he was far less comfortable with the idea of armed struggle against the Egyptian state. This may have been as much about not wishing to bring unnecessary retribution on his movement as it was about principles, given that jihad in its military sense was part of his overall vision for the Ikhwan, but he certainly tried to distance himself from the attacks that were carried out by the Nizam al-Khass against Egyptian targets. Qutb's uncompromising ideology was far removed from al-Banna's overriding pragmatism.

Yet Qutb's ideas touched a chord within many Egyptian Ikhwani who felt betrayed by the fact that they were being abused and repressed by the Nasserite regime that they had pinned their hopes upon and who were increasingly frustrated at the movement's gradual approach. The fact that Qutb was executed in prison in 1966 brought him the status of martyr and hero and gave him an even greater aura and authenticity. His ideology soon travelled beyond Egypt through figures such as the Syrian Ikhwani Marwan Hadid, who identified with the feelings of anger and despair articulated by Qutb and who spread Qutb's writings and ideas inside Syria. Similarly, Qutb ushered in a new era of radicalism within the Jordanian Ikhwan, in particular among the younger generation, something which prompted sudden outward displays of religiosity such as growing beards for men and wearing the hijab for women.[15] As explained in Chapter Four, Qutb's ideas also reached the Ikhwani in Europe, who were hungry for such new thinking. As Ayubi has argued, 'Qutb's ideas were to represent the main intellectual influence on the younger, militant Muslim Brotherhood.'[16]

While Qutb's radical thinking was making waves in Islamic circles around the world, it also prompted a major crisis within the Brotherhood as the more traditional older generation rejected his new ideas, which rang alarm bells for them. According to Ashur Shamis, some of the brothers who were in prison with Qutb were not happy with his 'separatist and confrontational' ideas, believing that they undermined the philosophy of the Brotherhood.[17] Yet given his status and importance, it was difficult to argue against him. The Murshid, Hassan al-Hodeibi, initially reacted well to Qutb's work, declaring that *Milestones* had vindicated all the hopes he had placed in Qutb, who now embodied 'the future of the Muslim *dawa*'.[18]

However, by the late 1960s al-Hodeibi was becoming increasingly concerned that Qutb was planting the *takfiri* seed within the Ikhwan. In 1969 he wrote his famous book *Du'aa La Qadat* (*Preachers not Judges*), primarily to refute the more militant ideas that were gaining currency within the movement. In the text al-Hodeibi argued against the idea that Egyptian society was in a state of *jahiliya*, asserting instead that it was in a state of *juhl* (ignorance) and simply needed to be educated in the tradition of the Ikhwan. Al-Hodeibi also argued against the ideas of Maududi, criticising his *al-hakimiyya* concept. Although there is a great deal of speculation surrounding this book and whether or not al-Hodeibi was pressured into writing it by the regime, the Ikhwan today uses it to demonstrate that the movement did not take up Qutb's ideas wholesale.[19]

Nonetheless, the Ikhwani continue to have an ambiguous relationship to Qutb. They may reject the concept of fighting against the state and Qutb's more radical ideas, but it seems they cannot relinquish him as a hero. He is considered one of the most important thinkers in the contemporary Islamic movement and as such there is a strong pride in him, all the more poignant because he died for his beliefs. Although there have been successive attempts by the leadership to distance themselves from his ideas – Omar al-Tilimsani in 1982 declared, 'Sayyid Qutb represented himself alone and not the Muslim Brothers'[20] – he continues to command huge reverence and respect within the movement. This even holds true for those of a more moderate bent. As Gilles Kepel has noted of Qutb's famous work *Milestones*, 'The most traditional of Muslim Brethren consider it a simultaneously fascinating and repellent text, some of whose assertions they consider admirable, others beyond the pale.'[21]

Yet another reason why the Ikhwan is so keen to somehow claim Qutb as its own is because he is essentially the only true scholar that the Ikhwan produced. Of course had he not been executed in 1966, Qutb might have gone on to separate himself from the Brotherhood, given that his ideas were so divergent from the original principles upon which the Ikhwan was founded. But as it stands, he is the only thinker whose ideas have really gone beyond the confines of the movement.

Many Ikhwani have tried to deal with this contradiction by claiming that Qutb's more radical ideas were misunderstood and taken out of context. Others blame the extreme repression and circumstances that forced him into taking such a radical stance. Some have also sought to give the impression that he abandoned his militancy just before he died. Farid Abdel Khaliq, the former secretary of Hassan al-Banna, was in prison with Qutb just prior to his death. He asserts that Qutb came to regret what he had done and was full of remorse for the pains he had caused the movement.[22]

Regardless of how one looks at the Ikhwan's relationship to Qutb, it is undeniable that his teachings ushered in a new wave of more militant thinking which served to radicalise not just the Ikhwan, but a whole generation of young militants. The Ikhwan's increasingly radical agenda in the 1970s, which sought to better position the movement in its challenge against the regimes of the day, was driven in large part by brothers who had taken up Qutbist ideas and co-ordinated themselves as Organisation 1965. The increased radicalism was also in line with the spirit of the time, itself a response to ongoing disappointment with the nationalist states that were proving even more repressive than their predecessors.

As such, the 1970s were a time of radicalisation during which oppositional politics were increasingly articulated through the discourse of Islam. In the Egyptian case of course the 1970s were also a time when the Ikhwan was bolstered by the cadres from the al-Jama'at al-Islamiya, who were not averse to the principle of violence but concerned only with its timing and usage.[23] The Ikhwan may not have taken the more extreme path of the many jihadist groups that began to flourish at this time (and that in some cases, such as al-Takfir wal-Hijra, were offshoots of the Brotherhood), but its whole outlook and discourse became more radical. The Ikhwan was just one of many opposition groups who sought an alternative to the state and a return to the mythical idea of a pure Islamist order, which they believed would act as a salvation to the deep-rooted problems of the day.

The Ikhwan in Afghanistan

Whilst the complexities surrounding Qutb and his ideas created divisions within the Ikhwan, the issue of war in Afghanistan following the Soviet invasion of 1979 was far more straightforward. This is because jihad is considered to be *fard al-ayn* (religious duty) when Muslims come under attack by an occupying power. The concept is enshrined in Islamic teachings and in the Qur'an. Reformist scholars of the late nineteenth century such as Muhammad Abdu and Rashid Rida, upon whose ideas the Brotherhood was based, argued that whilst peaceful co-existence was the normal state of affairs between Islamic and non-Islamic territories, jihad was still permissible as a defensive position.[24] This idea was certainly supported by al-Banna who was equally committed to jihad and who once said 'The *umma* is not frightened of death.'[25]

In the case of Afghanistan, a Muslim country under attack by a 'godless' communist force, the religious rulings were clear: fighting against the Soviet presence was considered a moral duty for many Muslims. Moreover, the conflict's religious legitimacy was bolstered by the many fatwas issued at the time calling on people to join the jihad. Such fatwas were issued not only by individual scholars but also by official religious establishments like Al-Azhar in Cairo.[26] Many of the Arab states tacitly supported the cause and some analysts have alleged that the Egyptian regime even released a number of radical Islamists from prison on condition that they continued their jihad in Afghanistan rather than at home.[27] Some Algerians have also suggested that the Algerian regime encouraged their nationals to join up: 'The government also helped send young Algerians to Afghanistan. Saudi Arabia paid for the tickets; they'd go to Mecca and then to Afghanistan.'[28]

The Ikhwan was as ready as any other group to support the Afghan jihad. Members of the Egyptian Ikhwan had developed ties with Afghan leaders decades before the conflict. During the 1930s the

Afghan ambassador to Egypt entrusted the education of his children to the Ikhwan through the circles of Hassan al-Banna. One of the ambassador's children, Sheikh Haroun al-Mujaddidi, became a well-known Muslim Brother who was imprisoned by Nasser in the 1954 clampdown.[29] Relations between Egyptian brothers and Afghan leaders also developed during the 1960s and 1970s.

The brother who was to play perhaps the most crucial role in the Afghan jihad, however, was the Egyptian Kamel Sananiri, who was a key facilitator in the conflict despite being thrown into prison in 1981, where he is believed to have died under torture. A member of the Nizam-al-Khass, Sananiri was one of those who came out of prison in the early 1970s with great aspirations for the Brotherhood as an international movement. He went to Afghanistan shortly after the Soviet invasion with the aim of co-ordinating the various Islamic groups operating there, and spent his time shuttling between Saudi Arabia and Afghanistan to provide a huge logistical support network for the fighters. His role was so great that al-Qa'ida ideologue Ayman al-Zawahiri paid particular homage to him in his book *Knights Under the Prophet's Banner*. Although generally dismissive of the Brotherhood, al-Zawahiri said:

> We were preceded to Peshawar by Kamel al-Sananiri, may he rest in peace. We could see that he had left his mark wherever we went. He had played a pioneering role in establishing the hospital where we worked and whenever we met with mujahideen leaders, they would speak of his assistance to them and his efforts to unite them. Although I never met him, his actions and contributions demonstrated his generosity and beneficial services in the cause of God.[30]

It was Sananiri who first persuaded Sheikh Abdullah Azzam to join the jihad. Azzam had joined the Brotherhood in Palestine at a very young age. After graduating from Sharia College in Damascus in 1966 he spent time in Amman but also in Cairo, where he studied at Al-Azhar and became close to the family of Sayyid Qutb.[31] Sananiri met with Azzam in 1980 whilst he was in Saudi Arabia; according to Dr Kamal Helbawy, who was also there at that time, Sananiri asked Azzam what he was doing there.[32] Azzam replied that he had been forced out of Jordan and had come to teach in the King Abdulaziz University in Jeddah. Sananiri reportedly told him that rather than stay in Saudi Arabia he should go to work in a university in Pakistan and that whilst there he should give some of his time to the Afghans.

Azzam was clearly persuaded by the Egyptian brother, for he soon found a teaching post at the International Islamic University in Islamabad and began travelling regularly to Peshawar and on occasions into Afghanistan itself. He also began to receive people from the Islamic movement and embarked upon a series of tours to collect money for the cause, including in the US. In 1984 Azzam decided to dedicate all of his time to the Afghan jihad, quitting his post at the university and setting up the famous Maktab al-Khadamat that would provide logistical support for the mujahideen. Azzam would become one of the most iconic Afghan Arabs, dubbed the father of the jihad.

In spite of Azzam's Brotherhood roots, it wasn't long before he began to fall out with the Ikhwan. According to his son Hudaifa, the reason for the split was that whereas Azzam was keen to accept anyone who was prepared to volunteer into the mujahideen's ranks, the Ikhwan wanted to restrict entry to those who were from the Brotherhood.[33] Hudaifa Azzam has also said that by the mid-1980s the Ikhwan had built up its own organisation in Peshawar, aimed specifically at taking control of the jihad.[34] This assertion is borne out by other veterans of the Afghan war. According to one Libyan Afghan veteran, in 1988 Mustafa Mashour and Mohamed Abu Nasser travelled to Afghanistan to ask Abdullah Azzam to close the Khalden camp because some of the Ikhwani recruits were returning to Egypt with a more militant ideology.[35] When Azzam refused, Mashour, reportedly under pressure from the Gulf states, which were becoming concerned at the ideas now doing the rounds in the camps, told Azzam that no one should be permitted to enter the camp without a reference from the Ikhwan.[36] Azzam of course refused, asserting that the camp was open to all Muslims and not just those from the Ikhwan, but this incident reflects the extent to which Mashour sought to bring the Afghan jihad under his control.

Dr Helbawy, meanwhile, sees the disagreement somewhat differently; he thinks that the real problem was that Azzam wanted the brothers to be more involved in the fighting. Azzam was 'going with a quicker step, a quicker pace than the Ikhwan'.[37] It is true that the Ikhwani were generally reticent to get involved in the fighting in Afghanistan, doing everything they could to facilitate the struggle, but preferring to engage in humanitarian work instead. It was almost as if they supported the ideological cause but considered themselves to be above the messy business of fighting. This reluctance to take up arms may have been because the Ikhwan has tended to be an elitist, middle-class organisation and therefore less inclined to fight than those of tougher stock. Whatever the reason, the Brotherhood has been strongly criticised within Islamic circles for its limited action on the battlefield. The Egyptian militant group al-Jama'at al-Islamiya, who were publishing their *Al-Murabitoun* magazine out of Afghanistan at that time, roundly condemned the Ikhwani for their unwillingness to engage in the fighting.[38] They were also criticised by those who went on to form al-Qa'ida for opting for the easy life, enjoying the luxuries of living in villas whilst their fellow volunteers were giving up their lives. The Ikhwani attitude towards the Afghan jihad exemplifies why they are so despised by those of a more militant bent, who consider them to be opportunists, ultimately more concerned with their own comforts and interests than with the greater cause.

The brothers defend their unwillingness to fight by asserting that they believed themselves to be more useful in performing other sorts of humanitarian duties. Kamal Helbawy, who was in charge of the Ikhwan's activities in Afghanistan and Pakistan from 1988 to 1994 and who was based in the Institute of Policy Studies in Pakistan during the conflict, asserts that he tried to convince Ikhwanis not to go and fight but rather to put their skills to better use. He explained:

> My own advice was not to go to fight jihad because ... many people can learn within three months how to fight and can go and fight, but a doctor who has been educated for twenty years, how can we train another doctor in his place? Or a nurse, or an engineer, or a teacher? ... The atmosphere of war is attractive but I was asking, what does Afghanistan need from us, not what would we like to do. One day a medical doctor came to me and said, 'I would like to go to fight.' I asked him why. He said 'because I want to fight jihad to go to paradise'. I said what you are doing can take you to paradise and all the work that we do is jihad ... Someone who is not a doctor can go ... Take others who are not needed here.[39]

However, some Ikhwani did get directly involved in the fighting. Helbawy has admitted, 'If any Muslim brother decided to fight on his own, then no one would stop him.'[40] Yet the idea that those Ikhwani fought as individuals rather than under the Muslim Brotherhood's banner is not entirely confirmed; others have suggested that the Brotherhood did organise some military activities for its members. Hudaifa Azzam has stated that the Ikhwan had two camps for training its fighters, one at Khost and the other at Ghazni.[41] According to him, these camps were top secret and only Ikhwani were allowed to enter, although they only held fifty volunteers each at maximum. Other sources have indicated that the Ikhwan did fight in Afghanistan. One website has posted what it claims is a question and answer session with the Ikhwan. This has the Ikhwan declaring: 'I don't know why the Ikhwan is always accused of NOT participating in the jihad there [Afghanistan]! Where is the Ikhwan who went there from all over the world? ... hundreds of the Ikhwan youth who participated as fighters, doctors, teachers ...'[42] It is impossible to verify this statement, given that it is not sourced and is not on any official Ikhwani website, yet it would appear that some members of the Brotherhood were more involved in the fighting than the movement often admits.

Fighting aside, the Ikhwan remains proud of the instrumental role it played in facilitating recruits from across the Middle East, for which it used its contacts with Saudi Arabia and the Pakistani Jama'at-e-Islami. The Ikhwan was one of the main linchpins in the jihad; as Olivier Roy describes it, the Afghan resistance was a 'joint venture between the Saudis, the Muslim Brotherhood and the Jama'at-e-Islami, put together by the ISI'.[43] The Brotherhood's role was multifaceted, and according to Helbawy, 'One of the major responsibilities of the Ikhwan was to co-ordinate the efforts of the mujahideen leaders, encourage them to consult among themselves and train new individuals who were not exclusively affiliated to their tribes or political parties.'[44] The Ikhwan used its skills and worldwide network of contacts to create a strong logistical support network for those doing the fighting. The importance of the conflict to the Brotherhood was such that key figures within the leadership regularly visited Afghanistan to give their backing to the mujahideen. Mustafa Mashour made many trips to Afghanistan to advise the fighters and to urge unity in their ranks.[45]

The Brotherhood in the Arab world also gave money to support the cause. The Ikhwani-dominated Egyptian Medical Syndicate organised and funded 95 per cent of the doctors working in Afghanistan, whether in relief agencies controlled by the Brotherhood or those independent of them.[46] In addition, the Ikhwani used the freedom they had in Pakistan to publish tracts and literature to promote both the cause of the Afghan jihad and their own ideology. Helbawy was in charge of producing a range of publications issued by the Institute of Policy Studies that was distributed across the Arab world. In Morocco, there was a system in place to reprint copies and to distribute them across the region.

In spite of the Ikhwan's desire to distance itself from the fighting in Afghanistan and the differences that developed between it and Azzam, as with Sayyid Qutb the Brotherhood is still keen to claim the father of the Afghan Arabs as its own. Just as with Qutb, some brothers have asserted that just before he died, Azzam suddenly realised his mistakes, acknowledging that the Brotherhood had been correct in its more measured outlook. According to Helbawy, a few days before Azzam was assassinated he came to Helbawy's house in Islamabad for breakfast with a number of other Islamist figures including the Yemeni Sheikh Abdulmajid Zidanai.[47] Azzam allegedly told Helbawy that he wanted the Ikhwan to participate more in the jihad. When Helbawy asked him whether he had been able to reach any agreement with the other factions who had participated with him, Azzam acknowledged that he hadn't, prompting him to declare, 'I wish I had done like you.'[48] Symbolically, Azzam then allegedly renewed his *baya* to the Brotherhood.

Such wistful stories read almost like the tales of the martyrs of the battlefield. Yet the Brotherhood's desire to reclaim Azzam is part of its bid to maintain credibility with its constituencies, which view figures like him as the real heroes of the Islamist movement.

At the same time, in the interests of demonstrating that they are a moderate and peaceful organisation, the Ikhwan prefers to direct the spotlight on to its humanitarian rather than military efforts in the Afghan jihad. As such the whole Afghanistan experience demonstrates yet another of the fundamental contradictions within the movement.

Jihad in Palestine and Iraq

Just as it supported the jihad in Afghanistan, the Ikhwan has supported fighting jihad in Palestine and more recently Iraq. Pronouncements by key Ikhwani leaders in support not only of the jihad but also of suicide operations have prompted much condemnation and accusations that they are supporting terrorism. Mehdi Akef is alleged to have stated in 2004:

> The Muslim Brotherhood movement condemns all bombings in the independent Arab and Muslim countries. But the bombings in Palestine and Iraq are a [religious] obligation. This is because these two countries are occupied countries, and the occupier must be expelled in every way possible. Thus, the movement supports martyrdom operations in Palestine and Iraq in order to expel the Zionists and the Americans.[49]

Whilst the brothers in Europe have tended to be more circumspect about such issues due to the political sensitivities of their environment, some have not shied away from openly declaring their support for jihad. Palestinian and former MAB leader Azzam Tamimi has said of those volunteers who go to fight in Iraq: 'They are responding to a duty because jihad for the sake of Allah is one of the main principles in our religion. Those who volunteer came from every part of the world and they are some of the goodness that the Prophet preached to us about when he said "the goodness in me and in my *umma* until the day of judgement".'[50] Similarly, Ahmed al-Rawi, former head of the FIOE, is reported to have stated: 'My opinion on the occupation [of Iraq] is that it is illegal. I couldn't call the resistance, even military resistance to the occupation, I couldn't consider it criminal.'[51] Moreover, one imam in the UK who followed the Ikhwan's ideology admitted that he would not try to dissuade anyone who came to him saying they wanted to go to fight in Iraq.[52]

Yet given the prevailing political and social climate in the Islamic world and the ideology that has underpinned the movement for so many decades, it would be extremely difficult for the Ikhwan to take any other stance. Firstly, as explained above jihad is considered a core religious duty not just by the Ikhwan but by the entire reformist Islamist trend that has come to dominate political Islam in the contemporary context. As part of this trend the Brotherhood cannot refute such concepts and holds them very close to its heart. It is true that jihad can be interpreted in various ways and can be a means of struggling through peaceful means, yet the Brotherhood has always interpreted jihad in its range of meanings and the concept of violent struggle has always been part of its religious teachings. As the former leader of the Jordanian Ikhwan, Abd al-Majid al-Dhunaybat, has expressed:

> Martyrdom operations are legitimate as long as the enemy targets civilians. Our ulema gave their religious opinion: They said these operations are religiously acceptable because they represent a reciprocal treatment. The Zionist enemy consists of people who are either in the military or preparing to join the military. Martyrdom-seekers offer the noblest forms of martyrdom. They sacrifice themselves knowing that they would meet God moments after their operations, and they realize that they wound the enemy in defence of their people and creed. Islamic history provides many examples of things similar to the martyrdom operations.[53]

Similarly Abdul Moneim Aboul Fotouh, once at the vanguard of the Egyptian Ikhwan's more progressive wing, said in April 2004 of jihad in Palestine and Iraq: 'This is a matter of religion, not politics. When a Muslim land is occupied, jihad becomes an individual duty for every man and woman, boy and girl. A woman goes out to jihad without her husband's permission and a child without his father's permission. In this matter there is no place for discussion or games.'[54]

Aboul Fotouh's assertion is of course highly questionable, in that the Ikhwan has used the jihad in both Palestine and Iraq as a means of rallying its supporters and bolstering its political standing. These two arenas of conflict have become key elements in its political agenda. In the Egyptian Ikhwan's reform initiative of March 2004, the section titled 'Most Important National Causes (Palestine and Iraq)' notably takes up three and a half pages, whilst the section titled 'In the Field of Combating Poverty' is only half a page long! The opening lines of the section on Palestine and Iraq read: 'Resistance against the Anglo-American and Zionist occupiers of Arab and Muslim lands is a legal right and duty imposed (on people under occupation) by Islam and guaranteed by Islam and guaranteed by international laws and treaties.'[55] As such the repeated assertion by the Ikhwan that jihad is simply a religious duty is arguably a means whereby the Brotherhood has sought to hide politics behind the mask of religion.

Moreover, fighting jihad has been core to the Ikhwan's political ideology since its very inception. Palestine was one of the first international causes to unite the Ikhwan and many brothers rushed to join the battle. Three battalions of Egyptian brothers went to fight in 1948 including Said Ramadan, who led a group of Ikhwani from Egypt to take part in the struggle. The Jordanian Ikhwan also sent its own battalion, as did the Syrians. Considering the difficulties of travelling at that time and the Ikhwan's limited membership it was remarkable that according to Hassan al-Banna, the Ikhwan had 1,500 volunteers inside Palestine at one time during the war.[56]

However, the Ikhwan's interest in Palestine pre-dates 1948; the Egyptian Ikhwan carried out propaganda activities on behalf of the Palestinians during the Palestinian revolt of 1936 and the Mufti of Jerusalem was in regular contact with al-Banna. The Ikhwan also formed a special committee headed by al-Banna to protest against Britain and defend the Palestinian cause, and a handful of Ikhwani took part in armed attacks against Jewish installations in Palestine during the revolt.[57] The cause of Palestine was also taken up by the first Syrian Ikhwani leader, Mustafa al-Sibai, who invested a great deal of effort into raising awareness of the plight of the Palestinians within Syria and beyond. Since that time, the cause has been central to the Ikhwan's political agenda and the call for Palestine's liberation is a key tenet of its public discourse. Moreover, the Ikhwan has been forthright in its support for Hamas, which itself grew out of the Brotherhood.

However, the call to liberate Palestine through violence is not unique to the Ikhwan or even to the Islamist camp. Given the deep resonance that the Palestinian issue has among Arab populations, Middle Eastern regimes have also railed against the occupation of Palestine and have sought to act as defenders of the Palestinian cause to bolster their legitimacy both domestically and in the Arab world. Defending Palestine went hand in hand with Arab nationalism. Yet it was also used by the conservative monarchies of the Gulf that sought to amplify the Palestinian issue for their own benefit. As such Palestine has become part of the discourse and rhetoric of the Arab world, with regimes and their opponents alike competing to make themselves appear as the legitimate and authentic defenders not only of Palestinians, but also of Muslims and Islam itself. Therefore in spite of the fact that Palestinians have been notoriously badly treated as individuals within the Arab world, the Palestinian cause has long been a means of tapping into popular sentiment and rallying support by those on all sides of the political spectrum.

As a result, the Ikhwan has sought to appeal to its grass roots support base with emotive calls demonstrating that it is fully behind the fight against Israel and that it is in some way 'its struggle'. Abd al-Majid al-Dhunaybat proudly declared:

> We want the jihad action to escalate and to involve the whole Muslim nation, not only the Palestinians. The enemy is a threat to the nation, not only to Palestine. Resistance against the enemy should not remain confined to the Palestinians; the entire nation must be involved. Resistance and the intifadah need the support of peoples to be able to continue.[58]

Similarly, during an appearance on Hizbullah's Al-Manar television channel, the former Deputy of the Egyptian Ikhwan Mohamed Habib announced:

> The truth is that the resistance, whether in Iraq or in Palestine, defends not only the holy places, the land, and the honour but also defends the nation's honour. They represent the first line of defence for the entire Arab and Islamic society and world. Therefore, the issue of martyrdom and of the martyrdom operations carried out by boys and girls, and also the operations carried out by the Iraqi resistance, these redeem self-confidence and hope, because a nation that does not excel at the industry of death does not deserve life.[59]

Among the Jordanian Ikhwani the cause of Palestine is even more fundamental and the need to be seen to be resisting Israel is perhaps most crucial. This is because of the huge number of Palestinian refugees who reside in Jordan and the fact that the Kingdom has been more directly affected by the fall-out of Israel's actions than any other state in the region. In addition, the ranks of the Jordanian Ikhwan have been swollen over the years by those of Palestinian origin. Whilst the Jordanian Ikhwan has long been divided into two currents – one that is more moderate, comprising those who are originally Jordanian, and the other the more hawkish Palestinian wing, which tends to be more representative of the grass roots of the organisation – it goes without saying that both currents share a complete aversion to any rapprochement with Israel. Their 1989 election platform stated: 'The Islamic movement believes that the liberation of all of Palestine is the most important and sacred duty ... The soil of Palestine is Islamic and belongs to the Muslims for eternity.'[60] When the Madrid peace conference on the Middle East opened in October 1991, the Jordanian Ikhwan termed the opening session as a 'day of mourning' and subsequently made clear its objection to all further peace deals with Israel, especially those that involved Jordan's Hashemite monarchy. The presence of so many Palestinians in the ranks of the Jordanian brotherhood has only increased the imperative for populist rhetoric.

Yet such grass roots appeals are not confined to those Ikhwan in the Middle East. Azzam Tamimi, who caused controversy in 2004 when he told the BBC that he would be willing to sacrifice himself for Palestine, is reported to have told a crowd at the ExpoIslamia convention in Manchester in 2006: 'Hamas is making sacrifices for you. We tell this government Hamas is not a terrorist group. It is elected by the people of Palestine. We are not terrorists. We are defenders of the truth. Fighting those who invade Muslims is a just cause.'[61]

It was in the context of this bid to be seen as defenders of Islam against Zionist forces that Mehdi Akef declared in 2006 that he was ready to send 10,000 fighters to Lebanon to fight alongside Hizbullah against Israel. Clearly such a proposition was totally preposterous; there was no way that Akef would have the intention or the capacity to muster such a force, yet alone send it to fight. Yet the pronouncement was aimed at capturing the mood of the street, which was firmly behind Hizbullah. In this case, too, the Ikhwan could do nothing other than back such a cause, despite the fact that Hizbullah are Shi'ite, because it had such enormous public support. One member of the Ikhwan told the US media: 'Of course we are supporting the resistance. We have no choice.'[62] Yet, as with the jihad in Palestine, the movement's action appears not to extend beyond making pronouncements that are aimed primarily at raising its own public profile.

In light of public sentiment within the Arab world towards the Palestinian issue, it would clearly be extremely difficult, if not impossible, for the Ikhwan to officially recognise Israel's right to exist; to do so would be tantamount to acknowledging the legitimacy of conquering Muslim land.[63] It would also shatter one of the core tents of the Brotherhood's ideology. Robert Leiken and Steven Brooke state that 'Every Muslim Brotherhood leader with whom we spoke claimed a willingness to follow suit should Hamas – the Palestinian offshoot of the Brotherhood – recognize the Jewish state.'[64] However, as they concede, 'Such earnest professions may be grounded in the confident assumption of Hamas recalcitrance.'[65] Even the most reform-minded Ikhwani maintain a degree of ambiguity about their stance on this issue when talking to Western commentators. During one interview, Abdul Moneim Aboul Fotouh declared: 'We as the Muslim Brotherhood know that the Jews in Israel are human beings ... and we know they should live, and should not be killed. Just the same as the Palestinians who are the original owners of the country should live and should not be killed.'[66] Later in the same interview he reportedly responded to a question about Hamas by saying: 'No, no, no! What they do is resistance, not violence. And what about Nelson Mandela? His movement had a military wing, too. We differentiate between resistance and violence.'[67] Clearly such ambiguity does little to assist the Ikhwan in its bid to prove to the world that it has fully renounced violence and can be trusted.

The issue of Iraq has similarly inflamed passions within the Ikhwan. Just as with Palestine, the Brotherhood has sought to demonstrate that it is defending the cause of Islam against the external aggressor. Although less symbolic than Palestine, not least because Saddam Hussein's Ba'athist regime was of a secular orientation and also repressed its own Muslim Brothers, the invasion of Muslim Iraq by Western powers was something that the Ikhwan could not fail to oppose in the strongest terms. Moreover, the issue of Iraq goes beyond Islam and is also related to Arab nationalism, something that the Brotherhood has been unable to shake off. For all that Saddam Hussein was secular, he was considered as a hero for attacking Israel in 1991 and he was also deemed to be the defender of the eastern flank of the Arab world against Persian domination. The Ikhwan may have launched some publicity stunts such as condemning the kidnapping of British hostage Norman Kember, who was abducted in Iraq in 2005, and calling for his immediate release (a fairly useless gesture given that the Ikhwan has no clout whatsoever with militants operating inside Iraq), it has in general supported the military struggle against US and British forces. Abdul Moneim Aboul Fotouh has said:

> We, as the Muslim Brotherhood and as the world leadership of the Muslim Brotherhood, support the armed resistance in Iraq against the American occupier, one hundred percent ... I personally, as all members of the Muslim Brotherhood in Egypt and around the world, wish to carry weapons against the American occupation in Iraq, just as we wish to carry weapons against the Zionist enemy in Palestine.[68]

It is easy to see why such statements are derided by those of a more militant bent, for in spite of his pronouncements, there is clearly no way that a figure such as the urbane Aboul Fotouh would ever dream of actually engaging in battle. Yet these kinds of statements are direct attempts to rally public support.

Although more measured in his response than Aboul Fotouh, Syrian leader Ali Saddredine al-Bayanouni has also made clear his belief that armed resistance is justified:

> We believe that Iraq is an occupied country. The Americans
> invaded to serve their own interests, not to liberate
> the Iraqi people. The chaos prevailing in Iraq today is a
> direct consequence of the occupation. Resistance against
> occupation is the legal and moral right of all people. The
> Iraqi Islamic Party has adopted peaceful resistance, but
> others are fighting through different means.[69]

Of course the Syrian Ikhwan may also be driven in their fervour by the
fact that Saddam Hussein provided shelter and refuge to various parts
of the Syrian Brotherhood when they fled from the al-Assad regime.

Whilst one wouldn't expect the Ikhwan to take any other stance,
the great irony in its position on Iraq is of course that, as described in
Chapter Three, the Iraqi Muslim Brotherhood in the form of the Iraqi
Islamic Party has been desperate to take part in the political process in
Iraq, something other parts of the Brotherhood consider to be a sham.
Clearly, for the Brotherhood, the propaganda opportunity presented
by the Iraq war has been more important than the views of their own
Iraqi Ikhwani in deciding what is best for the future of the country.

Anti-Westernism

Just as jihad has always been a core tenet of the Ikhwan's ideology,
so too has anti-Westernism. In view of the fact that the Ikhwan was
founded partly as a reaction to the colonial presence in Egypt, this
is hardly surprising. Much of the Ikhwan's support over the years has
been founded upon a sense that Westernisation and modernisation
were uprooting and degrading the very core traditions of Islamic
society. Although not averse to Western ideas and intellectual
traditions, al-Banna himself had a deep moral anxiety about the West
and the impact of Westernisation on Egyptian society. From the

early days, the Ikhwan promoted the message that 'Zionism aided by imperialism in the Arab world – the heart of Islam – and imperialism all over the Muslim world continue with impunity to act at will in the land of Islam.'[70] Such views were reiterated by other key Ikhwani scholars such as Imam al-Ghazali who in the 1950s lamented, 'the enemies of Islam had utterly wrecked the Islamic state'.[71] One of the reasons that some Ikhwani struggled to come to terms with Nasser's Arab nationalist republic was that they were confused by his apparent acceptance of secularised 'Western' values. Haj Abu Sen has said that he initially supported Nasser but when he visited Egypt for the first time following the revolution, he began to have second thoughts about him after seeing an advertisement featuring a scantily clad woman in one of the main squares in Cairo.[72]

Sayyid Qutb was also famously repulsed by Western cultural values and Western attitudes towards Islam. In *Milestones* he wrote:

> The Western ways of thought and all the sciences started ...
> with an enmity towards all religion and in particular with
> greater hostility towards Islam. This enmity towards Islam
> is especially pronounced and many times is the result of a
> well-thought-out scheme, the object of which is to first
> shake the foundations of Islamic beliefs and then gradually
> to demolish the structure of Muslim society.[73]

Qutb also displayed his total disgust and contempt for those Muslims who were attracted by the West: 'There are people – exponents of Islam – who are defeated before this filth in which *jahiliya* is steeped, even to the extent that they search for resemblances to Islam among this rubbish heap of the West, and also among the evil and dirty materialism of the East.'[74]

Although anti-Western rhetoric has softened somewhat over the years, and regardless of the fact that the Brotherhood allied itself with

Western powers against the communists in the war in Afghanistan, the essential beliefs underlying the discourse have not moved on very much. Pronouncements made by some members of the Ikhwan today are not that far removed from those issued by Hassan al-Banna. Mehdi Akef has allegedly referred to the United States as 'a Satan that abuses the region, lacking all morality and law'.[75] Abdul Moneim Abul Fotouh has said: 'The Middle East now is a clear example of Western violence. Even today we hear the voices of religious fundamentalism, a political dogma believed in and cultivated by the kings and presidents of the West.'[76]

Even one of the most reformist-minded Ikhwani, the Egyptian MP Issam al-Ariyan, declared in 2004: 'Throughout their history the Muslim Brotherhood have been an organisation or committee to resist the Western example through its different phases. This is the secret of the Ikhwan's presence.'[77]

The Ikhwan continues to cite Western aggression as the cause of all the ills of Muslim society not only in a political sense, but also in a cultural context. Mehdi Akef remarked in 2005: 'Our mission is immense, at the forefront of which is educating the lost youths on the streets and confronting the corruption that comes to us from the West to destroy our families and values.'[78] Akef also told the Arab media that 'the West desires to destroy the institution of family, whilst Islam strives to maintain the institution, because the family is what makes up, and is the essence of, the community'.[79] In a similar vein Aboul Fotouh has asserted: 'The West is preoccupied with material issues. Its democracy looks at the human being as a material entity. It overlooks the spiritual aspects that are there and cannot be denied.'[80] Moreover, as described in Chapter Four, Ikhwani in Europe have deep-seated concerns about Western values and how they will impinge on their own children and traditions. Although the language is far less aggressive than it was in the past, underlying rejectionist sentiments have not disappeared.

Of course some brothers do have a much more nuanced view of

the West. This is especially true of the reformist current within the Brotherhood. Aboul Fotouh for example observed that in Europe 'freedom of expression is guaranteed, in general. Human rights are respected. There is also a genuine respect for the opinion and will of the people. In most cases, the people elect the government they want to represent them. And they can hold that government accountable.'[81] Similarly, former deputy leader Mohamed Habib issued a statement in January 2008: 'There is a huge difference between our vision of the US administration, and the American people. A significant number of Americans oppose George Bush's policies, and millions of them took part in anti-Iraq war demonstrations.'[82] However, one has to wonder about the extent to which this statement was intended for a Western audience, given that it was issued in response to criticisms in the West that the Ikhwan was anti-American. Moreover, in spite of these more accepting comments, the Brotherhood continues to use this anti-Western discourse as a means of tapping into existing grievances and of presenting itself as the means whereby Islamic societies can save themselves from degradation.

Although anti-Western sentiment does not in any way equate with support for violence, such attitudes arguably create an environment in which a more militant mentality can flourish. Whilst the Brotherhood has broadly maintained its moderate stance, it has been accused repeatedly of being an incubator for terrorist ideology. As former Kuwaiti Education Minister, Dr. Ahmad al-Rab'i, has declared:

> The Muslim Brotherhood's problem is that it has no shame. The beginnings of all of the religious terrorism that we are witnessing today were in the Muslim Brotherhood's ideology of takfir. Sayyid Qutb's book *Milestones* was the inspiration and the guide for all of the takfir movements that came afterwards ... The founders of the violent groups were raised on the Muslim Brotherhood, and those who worked with

Bin Laden and al-Qaʻida went out under the mantle of the
Muslim Brotherhood.[83]

This opinion may be exaggerated but one cannot deny the fact that
Qutb's ideas inspired a generation of militants and it was through his
writings that the concept of *takfir* became more prominent. It is also
true that some of those who ended up joining more extreme groups
did pass through the ranks of the Ikhwan and that a number of militant groups such as Marwan Hadeed's Fighting Vanguard and Mustafa
Shukri's al-Takfir wal-Hijra sprang directly out of the Ikhwan.

More importantly, there has been a kind of tacit acceptance by the
Ikhwan of those with a more militant outlook and an unwillingness
to condemn or to expel them from the party ranks. In the Syrian case,
whilst the Ikhwan made it clear that it disagreed with the more violent
tactics of those of the Fighting Vanguard, it continued to fund the
group and to work with it when it suited it. Similarly, although Hassan
al-Banna criticised the Nizam al-Khass for engaging in acts of political
violence such as the killing of Judge Ahmed al-Khazindar Bey in 1948,
he did not take steps to dismantle the unit. The Brotherhood has been
more than willing to absorb those of a more militant bent within its
ranks, even displaying a tolerance of violence in some circumstances.
Murshid Maimoun al-Hodeibi is alleged to have welcomed the
assassination of Egyptian intellectual Faraj Foda, who was killed
for apostasy. Another key Ikhwani-oriented Egyptian, Mohamed
al-Ghazali, is alleged to have stated: 'The killing of Faraj Foda was, in
fact, the implementation of the punishment against an apostate, which
the State has failed to implement.'[84]

Given that the political and cultural goals and grievances of
the Ikhwan and the more militant groups are similar, it is easy to
see how someone within the Ikhwan could become frustrated by
the Brotherhood's slow approach and seek a faster, more proactive
way to achieve these goals. Yet to ascertain the extent to which the

Brotherhood influenced those who went on to take up more militant ideologies, or whether these individuals would have found their way to such ideological extremes regardless, is a near impossible task. To blame the Ikhwan for the actions of those who moved away from it is also somewhat unfair. Dr Kamal Helbawy has defended the Ikhwan on this issue:

> The impious and virtuous sons and fathers emerge from the same womb; the mothers and fathers are not responsible for this crime. This is why when the MB found out that there were youth in prisons and detention centres who had radical extremist thoughts and *takfir* tendencies, Brotherhood members who were also imprisoned clarified that they were not part of that movement.[85]

Yet it is reasonable to assert that the Ikhwan contributed to the general radicalisation that enveloped the Islamic world in the 1970s and 1980s. It is also true that prior to 9/11 there was less interest or differentiation between 'moderates' and 'militants' and there was a sense within the Brotherhood and the wider Islamist community that displaying the face of unity was of paramount importance. This was especially the case in Europe where in view of the small size of the Muslim community, radicals and moderates tended to mix and co-operate with each other and to do their utmost to conceal internal disputes within their own circles. However, since 9/11, when the world has been focusing intently on extremist elements, Ikhwani-oriented organisations have had to differentiate themselves more explicitly and publicly from those of a more radical bent. Therefore whilst the Brotherhood's flexible approach and apparent ambiguity towards violence may have meant that in the past they could be accused of unintentionally fostering more militant interpretations of Islam, in the present day such accusations would appear to be largely unfounded.

However, whilst the Brotherhood is clearly largely pacific, there are a number of issues in the movement's own past that it needs to take in hand. The Ikhwan's continued refusal to come to terms with the violence that the movement has supported or on occasions perpetrated throughout its long history needs to be addressed if it is to convince others that it has truly moved on. The opportunism that it has displayed over the years and the willingness that it has shown to resort to violence when expedient cannot simply be explained away as 'a response to repression'. The seeming desire to sweep these elements of the past under the carpet only serves to give the impression that the Brotherhood still believes its actions to have been somehow justified. Moreover its ideological ambivalence towards figures such Qutb, whose works are still part of the Brotherhood's educational curriculum, also needs to be tackled. Therefore whilst the Ikhwani have largely proved their pacific credentials in terms of their actions, a more robust ideological coming to terms with their own history would go a long way to convincing their detractors that they are truly a moderate and trustworthy movement that can carry the future of the Middle East in its hands.

The Arab Spring

From Opposition to Power

On 17 December 2011, Mohamed al-Bouazizi, a young Tunisian street vendor from the little known town of Sidi Bouzid, was to change the course of history. Al-Bouazizi had become so utterly frustrated by his repeated harassment at the hands of the local security services and by his dire personal circumstances that he set himself alight in protest. The young man's desperate act of defiance prompted the inhabitants of Sidi Bouzid to take to the streets to demand change. It wasn't long before the protests spread. Indeed, what started as a protest by Tunisia's long forgotten and underdeveloped interior soon reached the capital. Here Tunisians from all walks of life thronged into the streets to demand an end to the regime that had marginalised them both politically and economically for decades and that had left them feeling utterly disenfranchised. In the face of such profound and unprecedented public action, Tunisian President Zine El Abidine Ben Ali had no choice but to step down from power. On 14 January, the ageing president and his family fled to Saudi Arabia in disgrace and Tunisia turned a new page in its history.

The relative ease with which Ben Ali had been pushed out of power served as the spark to ignite the region. The fear of decades had suddenly been broken and people across the Arab world found it in themselves to take to the streets and to make their voices heard. Even in Libya where Colonel Qadhafi had maintained an iron grip for over four decades, it wasn't long before the east of the country had risen up to demand change. Although Libya's revolution turned out to be a much longer and bloodier process than that of Tunisia, people power finally won out, culminating in Qadhafi's grisly death in October 2011.

In Egypt, meanwhile, the events in Tunisia prompted young Egyptians to organise themselves and to take to the streets. Despite initially putting up resistance, President Mubarak soon saw that the tide of public anger had turned so thoroughly against him that he had no choice but to step aside. Although the Egyptian regime managed to hold on to power beyond Mubarak through the still powerful Supreme Council for Armed Forces (SCAF), in time even this body had to relinquish control to the forces that had emerged strongest out of the Arab Spring.

What was notable about all these revolutions was that they weren't driven by any overriding ideology. Rather, the Arab Spring represented the coming together of people from all walks of life, united by their shared desire to bring down the corrupt and authoritarian regimes that had dominated more or less since independence. However, somewhat ironically the main winners of these momentous events were the Islamist movements. After decades of suppression, the Arab Spring propelled what had been semi-clandestine or clandestine Islamist opposition movements directly into the political mainstream and in some cases into power.

Revolution in Egypt

When Egypt first became gripped by revolutionary fervour on 25 January 2011, the Muslim Brotherhood appeared as taken aback as the Mubarak regime by the sudden show of 'people power'. Despite the Brotherhood's being the largest and most established opposition movement in the country, it was the secular youth who, intoxicated by events in Tunisia, seized the moment and risked life and limb to try to bring revolution to Egypt. Indeed, the Brotherhood had been outmanoeuvred, overtaken by the so-called 'Facebook generation', who understood the enormity of what was unfolding in the region. As Egyptian youth flooded into Tahrir Square to demand change, the Brotherhood was left looking like an organisation that was not only behind the times but that had become as much a part of the furniture as the regime itself.

Not that the Brotherhood had been completely immune to the events that were shaking the region. The movement sought almost immediately to capitalise on the fall of the Ben Ali regime in Tunisia. Just a few days after Ben Ali fled in disgrace, the then Guidance Office member Mohamed Morsi issued a statement laying out five urgent demands to the Mubarak regime.[1] These demands included that the People's Assembly be dissolved and that free and fair elections be held; that the constitution be amended; that presidential elections take place; and that a new government of national unity be formed.[2] Morsi also warned that if the Mubarak regime did not respond positively to the demands of the Egyptian people, it could find itself sharing a fate similar to that of President Ben Ali. However, the Ikhwan, who had clearly failed to understand that this was not a time for making statements but a time for action, stopped short of actually demanding that Mubarak step aside. For the ever-judicious Brotherhood, such a step was a risk too far.

Participating in the Day of Rage, as 25 January had been dubbed, was deemed equally risky for the Brotherhood. Whilst some young Ikhwan members took part in the demonstrations as individuals, the movement did not list itself among the organisers of the protests and refused to give them its official backing. The fact that the country's most potent opposition force chose to shy away seemed like a contradiction in terms. However, there were good reasons for the Brotherhood's reluctance to get involved. Still uncertain at this stage as to whether the protestors would have the stomach to stick it out for long enough to actually bring down the regime, the Brotherhood did not want to risk taking any action that might see it lose the gains it had made over the past decades. It feared that the regime would retaliate hard and that it would be the main loser, scapegoated for the whole episode. The years of suppression seemed to have made self-preservation the Brotherhood's overriding preoccupation.

Moreover, the Brotherhood had never been a revolutionary movement. It had always maintained that it was not seeking to overturn established order but rather that it preferred to concern itself with reforming society to prepare it for the eventual establishment of the Islamic state. Joining the 'Day of Rage' was somehow too bold a revolutionary gesture for the Brotherhood.

However, as the protests gathered momentum and as it became apparent that the people were not going to back down, the Brotherhood came to the realisation that it could stand back no longer. If the people were going to overturn the Mubarak regime, the Brotherhood could not afford not to be part of the change. The movement knew it had to play catch up if it was to have any chance of playing a role in the country's future. As such its commitment to gradual reform was abandoned and the Brotherhood endorsed the protests scheduled for Friday 28 January and joined the demonstrations in an official capacity.

The movement was still reticent about putting itself at the forefront of the protests, preferring to send its members out to join the demonstrations but not taking any official leadership role. The movement was also more than willing to defer to Mohamed ElBaradei, the secular opposition figure who had become the unofficial figurehead of the protest movement. As Mohamed Morsi told the media at the time, 'we are not pushing this movement, but we are moving with it.

We don't wish to lead it but we want to be part of it.'[3] This message was clearly sent down the Brotherhood's chain of command and disseminated among its grassroots activists. As one young Brotherhood member in Tahrir Square parroted, 'We do not want to take over. Just the opposite. We only want to be a part of this, not control it.'[4]

Whilst much of this reluctance to get involved was still related to the movement's natural instinct for self-preservation, it was also because the Brotherhood didn't want to provide the regime with further ammunition with which to discredit the unfolding revolution. The Brotherhood had already been wrongly accused by the regime of having been behind the first day of protests, and it wasn't going to hand the authorities an own goal by putting itself in the foreground. As the Deputy to the Supreme Guide, Rashad al-Bayoumi, explained, 'we are keeping a low profile as an organisation. We are not marching with our slogans. We don't want this revolution to be portrayed as a revolution of the Muslim Brothers, as an Islamic revolution.'[5] The Brotherhood was well aware that if it took a leading role in the uprising, the regime would be able to dismiss it as little more than a bid by 'power crazy' Islamists to seize power. The Mubarak regime had long flagged the Islamist bogeyman as the only alternative to itself and had repeatedly used this threat to try to frighten the West. Thus the Brotherhood sought to ensure that the regime could not portray the protests as a bid by the movement to overturn the state and to seize power.

The Ikhwan was also concerned about how some of its fellow protestors would perceive its decision to join the revolution. The Brotherhood was well aware that underneath the newfound spirit of national unity that had been engendered by the uprisings, there were still plenty of young activists in Tahrir Square who were anxious about the Brotherhood and its intentions. In the words of one liberal activist, 'The Brothers ... They want it to be Islamic like Iran and this. But we don't want it to be like that. We are liberal.'[6] As such the Ikhwan was purposefully discreet during the uprisings and was careful not to brandish symbols that might unsettle other protestors. The slogans raised by the movement's members were purposefully all about change, freedom and social justice rather than the long-held motto, 'Islam is the solution'.[7]

Despite its low profile, the Brotherhood's presence in the demonstrations of 28 January and those that went on into February gave the uprising a new momentum. This was partly because for all that it might not have wanted to lead the revolution, the Brotherhood ensured that it put itself right at the heart of it. It did so by quietly taking on the role of arch organiser. Drawing on their years of experience as a social and welfare provision network, Brotherhood members strung up plastic sheeting in Tahrir Square to serve as tents, brought food and hot tea for their fellow demonstrators, distributed blankets and set up an emergency first aid clinic inside the square.[8] They also printed enormous banners depicting those young people who had been killed by Mubarak's regime. Most importantly, they rigged up the first microphones in the square, giving them control over the messages that were being pumped out to the demonstrators.[9] In conjunction with other opposition groups, Brotherhood members also took on the role of protector of the protestors, regulating entry and exit points to Tahrir Square, searching those who entered in order to prevent government thugs and intruders from infiltrating the demonstrations.[10] Indeed, the Brotherhood was in its element. As one youth activist, Mohamed Abbas, proudly declared, 'We are the best in Egypt to organise.'[11] Yet all this was done largely behind the scenes.

By early February, the Brotherhood's tone had changed again. Sensing that the protests were going to endure and that Mubarak couldn't last, the Ikhwan decided to up the ante and began calling for an end to the Mubarak regime. Having woken up to what was unfolding around them, and clearly feeling more secure of their support base, the brothers finally started speaking the same language as their fellow protestors, insisting that change could only be achieved if Mubarak's 'autocratic' regime be deposed.[12] Indeed, in characteristic fashion, the Brotherhood seized the moment and put itself to the fore. So much so that the Brotherhood even began talking in the name of the people. In one statement issued at the time, the movement asserted, 'the people refuse that this regime decides their destiny ... the people reject all the partial measures proposed by the head of the regime in his speech [given on 29 January] and do not accept anything less than the departure of the regime'.[13]

The Brotherhood's sudden call for Mubarak's downfall and its willingness to talk in the name of the people, some of whom had risked their lives while the Brotherhood remained on the sidelines, prompted some protestors to accuse the Brotherhood of muscling in and of trying to claim the revolution as its own. One protestor proclaimed, 'The Muslim Brotherhood wants to steal the success of this revolution ... They don't represent us.'[14] Such were the accusations that the Brotherhood was forced to issue a statement defending its actions and insisting that it had no private agenda and that it was not seeking to 'ride the current as some people are claiming'.[15]

Yet, for all the criticisms its actions provoked, the Brotherhood knew that if it wanted to shape Egypt's future, it had to make itself conspicuous. It was at this time that some of the movement's members began openly raising copies of the Qur'an in Tahrir Square.[16] Still profoundly aware of how it would be perceived both inside Egypt and abroad, the movement was careful to assert that it was not calling for change in order to take power itself. Even at this early stage, the Ikhwan began issuing statements that it was not seeking to take senior posts in the post-Mubarak phase. On 4 February 2011, Brotherhood spokesman Mohamed al-Beltagy told Al-Jazeera, 'We have said clearly we have no ambitions to run for the presidency, or posts in a coalition government.'[17] This was an assertion that the Brotherhood was to reiterate over and over again in the coming months.

The Brotherhood initially took an equally firm public stance on its attitude towards negotiating with the Mubarak regime. In the first days of February the movement was explicit that it would not even countenance engaging with the regime in any shape or form. Following newly appointed Vice President Omar Suleiman's announcement on 31 January that he was seeking dialogue with all political parties, the Brotherhood made it clear that it would not comply. Issam al-Ariyan declared on 1 February, 'Even after [Mubarak goes], we refuse to deal with Omar Suleiman.'[18] Similarly, in a statement posted on its website on 4 February, Mohamed Morsi announced, 'The Muslim Brotherhood categorically rejects any dialogue with the regime without any hesitation ... The people have brought down the regime and we see no point in any dialogue with an illegitimate regime.'[19]

However, by 5 February the Brotherhood had done a complete U-turn, announcing that it intended to participate in a dialogue with the Vice President. By 6 February Brotherhood representatives Mohamed Morsi and Saad al-Katatni were sitting around the table with Omar Suleiman and a handful of other opposition groups, including the Wafd party, Tagammu and members of a committee chosen by youth activist groups to discuss the possibility of setting up of a committee to look into changes to the most controversial articles of Egypt's constitution.

The Brotherhood tried to defend this sudden change of heart with some rather unconvincing excuses. Supreme Guide Mohammed Badie declared, 'We decided to take part in a round of negotiations in order to test the officials' seriousness about people's demands and their interests to respond.'[20] The Brotherhood also asserted that it had decided to engage in the negotiations to ensure that the people's demands were met. Saad al-Katatni, meanwhile, declared, 'We wanted the president to step down but for now we accept this arrangement ... It's safer that the president stays until he makes these amendments [to the constitution] to speed things up because of the constitutional power he holds.'[21]

However, the real reason for the Ikhwan's willingness to participate in the dialogue appears to have been related more to the Brotherhood's having concluded that if some kind of dialogue was going to go ahead, or some deal struck, it did not want to be left out. Indeed, for all the declared aspiration for a new Egypt, the Brotherhood, it seemed, would be happy to settle for a somewhat altered version of the old one, providing that it was given the space it wanted to operate. That the Brotherhood was willing to negotiate with the regime in this way was not that surprising, given its long history of forging alliances with the most unlikely of forces. From Iraqi President Saddam Hussein and former Syrian Vice President Abdul Halim Khaddam to the Egyptian President Anwar Sadat, the Brotherhood, as a worldwide movement, has never been averse to striking deals with the most authoritarian of characters and regimes when there has been an advantage to be had. Thus the Brotherhood saw no real contradiction in negotiating with the very regime it was trying to bring down. Indeed, the Brotherhood was seeking to keep one foot in Tahrir Square and the other with the regime.[22] As one analyst has observed, 'By virtue of their history, the Ikhwan were always with the regime, even when they confronted it and took part in a revolution against it.'[23] One thing was clear: the interests of the movement and its survival took precedence over the struggle for freedom and democracy.

The Brotherhood's willingness to enter into talks with the regime met with outrage among other parts of the opposition who had refused to negotiate with a power they believed had no legitimacy. It also prompted fury in Tahrir Square where protestors accused the Brotherhood of betraying the revolution. Banners and slogans were raised in the square on the day of the dialogue pronouncing, 'No negotiation, no representation before [Mubarak] leaving! No wisemen! No Brotherhood! The demands are in the Square.'[24] Many demonstrators viewed Omar Suleiman's offer of dialogue as little more than a bid to fragment the opposition and the Brotherhood's willingness to play ball as an act of treachery. Whilst the Brotherhood portrayed its participation in the dialogue as a valiant effort to 'place the people's demands on the table',[25] the protestors clearly saw things differently.

The Brotherhood's youth elements were not much enamoured with the willingness of their leadership to strike deals with the Mubarak regime either. Many Ikhwani young felt as though the Brotherhood leadership had risked compromising the whole revolution by its willingness to negotiate. These elements, along with other parts of the opposition, refused to compromise and continued to insist that they would not leave Tahrir Square until Mubarak had gone from office.

Under such pressures, the Brotherhood again found itself having to justify its actions. On 7 February it issued another statement asserting that it had entered into the dialogue in order to convey the people's demands to the Vice President.[26] The statement also stressed that the Brotherhood had done so 'while continuing the revolution' and that throughout the dialogue it had insisted that Mubarak should go.

Sensing that the dialogue was going nowhere and seeing the way in which the public mood was going, the Brotherhood began publicly denouncing the government for not doing enough. On 8 February, al-Bayoumi told the *Al-Hayat* newspaper, 'As initial signs indicate, nothing practical has happened. There were mere promises and pledges of reform, but they have not been implemented.'[27] However, the Brotherhood was still stating that it was open to dialogue with the regime.[28] On 10 February, Saad al-Katatni was quoted as saying, 'We will participate in the second round of the dialogue with Egypt's vice-president Omar Suleiman ... We have decided to take part in the talks to find a way out of the current crisis. No date has been set for the talks, but we believe they will be in the next few days.'[29]

By this point, events were moving faster than the Brotherhood. Thousands of protestors were still packed into Tahrir Square demanding Mubarak's departure. The protestors became even more determined following Mubarak's speech on 10 February in which the ageing leader promised not to run in the next presidential elections but refused to stand down. This prompted massive protests across the country and in Cairo demonstrators surrounded the presidential palace, the parliament and the state broadcasting building demanding the president's departure. Knowing that it was beaten, the regime concluded it had no choice and by the evening of 11 February Mubarak was gone.

Post-Mubarak

The Brotherhood was as jubilant as the rest of the protestors at Mubarak's departure. It was also equally explicit that Mubarak's removal was not the end of the road and that the army still needed to transfer power to a civilian authority for the revolution to be complete. However, the movement carried over the cautious approach it had employed during the uprising into the transition period. Once again the Brotherhood was quick to stress that it was not hungry for power and that it had no intention of dominating the post-Mubarak political arena. In a statement issued the day after Mubarak's departure, the Brotherhood declared that it would neither nominate a candidate for the presidency nor seek a majority in parliament.[30] A few days later, Issam al-Ariyan said, 'We are also not targeting to have a majority in the upcoming parliament. This is a time for solidarity, unity, we need a national consensus.'[31]

This concern not to frighten anyone off, least of all the still dominant military regime, was understandable. Ending up in confrontation with the military could spell disaster for the Brotherhood. If it was to ensure its role in the new Egypt, the movement's leadership knew that it had to play the game right. Doing so meant employing patience, moving gradually and, perhaps most challengingly, treading a difficult path between the military and the people. Despite its desire to see an end to the powerful military regime, the Brotherhood knew that being wholly on the side of the revolutionaries, who were still in Tahrir Square demanding that the Supreme Council for Armed Forces (SCAF) hand over power immediately, was a risky strategy that might backfire. Not only might such an approach result in further chaos and violence, it could still see the military retaliate and deny the Brotherhood any kind of legitimisation as a political actor. This would be a disaster for the movement that was determined to play its part in post-Mubarak Egypt. The Ikhwan calculated that its best option was to work with the SCAF to help it come up with an acceptable transition plan. This way, the Brotherhood believed, it could direct the transition and secure the best gains for itself in the unfolding process. However, the Brotherhood was also aware that it could not cosy up to the generals too much. This would risk alienating its supporters and losing the revolutionary credentials it had managed to chalk up despite being a latecomer to the uprisings.

The Brotherhood therefore had to navigate a careful path between the two camps, relying on its age-old strategy of forging temporary alliances of convenience and playing to both sides simultaneously. This way, the movement's leadership believed, the Brotherhood could manoeuvre itself gradually into a position of power. For all the Brotherhood's denials that it was seeking to dominate the post-Mubarak political arena, right from the outset its actions suggested otherwise. The Brotherhood jumped at the chance, for example, to participate in the committee of legal experts established by the SCAF immediately after Mubarak's departure. This committee, which comprised a small and select group of legal experts, was tasked with drawing up a set of recommendations for amending the constitution ahead of parliamentary and presidential elections. Lawyer and senior Brotherhood member, Sobhi Saleh, was appointed to the committee that was headed by Tariq al-Bishri, the former head of Egypt's administrative court, a known Brotherhood sympathiser.

Being part of this committee would enable the Brotherhood to have a direct say in how the transition would pan out. The committee proposed a series of amendments to regulate both presidential and parliamentary elections. The most crucial element for the Brotherhood in this respect, however, was that it could have a say in when the country's new constitution was to be drafted. Most political groupings in Egypt wanted a new constitution written before parliamentary and presidential elections took place. Conversely, the Brotherhood was intent on ensuring that elections occurred prior to the constitution writing process, and importantly, that they took place as soon as possible.

The Brotherhood's rush to hold elections had little to do with lofty ideals about the nature and machinations of the transition to democracy. Rather, being the most organised political grouping on the scene, the Ikhwan knew that it was best placed to succeed in any national poll. The Brotherhood's years of underground activism and the resulting networks it had established put it way ahead of its liberal and secular rivals, many of whom were new to the scene. As such, the Ikhwan wanted to ensure that there could be no delay in going to the polls.

Equally important to the Brotherhood was how the document was to be drawn up. The movement worked hard to ensure that the amendments specified that the constitution be drafted by members of a 100-member committee, to be elected by the People's Assembly and the Shura Council, the two houses in Egypt's parliament. The Ikhwan was eager for parliament to have the overall say in appointing the committee because it had calculated that it could win in parliamentary elections. It would thus be able to dominate the whole constitution drafting process and ensure that the resulting document have a strong Islamic flavour.

While an Islamic flavoured constitution was the last thing on the SCAF's mind, it was willing to work with the Brotherhood in return for the latter's supporting its roadmap. On 19 March, the proposed constitutional amendments were put to the people in a referendum.

Many political groupings, including those of a liberal bent, were desperate for the amendments to be rejected because they still wanted the constitution to come before the elections. However, having got the SCAF to agree to its transition plan, the Brotherhood was not going to squander its gains by allowing the people to vote 'no'. The movement mobilised its supporters by portraying the referendum as a choice between Islam and secularism, warning voters that opposing the amendments would be tantamount to rejecting Article II of the constitution of 1971, which describes Sharia as the principal source of legislation.[32] According to some reports, the Brotherhood resorted to even cruder tactics in order to convince people to vote 'yes', allegedly adopting slogans such as 'Voting yes, with Allah' or 'Voting no is siding with the Copts'.[33] By touching on such a raw nerve, the Brotherhood ensured that its supporters felt a kind of moral duty to come out and support the amendments.

The Brotherhood's efforts certainly paid off. A striking 77.3 per cent of voters came out in support of the changes. Although this was not all down to the Brotherhood, its efforts at mobilisation certainly helped swing the vote in the movement's favour. The results left the secular and liberal opposition reeling. They also left the liberal parties feeling as though they had been thoroughly stitched up by the military and the Brotherhood – the two big forces that had emerged out of the revolution. So much so that allegations began to surface that the SCAF and the Brotherhood had struck some kind of sinister backroom deal and that they were two sides of the same coin.

Perceptions to this effect were heightened by the fact that following Mubarak's departure, the Brotherhood pulled back from the ongoing demonstrations, distancing itself from the other revolutionary elements. When crowds flooded back into Tahrir Square at the start of April to demand that the SCAF move faster to hand over power, the brothers stayed away. Still they stayed away on 27 May when hundreds of thousands went back to Tahrir and when protests were held across the country in what was dubbed the 'Second Friday of Anger' or the 'Second Revolution'. The Brotherhood's absence also led some to conclude that the movement had hatched some kind of plot with the SCAF to share power.

Both the Brotherhood and the SCAF were quick to deny such allegations. Guidance Office member Saad al-Katatni asserted, 'It happened many times that our political stand coincidently went in the same direction of the military council's desires, but that doesn't necessarily mean we have a deal with them ... We don't care whether the military council is satisfied with our decisions or not.'[34] Indeed, accusations of a secret deal appear to be rather far-fetched. The two sides may have had some grudging respect for each other but they were hardly natural allies. Yet they somehow needed each other. With the Brotherhood being the largest and most potent force in the country, it was in SCAF's interests to get the movement on board and, more importantly, to convince it not to create further trouble on the streets. One retired general reflected later, 'The SCAF's goal at the time was to calm down the streets, and with the Brothers being the most organised and numerous group, they naturally felt it made sense to let them have a critical say.'[35]

Furthermore, in order for the SCAF to ensure it could direct the transition in the way it wanted, and, more importantly, to ensure the preservation of its own privileges, it was vital that it come to some kind of understanding with the Islamist movement it had fought so hard to suppress over so many decades. As one retired Egyptian army general put it, 'When you enter a new block, you usually look to see who is the strongest thug with whom you could have an understanding. The SCAF was the newcomer, and the thug was the Muslim Brothers.'[36]

For the Brotherhood, meanwhile, making itself indispensable to the SCAF, and working with rather than against it, was the surest way of getting what it wanted out of the transition process. Only this way could it ensure that the necessary constitutional foundations were put in place for it to be able to capitalise on its natural advantage. As one Egyptian analyst explained, 'The brothers do not want any obstacle to the elections because they are trying to achieve power through the ballot ... They are opposed to the immediate departure of the military as that would create turmoil in Egypt and delay the elections.'[37] Moreover, in the Brotherhood's view, co-operating with the SCAF was the most effective way to weaken it in the long term. As one Brotherhood member put it, 'How do you eat an elephant? One mouthful at a time.'[38] Thus the two sides came together in a kind of tactical and uneasy alliance of convenience.

The Brotherhood also knew that it needed to keep the SCAF sufficiently sweet to ensure that the latter would approve of its forming a political party. This was essential for the Brotherhood, as without a party it would not be able to contest the elections or enter the political scene in any meaningful way. Almost as soon as Mubarak fell, the Brotherhood's Shura Council announced its intention to set up a political arm. Then in April 2011 the Brotherhood set up the Freedom and Justice Party. Three members of the Guidance Office were appointed to lead this new political venture. Mohamed Morsi was appointed as party head, Issam al-Ariyan as its deputy and Saad al-Katatni as its secretary-general with all positions valid for a four-year term. On 18 May 2011, the Brotherhood formally submitted a request to establish the party, which boasted some 9,000 founding members.[39]

Setting up the Freedom and Justice Party was a bold and decisive move for a movement that had long been riven with internal debates over the rights and wrongs of establishing a political party. All the more so given that in the years prior to the revolution, the traditionalists, who advocated shying away from the political arena, had come to dominate. However, after some heated debates within the movement in which some brothers argued that the Brotherhood should remain as a *jama'a*, leaving its members free to join whichever political party they wanted, the objections to forming a political party, even among the party traditionalists, seemed to dissipate as quickly as Mubarak himself. Now that the opportunity of getting to power had become a reality, ideological concerns were put quickly to one side.

Not that the establishment of the Freedom and Justice Party was without its challenges. There was a great deal of discussion both inside and outside the movement about what the nature of the relationship between the party and the *jama'a* should be. The standard Brotherhood line on the subject was that the two entities would be completely separate.[40] However, old habits died hard. Supreme Guide Mohammed Badie seemingly saw no contradiction in the fact that party leaders were appointed by the Guidance Office. He also prohibited Brotherhood members from joining any party other than the Freedom and Justice Party.[41] The movement also wrote the party's platform and approved its bylaws.[42] For all its protestations to the contrary, it was clear that the party was going to be tightly controlled behind the scenes by the movement.

While this lack of separation was predictable enough, it still frustrated some more reformist-minded members who had hoped that the revolution would herald a newer, fresher and more open way of doing politics. Particularly aggrieved at the dominance of the old leadership over the new party were some Brotherhood youth elements. These young people tried to stand up to the Brotherhood machinery by holding public conferences at which they challenged the leadership's way of doing things. At one such meeting in April 2011, they demanded that the Brotherhood become an official Islamic society in order for the Freedom and Justice Party to operate as a truly independent body. They also called for a raft of reforms, including that the Brotherhood separate itself from the international *tanzeem*, and, most boldly, that it select a general controller other than the Supreme Guide. Some of these youth elements became so frustrated that they broke away and formed their own political parties, such the Hizb al-Tayyar Al-Masri (the Egyptian Current Party).

Just as it did with those Brotherhood members who broke away in the 1990s to form the al-Wasat party, the movement's leadership took a zero tolerance approach to these 'errant youth', expelling them from the movement making it clear that there was no room for disobedience within the ranks. Whilst much was made of these youth elements in the international media, where there were even suggestions that the Brotherhood might split apart, the movement proved as robust as ever. Indeed, a movement as large and solid as the Brotherhood could clearly withstand such shocks, which ultimately proved to be little more than an irritation. The message was clear: revolution or no revolution, the Brotherhood was not going to change its way of doing things.

Moreover, such matters were of trifling concern given what was at stake. The Brotherhood could see that after almost a century of semi-clandestine opposition, power was finally within its reach. Rather than get bogged down in soul searching about internal procedures and reform, something that risked weakening the movement, the Brotherhood focused all its energies on the more pressing task in hand. This was ensuring a victory in the upcoming elections that were scheduled for November 2011. This was the all-important moment for the Brotherhood that had to legitimise itself by turning its perceived popular support into tangible political gains.

However, as the elections approached, the Brotherhood found the SCAF to be a trickier partner than it had first anticipated. For all that the generals had been willing to work with the Ikhwan on the transition roadmap, as the elections approached the SCAF began to get increasingly alarmed at the prospect of a Brotherhood controlled parliament and a Brotherhood dominated constitution. The SCAF began to wonder whether it had made a mistake in rushing to work so quickly with the Brotherhood on the roadmap. Thus, the SCAF, that had already been frustrating both the Brotherhood and the revolutionaries by its repeated backtracking on agreed dates for its handing over of power, took a series of steps to try to ring-fence the

Ikhwan. Most notably, in July 2011, the SCAF issued a new parliament law which stipulated that 50 per cent of seats in the lower house of parliament be reserved for individual candidates, with the remaining 50 per cent to be elected under a party lists system. The law ruled too that in the Shura Council or upper house, 65 electoral constituencies would be reserved for individual candidates, while 28 would follow closed party lists. This was disastrous not only for the Brotherhood's Freedom and Justice Party, but for the other political parties and groupings. Under intense public pressure, the SCAF were forced in September to increase the share of party lists from 50 per cent to two-thirds of seats, but this would still work to limit the Brotherhood's presence and influence in the parliament.

The SCAF also upheld a constitutional provision introduced by President Nasser ruling that half of contested parliamentary seats be reserved for representatives of 'labourers and farmers.' What this had meant in practice in the last years of the regime was that these seats were taken by retired military officers and security personnel who turned themselves into farmers in order to enter government.[43]

Fearing that it was about to be denied its moment, the Brotherhood retaliated by playing it tactically, trying to outmanoeuvre the SCAF by finding other ways to dominate the political arena. In the early days after the fall of Mubarak, consistent with its cautious approach, the movement had insisted that it would only nominate candidates to 35 per cent of seats in the parliament. [44] By April 2011, a more self-assured Brotherhood had notched this figure up to 50 per cent. But by October 2011 the movement changed its tune and went full out for power. It announced that, through the alliance it had teamed up with – the Democratic Alliance for Egypt – it would be nominating candidates for all available seats.[45] There were ten other parties in this grouping, but the Freedom and Justice Party was the dominant player by far. It also supplied the vast majority of candidates nominated by the alliance for the elections.

At the end of September, the Brotherhood also upped the stakes by threatening to boycott the elections unless the SCAF amended the parliament law. However, it was careful not to push things too far. At the same time, it declined to give its backing to the mass protest that was held on 30 September to 'reclaim the revolution'. However, the pressure coming from all sides was such that the SCAF agreed in October to amend the law and to allow all seats to be contested through the party list system.

Whilst this was a triumph for the Brotherhood, the movement was soon to be disappointed again when, in November, the SCAF proposed a series of supra-constitutional principles. These principles, that had been circulating since August, included that the military budget remain confidential, that the military be granted the right to object to certain articles of the new constitution, and that if the parliament failed to draw up a new constitution within six months, the SCAF would be permitted to draw up a new assembly. Equally contentious for the Brotherhood was the proposal that the SCAF be granted the authority to hand pick 80 out of 100 members of the constitution writing committee.

Such an audacious attempt to deny the Brotherhood the power it craved was too much for the movement. With its interests threatened so directly, the Ikhwan once again took on the mantle of revolutionary and returned to the streets. The movement joined with other groups in Tahrir Square to demand the supra-constitutional principles be retracted. Demonstrating its seriousness, the Brotherhood set up its own stage in the square and mobilised its members to come out in force. The demonstrations were so large that there was talk of a second revolution. But it wasn't a second revolution that the Brotherhood was after. Rather, the movement wanted to demonstrate to the generals that without it on board, the SCAF was at the mercy of the masses.

In the face of such a mass outpouring of public anger, the SCAF had little choice but to announce that the supra-constitutional principles would no longer be binding, but would only be advisory. The SCAF also amended the principles so that the military would be placed directly under civilian government, asserting that it should 'abide by the constitutional and legislative regulations.'[46] Having got what it wanted, the Brotherhood agreed to pull its supporters from the streets and to enter into dialogue once again with the military. Indeed, sure of its own constituency, that did not include those who were still protesting in the square, the Brotherhood was determined to ensure that the all-important parliamentary elections would go ahead as scheduled.

Its judgement on the timing of the elections turned out to be correct. In the polls, which lasted from 28 November to 11 January 2012, the Freedom and Justice Party powered to victory with its coalition taking 235 seats, representing 47.2 per cent of the total. This made the Brotherhood the largest bloc by far. It turned out to be a disastrous election for the revolutionary and youth groups, and for the secular parties, who were left with almost nothing. The surprise result was that of the Salafist bloc, led by the al-Nour party, which came second with 120 seats. Indeed, despite the revolution's having starting out from a largely non-ideological base, it was the Islamists who were to reap the final rewards. But it was the Brotherhood specifically that played the whole post-Mubarak period with extreme skill and dexterity and that, despite its earlier protestations that it was not seeking a majority in parliament, had succeeded in manoeuvring itself into power.

However, the game was not over yet. There was still the presidency to play for. The Brotherhood had always insisted that it had no intention whatsoever of nominating a candidate for the presidency, but as the situation on the ground changed, once again it moved the goalposts and announced it was entering the race. In March 2012, the Freedom and Justice Party stunned Egypt when it declared that it was nominating its powerful Deputy, Khairet al-Shater, for the upcoming presidential elections. Some of this shock was a direct result of the fact that in June 2011, the Brotherhood had expelled prominent Brotherhood leader, Abdul Moneim Aboul Fotouh, after he had disobeyed orders and announced his intention to run for the presidency on an independent ticket. Issam al-Ariyan declared in June 2011, 'He has nothing to do with us now ... We cannot support anyone violating our decisions.'[47] While losing such a prominent figure was clearly a blow to the movement, the Brotherhood had always risen above personalities, proving that it had no time for those who promoted themselves or their ideas above the *jama'a* machinery. Moreover, Aboul Fotouh had always been somewhat of a loose cannon, whose more liberal views stretched the boundaries of what was acceptable to the Brotherhood's hierarchy. Yet Aboul Fotouh's expulsion was taken as a clear indication that the Brotherhood was serious about its promises not to field a presidential candidate.

But by March 2012 the Brotherhood was finding itself increasingly squeezed by the SCAF. It may have won the elections but it was frustrated at its inability to really exercise power. Most challenging was the SCAF's refusal to dissolve the government of Prime Minister Kamal Ganzouri and allow the Freedom and Justice Party to appoint a government of its own. The SCAF's intransigence made the Brotherhood feel as though it had been backed into a corner.

The SCAF had also begun issuing veiled threats to dissolve parliament, making the Brotherhood feel as though its hold on power was built on very fragile foundations. Thus al-Shater's nomination to the presidential race was a means for the Brotherhood to challenge the SCAF and to try to wrestle power away from it. As Mohamed Morsi explained, 'We have chosen the path of the presidency not because we are greedy for power but because we have a majority in parliament which is unable to fulfil its duties.'[48]

The decision to field a presidential candidate was not supported by all Brotherhood members. Some brothers were horrified at the move. Freedom and Justice Party MP, Mohamed al-Beltagi, wrote on his Facebook page, 'I oppose the Brotherhood's nomination of one of its own for the presidency ... It harms the Brotherhood and the nation, to have one faction assume all the responsibility under these conditions'.[49] According to Kamal Helbawy, who resigned from the movement on account of its nominating a presidential candidate, 52 members of the Shura Council had opposed al-Shater's nomination and the 56 who voted in favour only did so after significant pressure had been brought to bear upon them.[50] The decision also prompted a group of young IkhwanI, calling themselves, Sayha Ikhwania (Brotherhood Shout) to stage a sit-in in front of the Brotherhood's headquarters.

But fearing that the SCAF was moving to undermine the gains it had made, the Brotherhood's leadership felt it had no choice but to up its game. It wasn't long, however, before winning the presidential race became all the more pressing for the Brotherhood. On 5 April 2012 the Administrative Court suspended the constituent assembly that had been established to draft the new constitution. Its decision to do so was a direct response to the way in which the Brotherhood had handled the appointments to the assembly. With the parliamentary election victory under its belt, the Brotherhood had abandoned its ultra-cautious approach and the gloves came off.

Keen to get the constitution writing process completed before the presidential elections, not least because this way it could ensure that real power lay with the parliament rather than the presidency, the Brotherhood had set to work after its election victory to appoint the constituent assembly. In its rush to get the job done the way it wanted, the Brotherhood pushed things too far. Firstly, it nominated some 75 per cent of the 100 places in the assembly to Islamists, who hailed from the Salafist and Brotherhood currents. Whilst the Brotherhood had initially declared that it would not partner with the Salafists, once it saw an advantage in doing so, it moved to form a tactical alliance with them. Furthermore, out of the 100 seats, it insisted that 50 be given to parliamentarians, rather than those who hailed from outside the newly elected legislative body. Most of those parliamentarians it appointed were from the Freedom and Justice Party. The Brotherhood also drew up a reserve list, which also comprised around 75 per cent Islamist nominees.

Whilst the Brotherhood justified its choice of appointees by rightly insisting that the composition of the constituent assembly reflected the results of the parliamentary elections, its actions further alienated other political groupings. Twenty-five members of the constituent assembly, who represented the non-Islamist element, walked out on the grounds that the body was not sufficiently representative. They included not only liberal and secular elements, but more importantly representatives from the Coptic Church and from Al-Azhar (Egypt's official religious establishment). Indeed, the other political parties and groupings pulled together to protest at the 'Brotherhood's attempt to impose its hegemony over the constitution.'[51]

The obvious power grab made somewhat of a mockery of the Brotherhood's talk of national consensus. With the rest of the world watching, this should have been the time for the movement to demonstrate its democratic credentials and its desire to be inclusive, especially towards Egypt's minorities. But in the rush to gain the ultimate prize, and knowing that it would never have the same chance again, the Brotherhood seemed to forget itself, appearing to believe it could simply run roughshod over the objections of the other parties and constituencies. Freedom and Justice Party Secretary General, Saad al-Katatni, who was appointed as head of the constituent assembly rather disingenuously declared, for example, 'If anyone boycotts its meetings they will be replaced by others elected as reserves.'[52] Likewise, Brotherhood Secretary General, Mahmoud Hussein, declared that it didn't matter whether or not the constituent assembly was representative because as a body it would gather suggestions from all Egyptians![53] Displaying how much it was still caught up in the pre-revolution mindset, the Brotherhood also slipped back into conspiracy theory mode and claimed that the military had been behind the boycott.

Furthermore, the Brotherhood also seemed to believe that its win at the polls meant it had been somehow mandated by the Egyptians to provide an Islamic future for the country through the constitution. Khairet al-Shater told the *New York Times* in March 2012 for example that the elections had proved that Egyptians were demanding 'an explicitly Islamic state.' He added, 'The people are insistent ... All institutions should revise their cultures, their training programs and the way they build their individuals in the light of this real popular choice.'[54]

The suspension of this committee was therefore a serious blow to the Ikhwan's bid to consolidate its election gains and to turn them into real power. It also made winning the presidency a necessity. With the constitution in its existing form, it was the President who would wield all the power. Thus what started out as a bid to challenge the SCAF, turned into a race that the Brotherhood had to win. All the more so after 15 June when the SCAF formally dissolved parliament and stationed security forces around the building to bar MPs from entering the chambers without official notice.

By this point, however, the Brotherhood had been forced to field a new candidate. In another attempt to weaken the Brotherhood, al-Shater had been included in a list of ten presidential candidates banned from standing for the post. The reason for al-Shater's disqualification was because of a disputed criminal conviction. In 2008 al-Shater had been convicted by a military tribunal of money laundering and funding a banned group, namely the Brotherhood. The military tribunal sentenced him to seven years in prison. Despite the fact that al-Shater's lawyers argued that the Brotherhood leader had been granted a judicial pardon that covered all charges, the ban against him was upheld. Former intelligence chief, Omar Suleiman, who had proposed his candidacy in direct response to the Brotherhood's putting forward of al-Shater, and Salafist leader, Hazem Abu Ismail, were also included in the ban.

Undeterred, the Brotherhood quickly fielded a backup candidate, Mohamed Morsi. A seemingly unprepossessing engineering graduate who joined the Brotherhood while studying for his PhD in the US, Morsi rose through the movement's ranks and in 2000 was elected as a member of the People's Assembly. He served as the movement's parliamentary bloc leader until 2005, when he became leader of the Brotherhood's political division. Despite his lack of charisma, Morsi worked steadily towards the elections. When it came to the polls, he won 24.78 per cent of the vote in the first round, securing his position in a runoff against Ahmed Shafiq in the second round. On 24 June, Morsi was declared president, having won 51.73 per cent of the vote.

Although Morsi's victory was not as decisive as the Freedom and Justice Party's parliamentary election win, it was still a victory. By employing the tactics that had served it so well during its years in opposition, the Brotherhood had succeeded in turning its natural advantage into a tangible victory and after almost a century of opposition, the Brotherhood finally had Egypt in its hands.

The movement's transformation from semi-clandestine opposition group into ruling power had not happened the way that the movement's founder, Hassan al-Banna, or successive Murshids, might have wished or expected. The movement had always upheld that its main aim was to reform society from the bottom up. Yet the Brotherhood ultimately came to power through the shock of revolution, and a revolution which it could hardly claim as its own. However, in the event this seemed to matter little to the Brotherhood or its supporters. For them, the time had finally come.

It also seemed not to trouble the Brotherhood that it had come to power through the ballot box. Despite the fact that the movement had always displayed such resistance towards forming a political party and that the issue had caused some of the most serious ructions within the movement over previous decades, the Brotherhood proved more than willing to adapt itself to the prevailing climate. When the opportunity to get to power presented itself, the Brotherhood moved quickly and with typical pragmatism to capitalise on the unfolding situation.

The movement's ability to respond to the changing circumstances on the ground stood it in good stead. Despite not having taken part in the uprisings right from the beginning and despite coming under relentless criticism for the way in which it conducted itself during the revolution and beyond, the Brotherhood used its might and its experience to put itself right at the heart of the events. Indeed, the Brotherhood positioned itself to dictate the transition in the way it wanted, enabling it to secure the ultimate prize. Furthermore, despite the fact that the uprisings started out as a revolution of the youth, it was the Brotherhood's hardened old guard who proved shrewdest and toughest of all, and who were able to drive events in the way they saw fit. Indeed, for all the accusations that it had betrayed the cause, it was the Brotherhood who forced the revolution to its ultimate conclusion. That conclusion turned out to be the triumph of political Islam.

Brothers Next Door

The victory of political Islam was not unique to Egypt. For all that commentators may have believed that the non-ideological nature of the uprisings had ushered in a new era that had moved beyond Islamism, the Arab Spring proved otherwise. In Tunisia, where the Jasmine Revolution had been organised primarily by youth and secular elements, including those linked to the leftist trades unions, it was the Islamist party, An-Nahda, which had no real presence in the country at the time of the revolution, that emerged triumphant. An-Nahda won the largest majority in the October 2011 elections to the constituent assembly, winning 41 per cent of the vote. It also went on to form the government in coalition with two other parties.

Although An-Nahda is not officially part of the Brotherhood, it was born out of the same ideological tradition and shares the same broad ideological outlook. Some of An-Nahda's leaders are bound to the

Brotherhood's international structures through their membership in international Brotherhood-oriented organisations such as the International Union of Islamic Scholars. As such Tunisians proved as susceptible to the pull of reformist political Islam at the polls as the Egyptians.

An-Nahda's triumph was all the more shocking because Tunisia had always had a distinct image of itself as a modern, secular and open nation whose face was turned firmly and happily towards Europe. This was the legacy left by Habib Bourguiba, the country's first president following independence, who, for all his authoritarianism, was increasingly coming to be viewed with nostalgia by Tunisians who had become utterly frustrated at the ignoble excesses of President Ben Ali. Moreover, unlike in Egypt that had always been the cradle of political Islamism and where the Brotherhood was still able to operate on the ground despite being banned, the Tunisian regime allowed no space whatsoever for the forces of political Islam. Although An-Nahda had had a presence in Tunisia since the 1970s when it started out as the Mouvement de la Tendance Islamique (MTI), and although the regime had on occasion given it some breathing space, such as in 1989 when it was permitted to contest the elections, as a whole the movement was systematically suppressed. By the time of the uprising, An-Nahda had been reduced to little more than a movement in exile. It was also a movement that was ravaged by in-fighting and factionalism, with the Paris and London branches at each other's throats. Thus, when it came to the elections, although it had money, An-Nahda was not able to draw on the same kinds of networks that facilitated the Egyptian Brotherhood's ascent to power, making its victory all the more impressive.

Yet, similarly to the Brotherhood, An-Nahda played the transition phase with extreme skill. Most notably, it positioned itself to appeal to as wide a spectrum of voters as possible. Drawing on its reputation for moderation, engendered by the more progressive teachings of its leader Sheikh Rashid al-Ghannouchi who had long insisted that Islam and democracy were compatible, An-Nahda moved into the middle ground. Like the Egyptian Ikhwan, An-Nahda was equally keen not to frighten anyone off. It purposefully sought to reassure women, for example, asserting that it had no intention of modifying the personal status code or of imposing the hijab. It even went as far as to field a female candidate, Souad Abdul Rahim, who chooses not the wear the veil. Indeed, An-Nahda prioritised compromise giving the impression that it would be a reasonable and inclusive political player.

The party's long experience, especially outside of Tunisia, gave it an organisational advantage and a degree of media savviness. An-Nahda instructed its supporters not to go to the airport to greet al-Ghannouchi when he returned from his long exile for fear of creating images reminiscent of Ayatollah Khomeini's return to Iran.[55] Displaying similar pragmatism, when it became apparent that some of the more ideologically rigid elements within the party could not conceal their more conservative thinking, the party kept them away from the media.[56] An-Nahda was thus able to present itself as a unified body with a single cultural message despite the frictions and factions within the party between the radical and more moderate strands.

More importantly, An-Nahda positioned itself as the party that would restore traditional values and that would bring Islam and Arabism back to the heart of Tunisian society. In doing so it was careful to make it clear that it wanted to build a modern society, but also stressed that this society should be rooted in the country's 'authentic' identity. To this end, rather than raise controversial issues such as polygamy, party members focused on how to deal with social phenomena such as people being forced to marry late due to financial hardship and high divorce rates.[57] While such messages may not have appealed to all of the urban middle class, they certainly attracted enough Tunisians who felt alienated and troubled by the overt secularism of previous regimes.

Although An-Nahda was not the only party promising to shift the country back to its traditional Islamic and Arab identity (other parties, including those of an Islamist bent, promoted a similar message), it had a major advantage over its competitors: it was a known entity whose leaders had a special moral authority on account of the years they had spent imprisoned or in exile. Sheikh Rashid al-Ghannouchi in particular was a prominent and respected historical figure whose personal sacrifices were well known. As such he, and by extension the party, were held up as untainted by corruption and for many, as being synonymous with Islam. Thus An-Nahda entered the elections with a symbolic capital that far outstripped that of its rivals.

An-Nahda was therefore able to appeal to a cross section of Tunisian society. Not only did it receive the largest share of the vote in the poorer areas of the interior, especially in al-Ghannouchi's home area of Gabès, it managed to do well in the capital and notably in the more affluent areas of the coast, such as Sousse and Monastir, cities that had always been associated with the former regime. The key to much of An-Nahda's success was that it was able to connect with the masses. Whilst the liberal and leftist parties struggled to reach out beyond the urban elite, An-Nahda's message resonated with ordinary Tunisians, or at least with a large percentage of those who turned out to vote. The party was helped in this by the fact that it was able to use the country's mosques for political mobilisation. In so doing, it had the ear of the masses and, as it turned out, the masses proved receptive to the party and its message.

Meanwhile, political Islam was also coming out into the open in Libya. Although the Libyan Muslim Brotherhood was not to achieve the same kind of electoral success as its counterparts in Egypt and Tunisia, it still succeeded in turning itself from an outlawed and brutally repressed organisation into a credible political force and key shaper of post-Qadhafi Libya. This was an achievement given that of all the reformist political Islamist forces operating in the region, the Libyan Brotherhood was starting from the lowest base. Colonel Qadhafi's utter intolerance of any kind of political activism outside of the framework of his unique Jamahiriyah state, as well as his personal hatred for Islamists whom he referred to as *zinadaq* (heretics), had meant that the Brotherhood had not had any space to operate at all. The movement was largely wiped out inside the country in 1998 when, after having discovered the presence of some Brotherhood cells, the regime launched a mass arrest campaign. Over one hundred members of the movement were detained, including most of its leadership, and the rest forced to flee. Although the regime released over one hundred members of the movement in April 2006, as part of its bid to reform and rehabilitate Islamist prisoners, and although there were some contacts between the regime and the Brotherhood in the UK, the movement remained banned and its members closely monitored. Thus, like An-Nahda, by the time of the uprisings, the Libyan Brotherhood was little more than a movement in exile.

However, the Libyan Ikhwan rushed to play its part in the transition to the post-Qadhafi era. In November 2011, it held its first public conference inside the country, during which it elected Bashir al-Kebti as its new General Guide. Following in the footsteps of its Egyptian counterpart, it also moved to establish a political party. In March 2012, the Brotherhood launched its Justice and Construction Party in a high profile event in Tripoli at which Mohamed Sawan, from Misarata, was elected as party leader. Like the Egyptians, the Libyan Ikhwan maintained that the party was to be separate from the movement in order that the latter could operate in the fields of preaching, Islamic education and welfare provision.

Also in line with the Egyptians and with An-Nahda, the Libyan Brotherhood did its best to stress its moderate credentials. It extended membership of the Justice and Construction Party beyond the movement and was keen to emphasise its vision of Libya as a democratic civil state with an Islamic frame of reference. The Libyan Brotherhood was vague about exactly what it meant by such a frame of reference. However, it tried to impress upon the Libyans that it was inclusive and that it was nothing to be afraid of. As the movement's outgoing General Guide, Suleiman Abdelkader explained, 'We don't want to replace one tyranny with another. All together, we want to build a civil society that uses moderate Islam in its daily life ... our shared task is to protect Libya, to talk to each other instead of fighting.'[58]

When it came to the country's first national elections in over four decades, the Justice and Construction Party did not score the success it had hoped for. Although it was the second party, it only took 17 out of the 200 seats in the new National General Congress. There were many reasons for this failure, including the way the election law had been structured. Fearful that the Brotherhood would sweep the board given the choices electorates had made in both Tunisia and Egypt, and the fact that Libya is one of the most conservative and traditional societies in the region, the more liberal elements within the National Transitional Council, the interim ruling body established after the uprisings began, structured the law so that only 80 seats would go to political parties. The remaining 120 seats were reserved for individual candidates. Thus, whilst it did field some members as individuals, the Justice and Construction Party was only able to contest less than half the available seats.

However, the Brotherhood still fared considerably worse than the frontrunner, a broad based coalition led by former Planning Minister, Mahmoud Jibril, which took 39 seats. It is perhaps not surprising that the Brotherhood did not do better: the movement was little known inside Libya, its networks almost non-existent, given that it had never been able to get a real foothold inside the country. The movement was so emasculated that it was never able to produce any leader of particular note, or anyone with the stature of an al-Ghannouchi. As such it had no symbolic presence inside the country. In fact, the symbolic presence it did have was largely negative. Qadhafi had spent forty years railing against the Brotherhood, repeatedly warning of their plots to subvert the country and lumping them together in his discourse with more militant elements, tarring all Islamists with the same brush. Although the regime may have gone, some of its anti-Islamist sentiment seemed to have outlived it. A poll carried out by a Libyan research centre found that 40 per cent of respondents who did not vote for the Islamists chose not to do so because they were frightened of them; 45 per cent because they didn't know them; and only 8 per cent because they weren't convinced by their election programmes.[59] Given that the Brotherhood, like the other parties contesting the elections, had just eighteen days to campaign, it clearly came across as a movement that was neither known nor to be trusted.

The Brotherhood was also faced with the problem of how to distinguish itself from the myriad of parties that had entered the political arena. Given that Libya has no real secular currents and that even the liberal parties advocated Sharias being cited as the primary source of legislation in the new constitution, the Brotherhood struggled to differentiate itself as being the party that could make a real break with the past and return the country to its authentic Islamic identity. In addition, the Brotherhood was up against another important factor in Libyan society: tribalism. The Ikhwan were not able to supersede the country's powerful tribal forces who made their presence felt in the political arena primarily through those seats that were reserved for individual candidates.

Despite these challenges, however, the Justice and Construction Party still came out of the elections as a player and ended up with a number of portfolios in the country's first democratically elected government in decades, including that of Deputy Prime Minister. This achievement has less significance in the Libyan context than it would have elsewhere, given that the central authorities in Libya are so lacking in authority. One of the consequences of the Libyan revolution has been that the centre has given way to the periphery and the country is now home to a plethora of local power brokers, from tribes, regions and militias that all outweigh the power of the legitimately elected ruling bodies.

Compared to these elements, the Libyan Brotherhood is not a powerful force. But it is a force nonetheless and has successfully made the transition from clandestine opposition movement to mainstream political actor. Furthermore, the movement is already focusing its efforts on doing what the Brotherhood has always done best, namely making its presence felt on the ground. After years of being barred from such activities, the Libyan brothers are finally free to preach and to invest their resources into the movement's trademark charitable work. The movement is building a database of Libya's poor to help co-ordinate its welfare programmes and is also engaged in establishing youth training and employment projects.[60] As such, the Brotherhood and its political arm look set to be part of Libya's political and social landscape for the foreseeable future and are likely to grow in importance.

For all its non-ideological beginnings, therefore, the Arab Spring breathed new life into political Islamist movements, and into the Brotherhood in particular. This was all the more surprising, given that there was a growing sense among commentators in the years running up to the revolutions that political Islam had had its day. By the late 2000s, the Brotherhood, and what it stood for, was looking somehow outmoded and most definitely on the wane. The Egyptian Ikhwan in particular, ravaged by factionalism and in-fighting, seemed to be almost turning in on itself, resigned to its fate as the power that never was.

However, the Arab Spring provided a new opportunity that seemed to shake the lumbering movement out of the stasis it had become so bogged down in. The fact that the Arab Spring was not about ideas, that it was essentially a protest *against* the old regimes and the status quo rather than a protest *for* any specific alternative played straight into the Brotherhood's hands. It enabled the Brotherhood and An-Nahda to use their experience and superior organisational skills to move straight into the power vacuums that opened up with the toppling of the former regimes. In the absence of any new alternative, it was the Brotherhood and its reformist style of political Islam, rather than its more progressive competitors, that proved to be what the people wanted.

Conclusion

The Challenges Ahead

When the first edition of this book was published in 2010 it was unthinkable to imagine that after so many miserable decades of oppression, the Brotherhood and its affiliate An-Nahda would be catapulted to power in Egypt and Tunisia, that they would be part of the elected government in Libya, and that they would change the dynamics of the Middle East so profoundly. The Brotherhood has shifted from semi-clandestine opponent to legitimate political power almost overnight. For all that the transition has been fraught with difficulties, the movement has risen to the challenge, displaying no small degree of aplomb. Relying upon its traditional pragmatism and opportunism, it has played the transition period with skill and maturity and has proved a master at manoeuvring itself into power. Indeed, for all the talk that it was not seeking to rule, once it felt it had the people behind it, the Brotherhood moved quickly and strategically to gain power, elbowing out anyone who got in its way. Thus, for all that the Brotherhood had traditionally shunned revolution, the upheaval of the Arab Spring turned out to be its moment *par excellence*.

Yet getting to power, or becoming a mainstream political actor, was one thing. The Brotherhood in its various guises is now faced with the even more difficult business of operating out in the open and in some cases of governing. Indeed, the post-revolutionary reality is throwing up a series of trials that will seriously test the Brotherhood's mettle. How the Brotherhood and its counterparts will manage these challenges will be crucial to whether the movement is able to hold itself together and prove that it has the capacity to be part of the future.

One of the most important of these challenges is how the movement will reconcile its commitment to Sharia with its commitment to modern democracy. Whilst the Brotherhood has never aspired to an Islamic state ruled by theologians, it has always advocated a civil state that is run along strict Islamic principles and that is based upon Islamic Sharia. As Sayyid Qutb explains in his famous work, *Milestones*, 'The way to establish God's rule on earth is not that some religious men be given the authority to rule, as was the case with the rule of the Church, nor that men speak in the name of God, as is the case in a "theocracy" ... To establish God's rule means that His laws be enforced and that the final decision in all affairs be according to these laws.'[1] Indeed, respected Kuwaiti scholar Sheikh Abdullah Nafisi has remarked, 'Whoever thinks the Egyptian Ikhwan have any other goal than applying Sharia is mistaken.'[2] Even Rashid al-Ghannouchi, who is considered to be among the most progressive of Islamists, still refers to Sharia as the basis of his concept of Islamic democracy because 'no political theory can be considered Islamic if formulated outside the domain of Sharia. It would simply be illegitimate from an Islamic point of view.'[3]

As such, whilst it has long been content to participate in the electoral process and has jumped at the opportunity to contest elections following the Arab Spring, the Brotherhood has always demonstrated an ambivalent attitude towards modern multiparty democracy. Former Murshid Mustafa Mashour, for example, once commented, 'For now we accept the principle of party plurality, but when we will have Islamic rule we will either accept or reject this principle.'[4] Although Mashour was a renowned hardliner and was speaking in a previous era, his comments certainly raise questions about the Ikhwan's true intentions in the longer term. There is certainly misgiving in some quarters that the Brotherhood's willingness to work within the party system is little more than a stepping stone to power and that it will move to change the rules once it has the chance. While such suspicions are probably overplayed, not least because of the fact that the Brotherhood is not and can never be the only actor in the political arena in each of the countries where it has moved into the political mainstream, the movement and its affiliates have not always helped themselves in this respect. In November 2011, for example, Tunisian Prime Minister and senior An-Nahda member Hamdi Jibali caused uproar when, following his party's election victory, he told a group of An-Nahda supporters, 'My brothers, you are at a historic moment ... in a new cycle of civilization ... We are in the sixth caliphate, God willing.'[5] More strikingly, in November 2012, President Morsi, provoked outrage when he issued a series of decrees awarding himself far-reaching powers and preventing the courts from challenging any laws or decrees passed since he assumed office. Morsi was later forced to rescind the measures after widespread popular protests against the move. However, his actions raised serious questions about his commitment to the democratic process.

Even those members of the Brotherhood labelled as reformist and who had pushed hardest for political participation have expressed their doubts about 'Western' democratic models. Former Deputy General Guide Mohamed Habib once asserted, for example, Europe represents a model of democracy that is 'particular to European societies only'.[6] Similarly while still a member of the Brotherhood's Guidance Office, Abdul Moneim Aboul Fotouh declared that while democracy is positive for 'its own citizens in their respective countries. As for us and for our Arab and Islamic causes, it does not represent a reference; their model has no democracy or justice for us.'[7] In any case, both Habib and Aboul Fotouh, as well as other more reformist-minded members of the movement, have moved out from the Brotherhood finding its inflexibility too stifling.

Yet one of the problems that the Brotherhood has is that it has never been able to articulate a precise definition of the kind of democracy that it sees as appropriate to Muslim societies. In the years prior to the revolution, the movement issued a series of reform initiatives aimed at presenting a more progressive image in which it sought to tackle this thorny issue. However, despite its best intentions, the pronouncements on democracy in these initiatives remained vague. The 2004 reform programme of the Egyptian Brotherhood states, 'We, Muslim Brotherhood, stress our commitment to the regime as a democratic, constitutional, parliamentarian, presidential one, in the framework of Islamic principles.'[8] Yet the movement fails to spell out how this framework of 'Islamic principles' will work. In the same document, the Brotherhood also declares its support for, 'People representation through a freely elected parliament for a certain period following which elections are held again.'[9] However, later in the text under the section on legal reform the initiative stresses the Ikhwan's commitment to 'Changing the laws and purifying them to be in conformity with the principles of Islamic Sharia.'[10]

This lack of clarity about how the Ikhwan envisages the relationship between Sharia and the democratic political process has done little to assist it in its bid to be seen as a truly progressive and democratic movement. Rather, one is left with the impression that the Brotherhood is dealing with the issue by trial and error, something that is perhaps unsurprising given that the movement has always been primarily reactive. Furthermore, the Brotherhood has hardly been a bastion of democracy itself. Whilst members of the movement regularly assert that they have their own kind of democracy through the use of *shura* (consultation), some Islamic scholars have complained that the Ikhwan's talk of *shura* has become more propaganda than reality, and more mechanical than functional, given that the leaders do not allow any space for criticism or evaluation.[11] Indeed, what has characterised the movement over the years is that it has often been led, or at least controlled behind the scenes, by the same few faces who have remained in influential positions for lengthy periods.[12] Even the choosing of successive Murshids has seen the movement's own internal rules go out of the window, something that has frustrated many Ikhwani, especially from the younger generations. Likewise, Sheikh al-Ghannouchi has led An-Nahda since its inception despite complaints from some party members during his last years in exile in the UK that it was time for him to step aside.[13]

The Brotherhood may have been able to justify such behaviour in the past by the difficult circumstances it was forced to operate in and which necessitated a degree of secrecy. Now, however, the movement can no longer hide behind such explanations. The Brotherhood, or its political parties at least, have no choice but to do things out in the open and in the eye of full public scrutiny. Yet the Brotherhood is painfully aware that opening up and reforming its own way of doing things risks the coming to the fore of the factionalism that has dogged the movement for generations. If it abandons the principle of complete obedience in favour of true democracy within its ranks, the Brotherhood may inadvertently find itself a more factionalised and weaker organisation as a result. Thus while the Brotherhood is likely to engage in some cosmetic attempts at opening up and proving that it is operating in a more transparent fashion, it is unlikely to change the habits of a lifetime.

Moreover, while the Brotherhood leadership might have been keen to promote the concept of democratic principles in recent years, these ideas have rarely filtered down to the grass roots.[14] The reform platforms the movement came up with in the 2000s, for example, remained in the realm of the Guidance Office and the elite of the movement and the ideas expressed in them weren't incorporated into the movement's teaching. As one Egyptian commentator has observed, 'The Muslim Brotherhood presents a political discourse that asserts its acceptance of democracy and pluralism, but this is not clearly reflected in its literature, nor in its educational system. Many of the books they teach inside the organisation rely upon literature and books which Al-Jama'a claim they have gone beyond.'[15] The Ikhwan allegedly still teaches the works of some of its most conservative thinkers, including not only the works of Sayyid Qutb, but also Mustafa Mashour, including his book *Tariq al-dawa bayna al-isalah wal inhiraf* (*The Path of Al-Dawa: Between Reform and Deviation*) which teaches that any difference of opinion in ideology is something that has to be avoided at all costs.[16] As Tamam has observed, 'There isn't one book that consolidates democratic values. Rather they have books that reject differences and pluralism inside the Ikhwani idea itself.'[17] That there is such a limited culture of democracy or democratic tradition within the Brotherhood (and among its grass roots especially) is hardly surprising. The Ikhwan emerged in a part of the world that prior to the Arab Spring had little direct experience with democracy other than through the sham elections instituted by the former regimes. It is perhaps not surprising, therefore, that for the Ikhwan, democracy is still essentially about elections and voting rather than being a wider concept of democratic culture related to individual rights and freedoms. One of the Brotherhood's anxieties with liberal democracy is that it prioritises the individual over society, which for the movement has a negative impact on public morality. As Brotherhood spokesman, Mahmoud Ghazlan, has remarked, 'Ultimate sovereignty in Western democracy belongs to the people, and that gives them the right to legislate anyway they want, regardless of what is considered from a shar'i point of view as halal (licit) or haram (illicit), or even if it contradicted moral principles, such as not to commit adultery, homosexuality, alcohol, and gambling ... All these are deplorable issues, but still are considered legal in the West.'[18] Even al-Ghannouchi's concept of Islamic democracy asserts that Muslim societies can follow the same democratic political traditions and processes that are employed in the West, but that the 'Islamic contribution' should be 'primarily in the form of a code of ethics, a transcendent morality that seems to have no place in today's democratic practice ... What Islam provides is not only a set of values for self-discipline and for the refinement of human conduct but also a set of restrictions to combat monopoly and a set of safeguards to protect public opinion.'[19]

These anxieties over public morality have been present in the Ikhwan since its very beginnings. Hassan al-Banna's first forays into Islamic activism were through a series of Islamic societies that focused their efforts on preventing moral offences such as the Society for Moral Behaviour whose activities included composing and distributing 'secret and often threatening letters, to those they regarded as living in violation of the teachings of Islam'.[20] Moreover given that the Ikhwan is among the most conservative forces in the region, it is hardly surprising that such concerns feed right into the heart of its debates about democratic models. In the Egyptian Ikhwan's reform initiative of 2004, alongside the talk about the commitment to 'freedom of individual beliefs', the Brotherhood also asserts that cultural reform will be undertaken in 'papers, magazines, radio and television, so as to establish its material and work on Islamic values and principles ... This protects the individual from ignorance and Westernisation and does away with messing up with moral principles and falling into sins and trivialities.'[21]

Similar concerns have continued to preoccupy the Brotherhood into the post-revolution phase. In a statement posted on its website in November 2012, the Brotherhood declared, 'Sharia awakens faith, reforms behaviour, improves the general environment of the whole society, and polishes morals, through persuasion and education, with no coercion whatsoever.'[22] For all its talk of democracy therefore the Brotherhood remains intent on reforming the individual, suggesting that the movement sees no real distinction between being the guardian of morality and being the ruling power. This poses serious concerns not only for Egypt's liberal elements, but also for the country's minorities.

Given these concerns, all eyes have been watching how the Brotherhood and its counterparts have dealt with the constitution writing process. The challenge has perhaps been easier for the Libyan Ikhwan, where given the conservative and traditional orientation of the population that is almost exclusively Sunni Muslim, there is a broad consensus that Sharia should be cited in the constitution as the main source of legislation. However, there is still likely to be some disagreement among the various political players in Libya over the extent to which Sharia should be implemented and institutionalised.

An-Nahda, meanwhile, chose to play it safe. In line with its more progressive outlook, the party opted not to push for any change to Article One of Chapter One of the 1957 constitution, which states that Tunisia is 'a free, independent and sovereign state. Its religion is Islam, its language is Arabic.' An-Nahda's decision not to push for Sharia to be cited as the primary source of legislation was controversial, particularly among the more hard line elements within the party who objected to such a stance. However, the more moderate and dominant wing prevailed.

The Egyptian Ikhwan, however, faced a far more troublesome dilemma in this respect. This is because the Brotherhood found itself caught between two opposing camps with vastly divergent views on the constitution, neither of which the movement could afford to ignore. On one side were the secular liberals, who feared that enshrining a greater role for Sharia would limit personal freedoms and individual rights. With them were the Copts, who were particularly anxious about explicit references to the Islamic identity of the Egyptian state. On the other side of the debate were the Salafists, who were insistent that the constitution prioritise the role of Sharia even more forcefully and who went as far as to demand that Article Two of the old constitution which states that the 'principles of Sharia' are the main source of legislation be altered in order for the document to specify that Sharia be implemented in its entirety. To complicate matters further for the movement, it was not only the Salafists that the Brotherhood had to please on this front. Many of the movement's grass roots supporters were also expectant that the Brotherhood would move to implement Sharia law. Indeed, this is what many believed they voted for when they gave the Brotherhood their support in the elections.

As such the Brotherhood found itself having to tread a careful middle path. While ideologically and religiously the movement broadly supported the Salafists' position and would have liked to have backed the full implementation of Sharia law, in the end it sought to appease both sides by taking a characteristically gradual approach. Thus, while it did not seek to alter the wording of Article Two of the constitution, content to rely on 'principles of Sharia' being the main source of legislation, it pushed for the inclusion of a new article (Article 219) which stipulated that 'The principles of Islamic Sharia include general evidence, foundational rules, rules of jurisprudence, and credible sources accepted in Sunni doctrines and by the larger community.' It also pushed for the inclusion of a new clause stipulating that the official religious establishment of Al-Azhar should be consulted on matters related to Islamic law. Thus while it did not push for the full implementation of sharia law, it sought to amplify the Islamic nature of the constitution. This may have caused uproar among Egypt's secular elements, but it was a clear bid by the Brotherhood to maintain its religious legitimacy while working within the constraints it was being forced to operate in.

Maintaining its religious legitimacy has been more essential than ever for the Brotherhood. This is because the Arab Spring not only catapulted the Brotherhood into the mainstream, it also unleashed the Salafists, who have emerged as a powerful and growing force not only in Egypt, but across the region. Salafist currents in their various forms and shades were gaining in popularity prior to the Arab Spring. Indeed, the growth of Salafism was a key preoccupation for the Brotherhood at that time, with the movement fearing that the Salafists were muscling in on its natural constituency. The flourishing of the Salafists after the revolution, the decision by some Salafist elements to form political parties, and, in the Egyptian case, the surprise success of the Salafists in the parliamentary elections, have been a sobering wake up call for the Brotherhood. As one member complained, the Salafists in the form of the Al-Nour party are 'directly attacking our core'.[23]

The Salafists with their more rigid and 'purer' interpretation of Islam are serving as a serious pressure on the Brotherhood across the region. This is particularly the case in Tunisia where some Salafist groups have steadily upped the pressure on the ruling party. In perhaps the most extreme example, in November 2012, Salafist cleric, Nasr al-Din al-Alawi, appeared in a television interview alongside Interior Minister Ali Larayed in which the former called upon Salafist youths in Tunisia to declare jihad against An-Nahda.[24] But in all three countries the Salafists are condemning the Brotherhood for not being Islamic enough.

This leaves the Brotherhood in a serious dilemma. The movement is painfully aware that the more it concedes on core religious principles and the more it is forced by the demands of realpolitik to compromise on issues such as foreign policy, minority rights and the role of women, the more it risks losing some of its more conservative support base to the Salafist current. In order to get around this problem, the Brotherhood may ultimately choose to play it extra tough on issues of public morality, in the hopes that this will satisfy its support base and thereby give it the flexibility it needs in other spheres, such as the economy or foreign policy.

Yet foreign policy, or rather the Brotherhood's relations with the Western world, presents a particular challenge for the Brotherhood. Like the nationalist regimes before it, the Brotherhood has always relied upon anti-Westernism as a rallying cry and as a means of securing popular support. This does not mean that the movement has been averse to engaging with the US government where possible.

Even prior to the revolution, while it was spouting anti-US rhetoric, some Egyptian Brotherhood parliamentarians proved willing to meet with US diplomats. After the revolution, the Egyptian Brotherhood was equally keen to meet with US officials, clearly calculating that the regional and international legitimacy it stood to gain from being recognised by Washington outweighed the populist kudos it might have won from a premature clash with the US.[25]

Now, however, the Brotherhood has to forge a new relationship with the West and with the US in particular. This is particularly pertinent for the Egyptian Brotherhood. Given that Egypt receives around $1.5 billion dollars in US aid plus other support each year, the Brotherhood can hardly afford to turn its back upon such an important donor. Yet the movement knows that its support base remains largely sceptical at best about US intentions in Egypt and in the region more widely. The strategy adopted by the movement therefore has been to take a middle course, to demonstrate that it is not hostile to the US, but to make it clear that the Brotherhood intends to establish a more balanced and equal relationship with Washington than the former regime. During his election campaign, President Mohamed Morsi pledged to rework Egypt's relations with the US based upon 'independence of decision' and an end to 'subordination', asserting that he would 'seek to replace all political economic, military and other forms of subordination in the longer term, with new forms of relationships based on balanced joint gains'.[26] Indeed, Morsi has to prove to the Egyptian people that he can stand up to Washington when it counts. It is for this reason that in his first public speech following his election as President, Morsi vowed to free Omar Abdel Rahman, the blind Egyptian sheikh, imprisoned in the US after having been convicted of helping plan an attack on the World Trade Center in New York in 1993. Morsi knew that such a demand would be out of the question as far as the US was concerned, yet he knew he could get some popular mileage by raising it.

It is clear therefore that while the Brotherhood will continue to co-operate with Washington, it is not going to abandon its populist verbal assaults on the US. Likewise it will continue to use the Palestinian issue as a means of bolstering its popular support base. For all that it is bound by realpolitik to uphold Egypt's peace treaty with Israel and for all that it might see advantage in positing itself as a new mediator in the region, the Brotherhood cannot abandon its support for the Palestinians or for Hamas. Indeed, Morsi's first election campaign pledge in his list of foreign policy promises was to, 'Support the Palestinian people in their legitimate struggle to restore their rights, establish their own State and liberate their land.'[27] Given the mood on the streets, the movement has no real choice but to rely upon anti-Zionist and anti-Western rhetoric as a means of shoring up its popular support base. In fact, if the going gets tough, such rhetoric is likely to increase.

And things will get tough for the Brotherhood as it struggles to manage the needs and expectations of the populations who risked life and limb for their revolutions. This is particularly true in the Egyptian case. The Egyptian Ikhwan came to power on a ticket of Islam and poverty alleviation. It wasn't for nothing that the movement mobilised its charitable and welfare networks in the run up to the parliamentary elections to offer free or discount food and goods in some of Cairo's poorest neighbourhoods. Moreover, Morsi's campaign platform promised a 'Renaissance Project' to save Egypt from decline across the education, health, science and technology sectors. As such, many Egyptians are looking to the Brotherhood to solve their day-to-day problems of poverty, lack of jobs and dismal services.

Yet fixing the nuts and bolts of a society in which two fifths of the population live around the poverty line and are dependent on state subsidies (which eat up one third of the state budget[28]), and in which corruption is endemic and bureaucracy stifling, is not going to be easy. What makes it harder for the Brotherhood is that expectations are so high. As one Egyptian analyst explained, 'The expectations that he

[Morsi] would deal with all injustices quickly created an atmosphere of hopes that are very high and unrealistic.'[29] The Freedom and Justice Party's failure to meet some of these expectations has already prompted a wave of strikes and industrial action across a range of sectors. There have also been criticisms that the new President has failed to meet many of his ambitious list of sixty-four pledges, ranging from rubbish collection to improving Egypt's gridlocked traffic, that he vowed to achieve within his first 100 days of office.

Likewise, An-Nahda has struggled to respond to the needs and demands of a population that wants jobs and better services, as well as an end to corruption and to the stark regional inequalities that have dogged the country since independence. Like Egypt, Tunisia has seen a wave of public strikes and sit-ins and, despite its efforts, the government is proving unable to push economic reforms through quickly or forcefully enough. Whilst the Libyan Brotherhood, as a partner in the government is less in the firing line, it is still part of a ruling elite that is struggling to meet the everyday needs of the population, despite the country's enormous oil wealth.

How long those who gave the Brotherhood their vote will continue to support the movement has yet to be seen. The more the demands of governing force the movement to compromise on its core principles, the more it risks alienating its core support base. Indeed, the Brotherhood is still a movement that is rooted in its own traditions and in the past. Whether this large and lumbering force will be able to rise to the challenge of the modern age has yet to be seen.

Yet for the time being, this is still the Brotherhood's moment. For all that the movement has proved itself to be utterly self-serving, to have a questionable commitment to democracy in its wider sense, and to be unable to work economic miracles, for now, the Brotherhood and An-Nahda still seem to enjoy popular trust and support. While this is partly because the liberal and Salafist elements are in such disarray, meaning that there is still no credible alternative, it is also because the Brotherhood is more than a political party. It is a *jama'a*. Even An-Nahda has a role that extends beyond the realm of most conventional political parties. The Brotherhood did not come to power on account of its political or economic agenda alone. The Brotherhood's strength turned out to be what it had always been, its grass roots support base that sees in the movement a force that is morally untainted and that resonates with tradition and security. More importantly, perhaps, this grass roots continues to view the movement as synonymous with Islam.

Indeed, this is the real success of the Brotherhood. It has managed to posit itself as the authentic voice that can bring Islam to the core of every aspect of life, including politics. It is this 'authenticity' that enabled the movement to reach out beyond the revolutions and beyond the realm of elitist politics and to touch the masses. For the time being at least, the Brotherhood has proved itself more in tune with the people than either its political rivals or its predecessors could ever hope to be.

Acknowledgements

This book would not have been possible without the generous support of the Smith Richardson Foundation, who funded the research, and I would like to thank Nadia Schadlow in particular for backing this project. I would also like to give special thanks to all those Ikhwani and others from within the Islamist community and beyond who have been willing to be interviewed for this project. Particular thanks go to Dr Kamal Helbawy, who offered me great assistance and support throughout the project and whose frankness has been invaluable. I would also like to pay special tribute to the Syrian brother Sheikh Mohamed Hasnawi who sadly died during the course of this project. Sheikh Hasnawi demonstrated a particular generosity of spirit, openness and humility and made me feel particularly welcome during my stay in Amman. Thanks also go to Dr Issam al-Attar and to Adnan Saad Eddine for their kindness and support and for their particularly enlightening insights into the Ikhwan's history. Finally, I would like to thank Ahmed for his invaluable help with Arabic sources, for his comments on various drafts of the text and most of all for his enduring patience.

Notes

Introduction

1   I use the term 'Islamist' here and throughout the text to mean those who engage in political activism articulated through an Islamic discourse. This does not necessarily mean those who espouse violence.

Chapter 1

1   'The Fruitful Tree, The MB Call', on Ikhwanweb.com, 13 June 2007. See: http://www.ikhwanweb.com/Article.asp?ID=819&LevelID=1&Sectio nID=115

2   Ibid.

3   Mahmoud Abdelhalim, *Al-Ikhwan al-Muslimoun. Ahdath Sunat Al-Tareeq. Ru'iah Min al-Dakhil* (*The Muslim Brotherhood. The Events that Made History. An Insider's Vision*), Alexandria, 2004, Vol. 1, pp. 58–9.

4   '*Shahid Alla Aser, Al-Ikhwan al-Muslimoun Kama Yrahm Farid Abdel Khaliq*' (A Witness in Time, the Muslim Brotherhood as Seen by Farid Abdel Khaliq), on Al-Jazeera, Episode 1, 7 December 2003. Available in Arabic on http://www.aljazeera.net/NR/exeres/BF012F78-FC05-4E7B-839C-67E94CF195BA.htm

5   Ibid.

6   Richard P. Mitchell, *The Society of the Muslim Brothers*, Oxford 1993, p. 297.

7   François Burgat and William Dowell, *The Islamic Movement in North Africa*, Austin 1993, pp. 34–5.

8   Ibid.

9   T. Ramadan, *Aux Sources du Renouveau Musulman*, Lyon 2002, p. 362.

10   N. Ayoubi, *Political Islam: Religion and Politics in the Arab World*, London 1991, p. 90.

11   Brynjar Lia, *The Society of the Muslim Brothers in Egypt: The Rise of an Islamic Mass Movement 1928–1942*, Reading, 1998, p. 213.

12   'Shahid Alla Aser, Al-Ikhwan al-Muslimoun Kama Yrahm Farid Abdel
     Khaliq'. Episode 1, 7 December 2003.

13   Ibid.

14   Abdelhalim, Al-Ikhwan al-Muslimoun. Ahdath Sunat Al-Tareeq. Ru'iah Min
     al-Dakhil, Vol. 2, p. 360.

15   Muthakarat Dr Abdelaziz Kamel, Uthou fi al-Nizam al-Khass (The
     Memoirs of Dr Abdelaziz Kamel. Member of the Nizam al-Khass), July
     2007. Available in Arabic on http://www.paldf.net/forum/showthread.
     php?t=120458

16   'Shahid Alla Aser, Al-Ikhwan al-Muslimoun Kama Yrahm Farid Abdel
     Khaliq'. Episode 1, 7 December 2003.

17   Ibid.

18   Quoted in Lia, The Society of the Muslim Brothers in Egypt, p. 203.

19   According to Farid Abdel Khaliq, al-Banna went ahead and consulted with
     the party about the possibility of joining and subsequently decided to put
     the idea to the Ikhwan's Guidance Office. However, not wanting to influence
     the decision unduly he asked Abdel Khaliq to put forward the suggestion,
     which was ultimately rejected, as if it were his idea. See 'Shahid Alla Aser,
     Al-Ikhwan al-Muslimoun Kama Yrahm Farid Abdel Khaliq'.

20   See for example, Lia, The Society of the Muslim Brothers in Egypt.

21   'Shahid Alla Aser, Al-Ikhwan al-Muslimoun Kama Yrahm Farid Abdel
     Khaliq'.

22   See, for example Lia's description of how al-Banna bypassed his own
     Administrative Council when he disagreed with a decision they had made
     to set the wages of an imam and a handyman in the movement's mosque at a
     rate that al-Banna disapproved of and how he insisted upon the appointment
     of a Deputy of his choice. Lia, The Society of the Muslim Brothers in Egypt,
     pp. 61–2.

23   Abdelhalim, Al-Ikhwan al-Muslimoun. Ahdath Sunat Al-Tareeq. Ru'iah Min
     al-Dakhil, Vol. 1, p. 225.

24   Ibid.

25   Ibid.

26   Ibid.

27   Lia, The Society of the Muslim Brothers in Egypt, p. 251.

28   This group included a number of senior members of the Ikhwan including
     Mohamed Ali al-Mughlawi, who had been the Ikhwan's Secretary of the
     General Committee of Students and Workers, Mahmoud Abu Zayed
     Othman, who was the editor of the Brotherhood's weekly newspaper, and
     Mohamed Izzat Hasan.

29   See Lia, The Society of the Muslim Brothers in Egypt, p. 249.

30   Other members of the Nizam al-Khass included Ahmed Hassanein,
     Mahmoud al-Sabah, Mustafa Mashour, Ibrahim Al-Tayib, Yousef Talat,

262 THE MUSLIM BROTHERHOOD

Abdelrahman al-Sindi, Helmi Abdelhamid, Hosni Abdelbaqi, Said Sadeq, Ahmed Hijiazi and Mahmoud Asaf.

31 Abdelhalim, *Al-Ikhwan al-Muslimoun. Ahdath Sunat Al-Tareeq. Ru'iah Min al-Dakhil*, Vol. 1, pp. 178–9.

32 Lia, *The Society of the Muslim Brothers in Egypt*, p. 178.

33 Interview with Mehdi Akef, Cairo, May 2007.

34 Dr Mahmoud A'asaf, *Ma' Imam Shaheed Hasan al-Banna (With the martyred Imam Hasan al-Banna)*, Cairo, 1993, p. 154.

35 '*Shahid Alla Aser, Al-Ikhwan al-Muslimoun Kama Yrahm Farid Abdel Khaliq*'.

36 For example: in December 1945 a young nationalist, Huain Tawfiq, assassinated the Minister of Finance, Amin Othman Pashsa, who was widely accused of being a British agent.

37 Kamel, *Muthakarat Dr Abdelaziz Kamel, Uthou fi al-Nizam al-Khass*.

38 Mitchell, *The Society of the Muslim Brothers*, p. 68.

39 Abdelhalim, *Al-Ikhwan al-Muslimoun. Ahdath Sunat Al-Tareeq. Ru'iah Min al-Dakhil*, Vol. 1 p. 288.

40 Quoted in Dr Rifat Said, *Al-Irhab al-Mutaeslim (Islamicised Terrorism)*, Cairo, 2004, Vol. 1, p. 182.

41 Abdelhalim, *Al-Ikhwan al-Muslimoun. Ahdath Sunat Al-Tareeq. Ru'iah Min al-Dakhil*, Vol. 2, p.469.

42 Lia, *The Society of the Muslim Brothers*, p. 87.

43 Quoted in Sayed Khatab, 'Al-Hudaybi's Influence on the Development of Islamist Movements in Egypt', in *The Muslim World*, October 2001.

44 Lia, *The Society of the Muslim Brothers*, p. 88.

45 Omayma Abdel-Latif, 'Nasser and the Brotherhood', in *Al-Ahram*, 27 June–3 July 2002. Issue No. 592. Available on http://weekly.ahram.org. eg/2002/592/special.htm

46 Lia, *The Society of the Muslim Brothers*, p. 117.

47 It did so by declaring that the Brotherhood was a political party and therefore subject to the law of January 1953 which had abolished all such entities.

48 Lia, *The Society of the Muslim Brothers*, p. 148.

49 Barbara Zollner, 'Prison Talk: The Muslim Brotherhood's Internal Struggle', in *International Journal of Middle East Studies*, No. 39 (2007).

50 Interview with Ibrahim Ghuraiba, Amman, February 2007.

51 Interview with Dr Issam al-Attar, Aachen, December 2006.

52 '*Al-Ariyan Ya Tahadath An-Nashad Al-Tayar al-Islami bil Jamiat al-Misria.*' (Al-Ariyan Speaks about the Establishment of the Islamic Current in Egyptian Universities), Ikhwan Online, 8 June 2004. Available in Arabic on http://www.ikhwanonline.com/Article.asp?ArtID=7008&SecID=270

53 *Al-Ariyan Ya Tahadath An-Nashad Al-Tayar al-Islami bil Jamiat al-Misria.* (see fn 1, p. 37).

54 Hossam Tammam, *'Al-Murawaha Baina al-Hizb wa al-Jama'a ... Kaifa yara al-Ikhwan Anfisahum'* (Oscillating Between Party and Jama'a ... How the Ikhwan See Themselves), on Islamismscope, undated.

55 Abdul Moneim Aboul Fotouh, *Shehadat Abul Futuah* (Abul Futuah's Testimony), on Islam Online, 15 July 2009. Available in Arabic on http://islamyoon.islamonline.net/servlet/Satellite?c=ArticleA_C&cid=124818730 0655&pagename=Islamyoun%2FIYALayout

56 Ibid.

57 Ibid.

58 '*Al-Ariyan Ya Tahadath An-Nashad Al-Tayar al-Islami bil Jamiat al-Misria.*'

59 Tammam, *Al-Murawaha Baina al-Hizb wa al-Jama'a ... Kaifa yara al-Ikhwan Anfisahum.*

60 Aboul Fotouh, *Shehadat Abul Futuah.*

61 Aboul Fotouh, *Shehadat Abul Futuah.*

62 Tammam, *Al-Murawaha Baina al-Hizb wa al-Jama'a ... Kaifa yara al-Ikhwan Anfisahum.*

63 Ibid.

64 Mohamed Jamal Barot, *Likaila Takoun Dawat Abi Al-Futuah Sarkha fi Waad.* (So That the Call of Abu Futuah Doesn't Become a Shout in the Valley), Al-Hewar, 12 December 2003. Available in Arabic on http://www.ahewar.org/debat/show.art.asp?aid=19914

65 For detailed accounts of the Brotherhood's experiences in the unions and syndicates see Hesham Al-Awadi, *In Pursuit of Legitimacy: The Muslim Brothers and Mubarak, 1982–2000*, London, 2004; and Carrie Rosefsky Wickham, *Mobilizing Islam: Religion, Activism and Political Change in Egypt*, New York, 2002.

66 Barot, *Likaila Takoun Dawat Abi Al-Futuah Sarkha fi Waad.*

67 Interview with Youssef Nada, *Campione*, March 2007.

68 Salah Abdul Al-Maqsud. Quoted in Al-Awadi, *In Pursuit of Legitimacy: The Muslim Brothers and Mubarak, 1982–2000*, p. 92.

69 Ibid. p. 39.

70 Quoted in Meir Hatina, 'Restoring a Lost Identity: Models of Education in Modern Islamic Thought', in *British Journal of Middle Eastern Studies*, November 2006. Vol. 33 No. 2, pp. 179–97.

71 Tammam, *Al-Murawaha Baina al-Hizbwa al-Jama'a ... Kaifa yara al-Ikhwan Anfisahum.*

72 '*Qusat al-Hizb al-wasat bayna al-watani wal Ikhwan.*' (The Tale of the al-Wasat Party between the National Party and the Ikhwan), on Assam Sultan, 3 September 2009. Available in Arabic on http://www.youm7.com/News.asp?NewsID=132880

73 Quoted in parts one through eleven of serialised excerpts from Egyptian Al-Jihad Organisation leader Ayman al-Zawahiri's book *Knights Under the*

Prophet's Banner, in *Al-Sharq al Awsat*, 2 December 2001.

74 Abu Ala Ma'athi, *Hikayati Ma'a Ikhwan Wakasat al-Wasat* (My Story with the Ikhwan and the Tale of Al-Wasat), *Al-Fajr*, 1 January 2006. Available in Arabic on http://www.alwasatparty.com/modules.php?file=article&name=News&sid=285

75 Issam Sultan, '*Qusat al-Hizb al-wasat bayna al-watani wal Ikhwan*'.

76 Young Brothers. *The Jerusalem Report*, 18 April 1996.

77 Salah 'Abd al-Karim. Quoted in Joshua A. Stacher, 'Post-Islamist Rumblings in Egypt: The Emergence of the Wasat party', in *The Middle East Journal*, Summer 2002 Vol. 56 No. 3, p. 415.

78 Sultan, *Qusat al-Hizb al-wasat bayna al-watani wal Ikhwan*.

79 Ibid.

80 Bjørn Olav Utvik, 'Hizb al-Wasat and the Potential for Change in Egyptian Islamism', in *Critical Middle Eastern Studies*, Vol. 14, No. 3, pp 293–306, Fall 2005.

81 Ibid.

82 Sultan, *Qusat al-Hizb al-wasat bayna al-watani wal Ikhwan*.

83 These included Sabri Rida of the Port Said Engineers group, Dr Isam Hasan, Associate Professor of the Engineering Department of Cairo University, and Osama Ashraf Abd Al-Rahman, the treasurer of the Aswan Engineers Syndicate among others.

84 Interview with Mehdi Akef, Cairo, May 2007.

85 Sultan, *Qusat al-Hizb al-wasat bayna al-watani wal Ikhwan*.

86 Barot, *Likaila Takoun Dawat Abi Al-Futuah Sarkha fi Waad*.

87 Stacher, 'Post-Islamist rumblings in Egypt: the emergence of the Wasat party', p. 415.

88 See, for example, Patrick Poole in 'Symposium: The "Moderate" Muslim Brotherhood?' in *Front Page Magazine*, 21 December 2007. Available on http://www.frontpagemag.com/Articles/Read.aspx?GUID=B5E3F96C-FCD9-4D8D-BF40-ADE28BB2D168

89 Dr Amro al-Shobki, '*Mustakbal Jamat Al-Ikhwan Al-Muslimeen*' (The Future of the Muslim Brotherhood), in *Al-Ahram Strategic File*, Year 16, No. 163, May 2006.

90 Barot, *Likaila Takoun Dawat Abi Al-Futuah Sarkha fi Waad*.

91 Michael Emerson and Richard Youngs (eds.), *Political Islam and European Foreign Policy Perspectives from Muslim Democrats of the Mediterranean*, Brussels 2007, p. 67.

92 *Muslim Brotherhood Initiative. On the General Principles of Reform in Egypt*, 2004. Copy provided to author.

93 Al-Shobki, *Mustakbal Jamat Al-Ikhwan Al-Muslimeen*.

94 The movement's social base is comprised of a number of Islamic currents within Egyptian society including al-Azharites as well as apolitical religious

groups such as Ansar al-Sunna and Jamiyat al-Sharia who rally around the Ikhwan and who can be mobilised when necessary.

95 Dr Abdullah Nafisi (ed.), *Haraka Alislamia: Ruiat Mustakablia, Iwarq fi Alnaqd Althati* (The Islamic Movement: Future Vision. A Working Paper in Self-Criticism), Kuwait, 1989. Available in Arabic on www.alnefisi.com

96 Al- Awadi, *In Pursuit of Legitimacy: The Muslim Brothers and Mubarak, 1982–2000*, p. 65.

97 Tammam, *Al-Murawaha Baina al-Hizb wa al-Jama'a ... Kaifa yara al-Ikhwan Anfisahum.*

98 Nathan J. Brown and Amr Hamzawy, 'The Draft Party Platform of the Egyptian Muslim Brotherhood: Foray Into Political Integration or Retreat into Old Positions?', in *Carnegie Papers*, No. 89, January 2008.

99 Interviews with Ikhwani figures in the UK, 2007 and 2008.

100 Brown and Hamzawy, 'The Draft Party Platform of the Egyptian Muslim Brotherhood: Foray Into Political Integration or Retreat Into Old Positions?'

101 Ibid.

102 'Jumping the Gun', in *Al-Ahram Weekly*, No. 868, 25–31 October 2007.

103 Brown and Hamzawy, 'The Draft Party Platform of the Egyptian Muslim Brotherhood: Foray Into Political Integration or Retreat Into Old Positions?'

104 Akef speaks on internal conflict, elections, and the future. *Al-Masri Al-Youm*. 25 October 2010.

105 http://ww.moheet.com/show_files.aspx?fid=332988

106 Ibid.

107 Ibid.

108 Ibid.

109 Ibid.

110 'Egypt's Muslim Brotherhood Reportedly Picks New Leader'. *Al-Hayat*, 13 January 2010.

111 Quoted in 'Continuing on the Path of Qutb: Dr Mohamed Badei, the New Supreme Guide of the Muslim Brotherhood?', *Investigative Project on Terrorism*, 15 January 2010.

112 The regime's obvious intention to contain the group was evidenced in part by its 2007 constitutional amendment removing a previous requirement that the elections be monitored by members of the judiciary

Chapter 2

1 Brynjar Lia, *The Society of the Muslim Brothers in Egypt*, Reading, 1998, p. 155.

2 Dr Umar F. Abd-Allah, *The Islamic Struggle in Syria*, Berkeley, 1983, p. 94.

3 Ibid., p. 92.

4 Ibid.

5   Ibid.
6   Ibid.
7   Ibid.
8   Interview with Mohamed Hasnawi, Amman, February 2007.
9   Interview with Issam al-Attar, Aachen, December 2006.
10   Ibid.
11   Interview with Issam al-Attar, Aachen, December 2006.
12   Ibid.
13   Interview with Adnan Saad Eddine, Amman, February 2007.
14   *Dr Hassan al-Huwaidi, naib al-musrhid al-am yekshif al-mujtamaa: Kusat al-Ikhwan al-muslimeen fi Suria...min an-nasha hata al-manfa* (Dr Hassan Al-Huwaidi, the Deputy of the Supreme Guide reveals to *Al-Mujtamaa*: The Story of the Muslim Brotherhood in Syria from the Beginning Until Exile), in *Al-Mujatmaa*, No. 1741, 3 March 2007. http://www.almujtamaa-mag.com/Detail.asp?InSectionID=1307&InNewsItemID=217090
15   Interview with Mohamed Hasnawi, Amman, February 2007.
16   Maktabat Wahba, *Said Hawa hathihi tajrubati ... Wa-hathahi shahadati* (Said Hawa: This is my experience and this is my testimony), Cairo 1987.
17   *Al-Kharta siassia suria 6* (The Syrian Political Map 6, Ismail Ahmed), in *Al-Hewar*, 26 June 2005. http://www.ahewar.org/debat/show.art.asp?aid=39999
18   Hanna Batatu, 'Syria's Muslim Brethren', in *Merip Reports*, November–December 1982.
19   Ibid.
20   See: http://ahmedzaidan.maktoobblog.com
21   Ismail Ahmed, *Al-Kharta siassia suria 6*.'
22   Mohamed Jamel Barot, *Yathrab al-jadida, alharakat alislamia alrahna* (*The New Yathrab, The Current Islamic Movement*), London, 1994.
23   Ibid.
24   Barot, *Yathrab al-jadida*.
25   Adnan Saad Eddine, *Mesirat jama'at al-Ikhwan al-Muslimeen fi Suria* (*The Journey of the Syrian Muslim Brotherhood*), private publisher, July 1998.
26   The exact nature of the events that prompted this confrontation is still unclear. According to some sources, a young man from Hamah was killed by the police in 1964 after he beat one of his teachers to death for speaking out against Islam. When he found out about the incident Hadid is alleged to have declared: 'The boy was a Muslim and the teacher was a disbeliever! His blood is permissible! As for the Muslim, then his blood must be avenged!' (Sheikh Abdullah Azzam, *The Soul Shall Rise Tomorrow: The Story of Marwan Hadid*, pp. 21–5. Available on http://forums.islamicawakening.com/showthread.php?t=2222). This allegedly provoked a major demonstration against the regime. However, other versions have it that

the trouble began when a young schoolboy in Hamah erased the Ba'athist slogan in his classroom and replaced it with the words: 'The Atheist Ba'ath are Against God!' ('A Cure for Sick Brothers', *Time Magazine*, 1 May 1964). When the boy was sentenced to a year's hard labour for his actions, a mob of young activists, led by Hadid, reportedly went into the streets. Whichever version is correct, the resulting demonstration against the regime prompted the security services to open fire on the crowd, forcing Hadid and his group to take refuge in the Sultan mosque.

27 'A Cure for Sick Brothers', in *Time Magazine*, 1 May 1964.

28 Eddine, *Mesirat Jama'at al-Ikhwan al-Muslimeen fi Suria*.

29 'Ali al-Bayanouni: The Muslim Brothers in Syria. Part I. Special Visit', Al-Jazeera, 26 November 2005. Available in Arabic on http://www.aljazeera.net/NR/exeres/B990668B-5CA6-4DC9-B16A-6828149AE0EA.htm

30 Taken from e-mail correspondence with Obeida Nahas in December 2007.

31 'Ali Al-Bayanouni: The Muslim Brothers in Syria. Part I. Special Visit'

32 Interview with Ali Saddredine Al-Bayanouni, London, 2006.

33 'The Battle within Syria: An Interview with Muslim Brotherhood Leader Ali Al-Bayanouni', in *Terrorism Monitor*, Volume 3, No. 16, 11 August 2005.

34 Interview with Adnan Saad Eddine, Amman, February 2007.

35 Eddine, *Mesirat Jama'at al-Ikhwan al-Muslimeen fi Suria*.

36 Interview with Mohamed Hasnawi, Amman, February 2007.

37 Eddine, *Mesirat Jama'at al-Ikhwan al-Muslimeen fi Suria*.

38 Interview with Mohamed Hasnawi, Amman, February 2007.

39 Eddine, *Mesirat Jama'at al-Ikhwan al-Muslimeen fi Suria*.

40 Barot, *Alharakat alislamia alrahna*.

41 Interview with Adnan Saad Eddine, Amman, February 2007.

42 Interview with Mohamed Hasnawi, Amman, February 2007.

43 Eddine, *Mesirat Jama'at al-Ikhwan al-Muslimeen fi Suria*.

44 Interview with Mohamed Hasnawi, Amman, February 2007.

45 Eddine, *Mesirat Jama'at al-Ikhwan al-Muslimeen fi Suria*.

46 Ibid.

47 Robert Fisk, *Pity the Nation*, Oxford, 1990, p. 181.

48 Abd-Allah, *The Islamic Struggle in Syria*, p. 117.

49 Quoted in Batatu, 'Syria's Muslim Brethren'.

50 'Ali Al-Bayanouni: The Muslim Brothers in Syria. Part I. Special Visit', Al-Jazeera, 24 November 2005.

51 Interview with Obeida Nahas, London, December 2007.

52 Ibid.

53 Interview with Mohamed Hasnawi, Amman, February 2007.

54 Ibid.

55 Interview with Obeida Nahas, London, December 2007.

56 Barot, *Yathrab al-Jadida*, p. 171.

57 Alasdair Drysdale, 'The Asad Regime and its Troubles', in *Merip Reports*, November/December 1982.

58 Quoted in http://globaljihad.net/view_page.asp?id=237

59 'The Battle within Syria: An Interview with Muslim Brotherhood Leader Ali Al-Bayanouni'.

60 'Ali Al-Bayanouni: The Muslim Brothers in Syria. Part I. Special Visit'.

61 *Dr Hassan al-Huwaidi, naib al-musrhid al-am yekshif al-mujtamaa: Kusat al-Ikhwan al-muslimeen fi Suria ... min an-nasha hata al-manfa.*

62 Interview with Adnan Saad Eddine, Amman, February 2007.

63 Eddine, *Mesirat Jama'at al-Ikhwan al-Muslimeen fi Suria.*

64 Author attempted on several occasions to see a copy of this report but was denied this request.

65 Eddine, *Mesirat Jama'at al-Ikhwan al-Muslimeen fi Suria.*

66 Ibid.

67 Ibid.

68 Ibid. In the same book Eddine also claimed that a number of those who perpetuated the violence were from Homs and that they were influenced and financed by another brother who lived in the Gulf who used to send him letters advocating the killing of specific people in Syria and warning him against Adnan Aqla. He claimed too that this same brother used to declare in his writings that jihad is nasty work but in fact he 'pushed the whole group to their deaths'.

69 *The Political Project for the Future: Syria. A Vision of the Muslim Brotherhood Group in Syria. 425 AH–2004 AD.* Copy given to author in 2007.

70 Ibid.

71 Ibid.

72 Ibid.

73 Ibid.

74 Ibid.

75 'Syrian Muslim Brotherhood Discusses Call for Leadership Change,' *BBC Monitoring International Reports*, 19 August 2005. Available on http://faculty-staff.ou.edu/L/Joshua.M.Landis-1/syriablog/2006/03/Al-Bayanouni-khaddam-link-up-_114264946582158617.htm

76 Michael Jacobson, 'An Islamist Syria is Not Very Probable', in *The Daily Star* (Beirut), 29 April 2005, http://www.washingtoninstitute.org/templateC06.php?CID=823

77 'Muslim Brotherhood Leader Offers Support to Syrian Defector', *Financial Times*, 6 January 2006.

78 Quoted in Gary Gambill, 'The Syrian Muslim Brotherhood', in *Mideast Mirror*, Vol. 1, No. 2, April/May 2006.

79 Interview with Abdel Khalim Khaddam, Paris, December 2007.

80 Interview with Obeida Nahas, London, December 2007.

81 'Former Political Enemies Join in Exile to Push for Change in Syrian Leadership', *New York Times*, 23 May 2006.

82 'Interview with Syria's Muslim Brotherhood Leader', Ikhwanweb, 16 February 2006 http://www.ikhwanweb.com/Article.asp?ID=4799&SectionID=0

83 *Al-Diyar*, 4 June 2006.

84 For the full list of founding members see: http://www.savesyria.org/english/structure.htm

85 'Syrian Muslim Brotherhood Withdraws from Opposition Group', in *Al-Sharq al-Awsat*, English edition, 6 April 2009.

86 Given its inability to champion the Palestinian cause in a way that can match the efforts of the Syrian state, the Syrian Ikhwan has taken to slinging cheap shots at the Ba'athist regime in a bid to inflame sectarian tensions. Following the sensitivities over Shi'ism that have developed across the Arab world in the aftermath of the 2003 invasion of Iraq, the Syrian brothers have tried to portray the Alawite regime's growing closeness to Tehran as proof of its being a puppet in the hands of the Iranian regime. In 2007 al-Bayanouni declared that the Syrian regime had 'become an instrument in the hand of Iranian politics'. Similarly, Mohamed Tayfour asserted, 'Syria is being flooded with Shi'ite religious propaganda; secondly, the Iranians are in control of the Syrian economy – so much so that Syrian institutions, government ministries, and industries have all passed into Iranian hands ... Syria has fallen under Iranian occupation.'

87 'Syrian Muslim Brotherhood Withdraws from Opposition Group'.

88 Ibid.

89 Al-Bayanouni, 'Syria is Just an Instrument in Iran's Hand', on Ikhwanweb, 2 December 2007.

90 'Mistrust of Syria's Muslim Brotherhood Lingers', Reuters, 12 November 2012.

91 'Syrian Muslim Brotherhood: Pledge and Charter on Syria', available on http://carnegie-mec.org/publications/?fa=48390

92 Ibid.

93 'Syrian Muslim Brotherhood Leader: Christian or a Woman Can Be President; Alexandretta Is Not Syrian', Dubai TV. 11 June 2012. Clip available on You Tube at http://www.youtube.com/watch?v=MuhtL6wc3wU

94 'Mistrust of Syria's Muslim Brotherhood Lingers', Reuters. 12 November.

Chapter 3

1 Interviews with Dr Kamal Helbawy during 2006 and 2007.

2 Interview with Dr Hassan al-Huwaidi, Amman, February 2007.

3 'Jordanian Muslim Brotherhood leader on relations with regime, Hamas', on *BBC Monitoring Middle East*, 14 March 2006.

4   Interview with Abdul Moneim Aboul Fotouh, Cairo, April 2007.
5   E-mail correspondence with Youssef Nada, October 2007.
6   See Patrick Poole, 'The Muslim Brotherhood Project', *Front Page Magazine*, 11 May 2006.
7   From a report in *Khaleej Times*, 26 January 1996. Quoted in *Strategic Analysis*, Vol. 22, No. 8, November 1998
8   Robert S. Leiken and Steven Brooke, 'The Moderate Muslim Brotherhood', *Foreign Affairs*, March/April 2007.
9   Xavier Ternisien, *Les Frères Musulmans*, Paris 2005, p. 127.
10   Interview with Dr Mohamed Habib, Cairo, May 2007.
11   Interview with Adnan Saad Eddine, Amman, February 2007.
12   Interview with Issam al-Attar, Aachen, December 2006.
13   Interview with Dr Ibeahim Gharaiba, Amman, February 2007.
14   Hassan al-Turabi, *'Al-Bud Alami Lil-Haraka Al-Islamia: Al-Tijerba Al-Sudania'* ('The International Dimension of the Islamic Movement'), in Dr Abdullah Nafisi (ed.), *Haraka Alislamia: Ruiat Mustakablia, Iwarq fi Alnaqd Althati* (The Islamic Movement: Future Vision. A Working Paper in Self-Criticism), Kuwait, 1989. Available in Arabic on www.alnefisi.com.
15   Ibid.
16   Interview with Ibrahim Ghuraiba, Amman, February 2007.
17   Interview with Dr Issam al-Attar, Aachen, December 2006.
18   Adnan Saad Eddine, *Mesirat Jama'at al-Ikhwan al-Muslimeen fi Suria* (*The Journey of the Syrian Muslim Brotherhood*), private publisher, 1998, p. 18.
19   Interview with Dr Issam al-Attar, Aachen, December 2006.
20   Ternisien, *Les Frères Musulmans*.
21   Hossam Tammam, *Al-Tanzeem Al-Dawli lil Ikhwan: Al-Wa'ad, Wal Misira, Wal Ma'al*? (The International Tanzeem: The Promise, the Path and its Future?), 20 September 2004. Available in Arabic on http://www.ahewar.org/debat/show.art.asp?aid=23729
22   The Ikhwan's former Supreme Guide, Maimoun Al-Hudaibi, worked as a personal consultant to Prince Nayef Abdul Aziz. King Fahd's personal physician was also a Muslim Brother. Sayyid Qutb's brother Mohammed worked as an academic in the Saudi Kingdom and wrote a number of texts for the school curriculum there.
23   *'Al-Mushid alam al Ikhwan al-muslimeen: nouayid tershia Mubarak wa atammana al-jillous mahahoo'*, (The Supreme Guide of the Muslim Brothers: I Support the Candidacy of Mubarak and I Wish I Could Sit with Him), *Akhbar el-Yom*, 20 July 2005. http://www.akhbarelyom.org.eg/akhersaa/issues/3691/0501.html
24   Interview with Dr Alamin Osman, London, 2006.
25   Interview with Dr Issam al-Attar, Aachen, December 2006.
26   Interview with Dr Kamal Helbawy, London, May 2005.

27 Interview with Abu Ala Madhi, Cairo, May 2007.
28 Interview with Dr Rifat Said,Cairo, May 2007.
29 Nafisi (ed.), *Haraka Alislamia: Ruiat Mustakablia, Iwarq fi Alnaqd Althati*
30 Ibid.
31 Ibid.
32 Interview with Ibrahim Ghuraiba, Amman, February 2007.
33 Interview with Dr Alamin Osman, London, 2006.
34 Ibid.
35 Tammam, *Al-Tanzeem Al-Dawli lil Ikhwan: Al-Wa'ad, Wal Misira, Wal Ma'al?*
36 Nada has been somewhat of a controversial figure, as whilst he describes himself as the Brotherhood's Commissioner for International Political Relations, the Ikhwan does not publicly recognise him as such. Following an interview he conducted with the Al-Jazeera channel, the Ikhwan issued a number of statements denying that any such post existed. Egyptian member of the Guidance Office Abdul Moneim Aboul Fotouh is alleged to have said: 'I appreciate Youssef Nada but there is no administrative post called the Commissioner of International Political Relations.' (Hossam Tammam, *Tahawilat Al-Ikhwan al-Muslimoun (The Transformation of the Muslim Brotherhood)*, Cairo, 2006, p. 103). Rather his role is informal and his influence appears to arise from his close links to successive Murshids. As he explained, 'I come with an idea and I consult with the Murshid or the Murshid approaches me to do something for the Brotherhood.' (Interview with Youssef Nada, *Campione*, March 2007). Former Deputy to the Murshid Mohamed Habib explains that Nada is entrusted with jobs because of his 'capacity, contacts and ability'. (Interview with Mohamed Habib, Cairo, April 2007.)
37 Youssef Nada, interview with Al-Jazeera, *'Al-Ilakat Al-Dowlia Kama Yaraha Al-Ikhwan'* ('International Relations as Seen by the Ikhwan'), Episode 1, 2002. Available in Arabic on http://www.aljazeera.net/NR/exeres/56CCF13A-B3AB-4398-83E4-1A9C40AB5B42.htm
38 'Cleric Held Shares in Bank with Terror Links', *The Observer*, 11 July 2004.
39 Youssef Nada, interview with Al-Jazeera, *Al-Ilakat Al-Dowlia Kama Yaraha Al-Ikhwan*.
40 See, for example, Sylvain Besson, *La Conquête de L'Occident: le projet secret des Islamistes*, Paris, 2005.
41 English translation available in Patrick Poole 'The Muslim Brotherhood Project', *Front Page Magazine*, 11 May 2006.
42 Interview with Youssef Nada, *Campione*, March 2007.
43 *'Awraq Urdania fi Assoulia wa Siasa'* ('Jordanian Files on Fundamentalism and Politics'), in *Al-Sharq al-Awsat*, 11 October 2005. Available in Arabic on http://www.aawsat.com/details.asp?issueno=9814&article=327764

44 Statement of Jama'at al-Ikhwan al-Muslimeen, *Majallat Liwa*, August 1990.
45 'Ali Al-Bayanouni: Negotiation between the Ikhwan and the Authorities', interview II, Al-Jazeera, 3 December 2005.
46 Statement of Jama'at al-Ikhwan al-Muslimeen, *Majallat Liwa*, 2 August 1990.
47 Ibid.
48 Martin Kramer, 'Islam vs. Democracy, in *Commentary*, January, 1993. Available on http://www.geocities.com/martinkramerorg/IslamvsDemocracy.htm
49 Interview with Dr Kamal Helbawy, London, May 2005.
50 Interview with Adnan Saad Eddine, Amman, February 2007.
51 *Awraq Urdania fi Assoulia wa Siasa*.
52 Statement of Jama'at al-Ikhwan al-Muslimeen, *Majallat Liwa*, 5 August 1990.
53 *Awraq Urdania fi Assoulia wa Siasa*, [see fn 2, p.120].
54 Statement of Jama'at al-Ikhwan al-Muslimeen, *Majallat Liwa*, 6 August 1990.
55 *Awraq Urdania fi Assoulia wa Siasa*, [see fn 2, p. 120].
56 Statement of Jama'at al-Ikhwan al-Muslimeen, *Majallat Liwa*, 15 September 1990.
57 Ibid.
58 Ibid.
59 Letter from Mustafa Mashour to the Kuwaiti people, *Majallat Liwar*, No. 9, November 1990.
60 Wendy Kristianasen, 'Kuwait's Islamists, Officially Unofficial', in *Le Monde Diplomatique*, June 2002.
61 *Awraq Urdania fi Assoulia wa Siasa*, [see fn 2, p. 120].
62 Interview with Dr Kamal Helbawy, London, May 2005. NB Helbawy worked at the Institute of Policy Studies in Islamabad.
63 *Itha'at: Sheikh Saud Al-Nasser Al-Sabah* (Spotlight: Sheikh Saud Al-Nasser Al-Sabah), on Al-Arabiya, 5 January 2005. Available in Arabic on http://www.alarabiya.net/programs/2005/01/07/9353.html.
64 *Awraq Urdania fi Assoulia wa Siasa*, [see fn 2, p. 120].
65 *Itha'at: Sheikh Saud Al-Nasser Al-Sabah*, [see fn 2, p. 123].
66 Busuleimani and Nahnah were happy to become part of this international movement whilst others within their group rejected the idea of being tied so formally to Cairo. However, it wasn't long before Nahnah had competition from another well-known Islamist, Abdallah Djaballah, who considered that he should represent the Algerian Ikhwan instead of Nahnah. Djaballah appealed to Cairo to review the situation. However, the international organisation had the final say and gave the leadership position to Nahnah, who promptly gave *al-baya* to Omar al-Tilmisani. Nahnah then began using the formal slogans of the Ikhwan and called on his followers to give their allegiance to Cairo.
67 *Al-Amoush al-Ikhwan al-Muslimoun bi haja ila perestroika* (Al-Amoush: The

Muslim Brotherhood are in a need of a perestroika), in *Al-Ghad* newspaper, 9 July 2007. Available in Arabic on http://www.alghad.jo/?news=186069.

68 Wendy Kristiansen, 'A Row in the Family', in *Le Monde Diplomatique*, April 2000. Available on http://mondediplo.com/2000/04/03tanzim

69 The Al-Wasat affair was when a group of Egyptian Ikhwan split from the Brotherhood to form their own political party. See Kristiansen, 'A Row in the Family'.

70 Ibid.

71 Interview with Dr Kamal Helbawy, London, June 2007.

72 Mohammed Al Shafey, 'Have the Muslim Brotherhood Gone Global?', in *Asharq Al-Awsat*, 12 May 2007.

73 Interview with Dr Hassan al-Huwaidi, Amman, February 2007.

74 Interview with Ali Saddredine Bayanouni, London, May 2006.

75 Ibid.

76 Interview with Mohamed Habib, Cairo, May 2007.

77 *Al-Amoush al-Ikhwan al-Muslimoun bi haja ila perestroika*, [see fn 2, p. 125].

78 Interview with Fareed Sabri, London, May 2006.

79 Interview with Mehdi Akef, Cairo, May 2007.

80 Ibid.

81 Interview with Fareed Sabri, London, May 2006.

82 Ibid.

83 Interview with Mehdi Akef, Cairo, May 2007.

84 Ibid.

85 Interview with Mohamed Habib, Cairo, April 2007.

86 See http://yhoo.it/SgnDQ2 13 July 2012 and also see http://www.aawsat. com/leader.asp?section=3&article=686218&issueno=12281

87 See for example, http://www.youtube.com/watch?v=xS36Ueyji_o&feature =relmfu

Chapter 4

1 Interview with Dr Kamal Helbawy, London, January 2008.

2 Lorenzo Vidino has stated, 'Unlike the larger Islamic community, the Muslim Brotherhood's ultimate goal may not be simply "to help Muslims be the best citizens they can be", but rather to extend Islamic law throughout Europe and the United States.' See Lorenzo Vidino, 'The Muslim Brotherhood's Conquest of Europe', in *Middle East Quarterly*, Winter 2005. See also Sylvain Besson, *La conquête de l'Occident: Le projet secret des Islamistes*, Paris, 2005.

3 The MTI's agenda was not only to reassert the Islamic and Arab way of life, but it also rejected Tunisia's Francophile elite, which it condemned for being

Westernised.

4   Gilles Kepel, *Les banlieues de l'Islam*, Paris, 1991, p. 265.

5   Ibid. pp. 259–60.

6   Ibid. p. 272.

7   Following this letter, and in response to growing sensitivities over the issue, in 1990 Interior Minister Pierre Joxe set up a Conseil de reflexion sur l'Islam de France (CORIF). This was designed as a consultative group that would enable the French state to open channels with representatives of the Muslim community. Although the council achieved little and was soon suspended on account of internal differences, for the UOIF being in this body was crucial, as it had at last given them an opening into the very heart of the French establishment.

8   Amghar, 'Les mutations de l'Islamisme en France'.

9   W. A. R. Shadid and P. S. Van Koningsveld, *Political Participation and Identities of Muslims in Non-Muslim States*, Leuven, 1996, p. 98.

10   Ternisien, *La France des mosques*, p. 191.

11   Kepel, *Allah in the West*, p. 199.

12   Ternisien, *La France des mosques*, p. 151.

13   Interview with Mohsen N'Gazou, Marseille, July 2006.

14   Interview with Bernard Goddard, Paris, June 2006.

15   Interview with Sheikh Ahmed Jaballah, Paris, June 2006.

16   Ternisien, *La France des mosquees*, p. 157

17   Quoted in 'The True Face of the UOIF', Simon Wiesenthal Centre.

18   Interview with Lhaj Thami Breeze, Paris, June 2006.

19   Quoted in Darif, *Bricolages identitaires des Musulmans dans l'espace politique français: cas de UOIF*.

20   Interview with Mohsen N'Gazou, Marseille, July 2006.

21   Interview with Moulay Abderrahmane Ghoul, Marseille, July 2006.

22   Interview with Soheib Bensheikh, Marseille, July 2006.

23   Interview with Lhaj Thami Breeze, Paris, June 2006.

24   Ibid.

25   'Qu'est ce que l'UOIF?', in Paris, 2006, p. 19

26   Interview with Sheikh Ahmed Jaballah, Paris, June 2006.

27   Helle Merete Brix, 'Among the Believers', in *Sappho*, 1 June 2007. Available on http://www.sappho.dk/Den%20loebende/bourgetengelsk.html

28   Interview with Mohsen N'Gazou, Marseille, July 2006.

29   Ibid.

30   Xavier Ternisien, 'Enquête sur ces Musulmans qui inquiètent l'Islam de France', in *Le Monde*, 13 December 2002.

31   Interview with Sheikh Abdelhadi, Marseille, July 2006.

32   Ibid.

33   Ibid.

34 Interview with former UOIF member who preferred to remain anonymous, Paris, December 2006.

35 Interview with former French Interior Ministry Official, Paris, June 2006.

36 Interview with Mohsen N'Gazou, Marseille, July 2006.

37 'Balancing Reactions', in *Al-Ahram*, 26 February–3 March 2004, No. 679.

38 Ibid.

39 'France hijab ban takes effect', on Al-Jazeera.net. 4 September 2004. Available on: http://english.aljazeera.net/English/archive/archive?ArchiveId=6217

40 Ibid.

41 Dominic McGoldrick, *Human Rights and Religion: The Islamic Headscarf Debate in Europe*, Oxford, 2006, p. 96.

42 '*Muslimo Fransa Yatasdoun li Fernasat Al-Islam*' ('French Muslims Challenge Francophised Islam'), on Al-Motamar, 18 August 2006. Available on http://www.almotamar.net/news/33926.htm

43 Interview with Lhaj Thami Breeze, Paris, June 2006.

44 Interview with Dr Kamal Helbawy, London, January 2008.

45 Ibid.

46 Ibid.

47 Ziauddin Sardar, 'Searching for secular Islam', in *The New Humanist*, Vol. 119 No. 5, September/October 2004. Available on http://newhumanist.org.uk/798 (Accessed January 2008).

48 Interview with Dr Kamal Helbawy, London, January 2008.

49 Interview with imam at the Muslim Welfare House, London, 2004.

50 Interview with Dr Kamal Helbawy, London, January 2008.

51 Ibid.

52 See http://mssuk.net/pastactivities/pre2001.htm

53 Ziauddin Sardar, *Desperately Seeking Paradise. Journeys of a Sceptical Muslim*, London, 2004, p. 35.

54 Ibid.

55 E-mail correspondence with Ashur Shamis, January 2008.

56 Interview with Dr Kamal Helbawy, London, January 2008.

57 Ibid.

58 Ibid.

59 Ibid.

60 *Al-Tandeem al-Dawli lil ikhwan: al-wahd messira wal ma'al?* [The International Organisation of the Ikhwan: The Promise, the History and the Outcome?], 20 September 2004. Available on http://www.rezgar.com/debat/show.art.asp?aid=23729

61 Quoted in 'Who Speaks for the Ikhwan', in *Crescent International*, 1–15 January 1982.

62 Quoted in Ibid.

63 Kamal El-Helbawy, 'A Message from Muslim Brotherhood Information Centre London, and the Spokesman for Muslim Brotherhood in the West', 19 February 1996. Available on http://lists.asu.edu/cgi-bin/wa?A2=ind9602 d&L=muslims&T=0&O=D&P=65

64 Interview with Dr Kamal Helbawy, London, January 2008.

65 British Muslims Monthly Survey, Vol. 6, No. 3, March 1998.

66 See MAB website: http://www.mabonline.net

67 British Muslims Monthly Survey, Vol. 6, No. 3, March 1998.

68 Interview with Ahmed Sheikh, London, 2006.

69 Ibid.

70 'MAB Responds to Vile Attack': statement by the MAB, 13 August 2004.

71 http://www.publications.parliament.uk/pa/cm200304/cmhansrd/ vo031218/debtext/31218-18.htm

72 'The Federation of Student Islamic Societies and the Muslim Association of Britain. An Alliance for Workers' Liberty Briefing', April 2005, Appendix B. Available on http://66.102.9.104/search?q=cache:7yjVpiroxDkJ:www.free-education.org.uk/Appendix_B_PDF.pdf+muslim+association+of+britain+ja mal&hl=en&ct=clnk&cd=1&gl=uk&ie=UTF-8 (Accessed January 2008).

73 'Open up a Dialogue', *The Weekly Worker*. No. 463. 16 January 2003. Available on http://www.cpgb.org.uk/worker/463/dialogue.html

74 Interview with Ahmed Sheikh, London, 2006.

75 'The Muslim Association of Britain. The Centre for Social Cohesion', undated. Available on http://www.socialcohesion.co.uk/pubs/mab.php

76 Ian Johnson, 'A Mosque for ex-Nazis became Center of Radical Islam', *The Wall Street Journal*, 12 July 2005.

77 Ibid.

78 Lorenzo Vidino, 'The Muslim Brotherhood's Conquest of Europe', in *Middle East Quarterly*, Vol. 12, No. 1, Winter 2005.

79 Interview with Dr Rifat Said, Cairo, May 2007.

80 Interview with Mehdi Akef, Cairo, May 2007.

81 Johnson, 'A Mosque for ex-Nazis became Center of Radical Islam'.

82 Interview with Mehdi Akef, Cairo, May 2007.

83 See http://de.wikipedia.org/wiki/Ibrahim_El-Zayat

84 See http://ammanmessage.com/index.php?option=com_content&task=vie w&id=40&Itemid=34

85 See http://de.wikipedia.org/wiki/Ibrahim_El-Zayat

86 Interview with Ibrahim El-Zayat, Cologne, December 2006.

87 'Islam and Identity in Germany', Europe Report No 181, 14 March 2007. Available on http://66.102.9.104/search?q=cache:A_otya3lJgMJ:www.flwi. ugent.be/cie/documenten/islam_in_germany.pdf+milli+gorus+Cem+germ any+igd&hl=en&ct=clnk&cd=1&gl=uk&ie=UTF-8

88 Interview with Oguz Ücüncü, General Secretary Millî Görüş. Cologne.

December 2006.

89 Interview with Ibrahim El-Zayat, Cologne, December 2006.

90 Ibid.

91 Johnson, 'A Mosque for ex-Nazis became Center of Radical Islam'.

92 See http://www.ikhwanweb.com/Article. asp?ID=752&SectionID=121

93 Interview with Ibrahim El-Zayat, Cologne, December 2006.

94 Ibid.

95 Ibid.

96 Ibid.

97 Ibid.

98 Ian Johnson, 'Islamic Justice Finds a Foothold in Heart of Europe', *The Wall Street Journal*, 4 August 2005.

99 Ibid.

100 Interview with Ibrahim el-Zayat, Cologne, December 2006.

101 Quoted in Kent Olsen, 'Quran reported to the Police in Germany', *Jyllands-Posten*, 18 April 2006. Available on http://www.islam-watch.org/SpecialEvents/KoranReported.htm

102 *Deutsche Welle*, 27 Sep 2006, Available in Arabic on http://www.dw-world. de/popups/popup_printcontent/0,,2186411,00.html

103 Ibid.

104 '*Verfassungsschutz Informationen. Bayerisches Staatsministerium des Innern*', 2007. Available in German on http://www.verfassungsschutz.bayern.de/imperia/md/content/lfv_internet/service/halbjahresbericht_2007.pdf

105 Testimony of Matthew Levitt, 'Islamic Extremism in Europe. Beyond al-Qaeda: Hamas and Hezbollah in Europe', Joint Hearing of the Committee on International Relations and Subcommittee on Europe and Emerging Threats, US House of Representatives, 27 April 2005.

106 Ian Johnson, 'How Islamic Group's Ties Reveal Europe's Challenge', *The Wall Street Journal*, 29 December 2005.

107 Ibid.

108 'In Germany, Harder Line Looms; Bavarian Probes into Muslim Groups May Foretell Deeper Scrutiny', *The Wall Street Journal*, 16 September 2005.

109 Ibid.

110 Ibid.

111 Interview with Ibrahim El-Zayat, Cologne, December 2006.

112 Ibid.

113 Interview with Dhaou Meskine, Paris, December 2007.

114 Ibid.

115 Interview with Ahmed al-Rawi, *Mufakarat al-Islam* (Islam Memo), 21 June 2006. Available in Arabic on http://www.islammemo.cc/article1.aspx?id=5172

116 Interview with Libyan Ikhwani, Manchester, October 2004.

117 Interview with Mohsen N'Gazou, Marseille, July 2006.
118 Quoted in Ternisien, *Les Frères Musulmans*, pp. 110–11.
119 Besson, *La conquête de l'Occident: le projet secret des Islamistes*, p. 100.
120 'A Rare Look at Secretive Brotherhood in America', in *The Chicago Tribune*, 19 September 2004.
121 Interview with Mohsen N'Gazou, Marseille, July 2006.

Chapter 5

1   Dr Rachel Ehrenfeld and Alyssa A. Lappen, 'The Truth about the Muslim Brotherhood', *Front Page Magazine*, 16 June 2006.
2   Evan Kholmann, quoted in Mary Crane, *Does the Egyptian Muslim Brotherhood have Ties to Terrorism?*, Council on Foreign Relations, 5 April 2005.
3   Interview with Rifat Said, Cairo, May 2007.
4   Martin Bright, 'Talking to Terrorists', *New Statesman*, 20 February 2006.
5   *Al-Gomhuriya*, 23 June 2007. Quoted in 'Warnings in the Egyptian Press: The Muslim Brotherhood in Egypt is Going the Way of Hamas in Gaza', *Memri Special Dispatch*, No. 1638, 28 June 2007.
6   *Al-Gumhuriya*, 13 December 2006. Quoted in L. Azuri, 'Relations Worsen Between the Egyptian Regime and the Muslim Brotherhood', *Memri Special Dispatch*, No. 321, 2 February 2007.
7   Interview with Mustafa Mashour, 'Soldiers of the Sharia', in *Al-Ahram Weekly*, No. 247, 16–22 November 1995. Available on http://weekly.ahram.org.eg/archives/parties/muslimb/sharia.htm
8   Interview with Mehdi Akef, Cairo, May 2007.
9   Brynjar Lia, *The Society of the Muslim Brothers*, Reading, 1998, p. 83.
10   'Jordan Says Legal Action to be Taken against Four IAF MPs on Incitement', *The Middle East Reporter*, 13 June 2006.
11   Muhammad Hafiz Diyab, *Sayyid Qutb: Discourse and Ideology*, Cairo, 1988.
12   Nazih Ayubi, *Political Islam*, London, 1991, p. 137.
13   Mohamed Jamal Barout, *Yathrab al-Jadida* (The New Medina), 1994.
14   Quoted in Ayubi, *Political Islam*, p. 140.
15   Interview with Ibrahim Ghuraibya, Amman, February 2007.
16   Ayubi, *Political Islam*, p. 142.
17   Interview with Ashur Shamis, London, March 2007.
18   Gilles Kepel, *Muslim Extremism in Egypt: The Prophet and the Pharaoh*, Berkeley, 1993, p. 30.
19   Some, such as Rifat Said, have claimed that al-Hodeibi wrote the book under duress, asserting that he was insufficiently versed in Sharia to have been able to write it. According to Said, the book was produced under the instructions

of General Fouad Allam, who had a draft written by al-Azhar that he gave to al-Hodeibi to pass off as his own. (Interview with Rifat Said, Cairo, March 2007.)

20 Gilles Kepel, *The Roots of Radical Islam*, London, 1985, p. 64.

21 Ibid., p. 36.

22 Interview with Farid Abdul Khaliq, Cairo, March 2007.

23 Abdul Moneim Aboul Fotouh, *Shehadat Abul Futuh* (Abul Futuah's Testimony). Islam Online, 15 July 2009. Available in Arabic on http://islamyoon.islamonline.net/servlet/Satellite?c=ArticleA_C&cid=124818730 0655&pagename=Islamyoun%2FIYALayout. For a more detailed discussion of this issue see Chapter One.

24 Rudolph Peters, *Jihad in Classical and Modern Islam*, Princeton, 1996.

25 Abdelaziz Ramadan Al-Haya Al-Maseria Al'Ama Lilkitab, *Jama'at al-Takfir fi Misr. Al-Oosoul Tarikhia wa Fikeria* (Takifiri Groups in Egypt: Intellectual and Historical Origins), Cairo 1995, p. 77.

26 Dr Nashat Hamid Abdel al-Majid, *Asbab nashat al-Afghan al-Arab* (The Reasons Behind the Creation of the Afghan Arabs), on Islam Online, 7 October 2001. Available on www.islamoneline.net

27 W. Laqueur, *No End to War*, New York, 2003, p. 52.

28 Interview with members of the Parti Algérien pour la Démocratie et le Socialisme (PADS). Ellen Ray and Lenora Foerstal, 'Algeria: Theocracy by Terror?', on Covert Action, October 1998. Available on http://www.covertaction.org/content/view/109/75/

29 'The Muslim Brotherhood in Afghanistan', in *Islamism Digest*, Vol. 2 No. 10, October 2007.

30 Ayman al-Zawahiri, *Knights under the Prophet's Banner*, 2001.

31 Biography of Sheikh Abdullah Azzam (Shaheed), undated. Available on http://www.religioscope.com/info/doc/jihad/azzam_defence_2_intro.htm

32 Interview with Dr Kamal Helbawy, London, May 2007.

33 Interview with Hudaifa Azzam, Amman, February 2007.

34 Ibid.

35 Interview with Noman Bin Othman, London, April 2007.

36 Ibid.

37 Interview with Dr Kemal Helbawy, London, May 2007.

38 Ibid.

39 Ibid.

40 'The Muslim Brotherhood in Afghanistan', in *Islamism Digest*, Vol. 2, No 10, October 2007.

41 Interview with Hudaifa Azzam, Amman, February 2007.

42 Muslim Brotherhood Movement Homepage, http://www.ummah.net

43 Olivier Roy, *Afghanistan, from Holy War to Civil War*, Princeton 1995.

44 'The Muslim Brotherhood in Afghanistan'.

45 Mustafa Mashour obituary, *Impact International*, Vol. 32, No. 12, 2002.
46 'The Muslim Brotherhood in Afghanistan'.
47 Interview with Dr Kemal Helbawy, London, May 2007.
48 Ibid.
49 Al-Arabi (Egypt), 18 January 2004. Quoted in 'New Muslim Brotherhood Leader: Resistance in Iraq and Palestine is Legitimate; America is Satan; Islam Will Invade America and Europe', *Memri Special Dispatch Series* No. 655, 4 February 2004. Available on http://www.memri.org/bin/articles. cgi?Area=egypt&ID=SP65504#_edn1
50 Al-Jazeera, 10 January 2005. http://www.aljazeera.net/NR/ exeres/18673EC8-1EB6-4844-BFAF-7331D5A6CD34.htm
51 'British Muslim says Troops are Fair Target', *The Sunday Times*, 31 October 2004.
52 Interview with imam, London, 2005.
53 'Jordan: Muslim Brotherhood Leader On 'Martyrdom' Attacks, Iraq, Local Issues', on BBC Monitoring. 6 October 2002.
54 Quoted in 'Dr Abdelmonem Abu Futuah, an Egyptian Muslim Brotherhood Leader, Volunteers to Carry Out Attacks Against American Forces in Iraq', (Al-Jazeera TV) *Memri*, Clip 44. 25 April 2004.
55 'Muslim Brotherhood Initiative on the General Principles of Reform in Egypt', Cairo, 2004. Obtained from the Brotherhood's headquarters in Cairo.
56 *Zawal Isra'il Hatmiyya Qur'aniya* (The Destruction of Israel is a Qur'anic Imperative), no publisher or place of publication, 1988. Quoted in Ziad Abu Amr, *Islamic Fundamentalism in the West Bank and Gaza*, Indiana, 1994, p. 2.
57 Abu Amr, *Islamic Fundamentalism in the West Bank and Gaza*, p. 2.
58 'Jordan: Muslim Brotherhood Leader On "Martyrdom" Attacks, Iraq, Local Issues', BBC Monitoring. 6 October 2002.
59 Deputy Leader of Muslim Brotherhood in Egypt: 'A Nation that does not Excel at the Industry of Death does not Deserve Life', *Memri*, 8 April 2004.
60 Quoted in Nachman Tal, *Radical Islam in Egypt and Jordan*, Brighton, 2005, p. 199.
61 'Firebrand Islamic academic: "Dying for your Beliefs is Just"', in *The Daily Mail*, 21 August 2006.
62 'Leading Saudi Sheik Pronounces Fatwa against Hezbollah', in *The New York Sun*, 20 July 2006.
63 Abu Amr, *Islamic Fundamentalism in the West Bank and Gaza*, p. 23.
64 Robert S. Leiken and Steven Brooke 'The Moderate Muslim Brotherhood', in *Foreign Affairs*, March/April 2007.
65 Ibid.
66 Helena Cobban, interview with Dr Abul Moneim Aboul Fotouh, *Just*

World News, 23 February 2007. Available on http://justworldnews.org/archives/002404.html (accessed February 2008).

67 Ibid.

68 Quoted in 'Dr Abdelmonem Abu Futuah, an Egyptian Muslim Brotherhood Leader, Volunteers to Carry out Attacks against American Forces in Iraq'.

69 Mahad Abedin, 'The Battle within Syria: An Interview with Muslim Brotherhood Leader Ali Bayanouni', in *Terrorism Monitor*, Vol. 3, No. 16, 11 August 2005.

70 Richard P. Mitchell, *The Society of the Muslim Brothers*, Oxford, 1993, p. 211.

71 From Al-Ghazali, *Al-Islam wa'l-istibdad al-siyasi 1950-51*. Quoted in Mitchell, *The Society of the Muslim Brothers*, p. 211.

72 Interview with Haj Abu Sen, London, September 2007.

73 Sayyid Qutb, *Milestones*, New Delhi, 1964, p. 116.

74 Ibid., p. 139.

75 Quoted in 'New Muslim Brotherhood Leader: Resistance in Iraq and Palestine is Legitimate; America is Satan; Islam Will Invade America and Europe', in *Al-Arabi*, 18 January 2004.

76 'Abdul Moneim Abul Fotouh. The Muslim Brotherhood Comments on "Gray Zones", Carnegie Paper', on Ikhwanweb, 16 July 2006.

77 Hossam Tammam, *Tahawilat Al-Ikhwan al-Muslimoun* (The Transformation of the Muslim Brotherhood), Cairo, 2006, pp. 146–7.

78 'Interview with Muslim Brotherhood's Supreme Guide, Mehdi Akef', *Al-Sharq Al-Awsat*, 16 December 2005.

79 Fadi Fahem, 'World in Need of Islamic Principles and Morals: Akef', *Khaleej Times*, 2 September 2005.

80 Michael Emerson and Richard Youngs (eds.), *Political Islam and European Foreign Policy Perspectives from Muslim Democrats of The Mediterranean*, Brussels, 2007.

81 Ibid.

82 'Habib: Muslim Brotherhood is Not Anti-American', on Ikhwanweb, 14 January 2008. Available on http://www.ikhwanweb.com/Article.asp?ID=15359&LevelID=1&SectionID=146

83 'Former Kuwaiti Education Minister: All of al-Qa'ida's Terrorism Started from the Ideology of the Muslim Brotherhood', in *Memri Special Dispatch Series 941*, 26 July 2005.

84 Ana Belén Soage, 'Faraj Fawda, or the Cost of Freedom of Expression', in *Middle East Review of International Affairs*, Vol. 11, No. 2, June 2007.

85 Mohammed Al-Shafey, 'Have the Muslim Brotherhood Gone Global?', in *Al-Sharq al-Awsat*, 12 May 2007.

Chapter 6

1   Statement on Ikhwanonline website, 19 January 2011.
2   The five demands in full were as follows: to revoke the state of emergency; to dissolve the People's Assembly and to hold free and fair elections; to amend the 'defective constitutional articles [Articles 76, 77 and 88] which led to the rigging of the last elections and which will affect the upcoming presidential elections'; to hold the presidential elections according to the above amendments; to fire the government and to form a new government of national unity that is responsive to the demands of the Egyptian people.
3   Nobel Peace Winner Returns to Egypt to Lead Anti-Government Protest Movement, Associated Press, 27 January 2011.
4   Charles Sennott, 'Inside the Muslim Brotherhood: Part 1. Special report: The Brotherhood's Role in Egypt's Revolution,' Frontline, 21 February 2011. http://www.globalpost.com/dispatch/egypt/110220/inside-the-muslim-brotherhood
5   'The Revolution Will Continue Until Our Demands Are Met,' Spiegal Online, 7 February 2011.
6   Sennott, 'Inside the Muslim Brotherhood: Part 1. Special report: The Brotherhood's Role in Egypt's Revolution'.
7   Amani Tawile, 'Al-Ikhwan Wal Thawra Misria A Mostaqbel?' ('The Brotherhood and the Egyptian Revolution. What Future?), The Arab Center For Research and Policy Studies, Doha, 3 March 2011
8   Sennott, 'Inside the Muslim Brotherhood: Part 1. Special report: The Brotherhood's Role in Egypt's Revolution.'
9   Ibid.
10 Mariz Tadros, *The Muslim Brotherhood in Contemporary Egypt: Democracy Redefined or Confined?*, London, 2012, p. 35
11 'Frontline Examines Muslim Brotherhood's "Strong, Layered" Role in Egypt', PBS, 22 February 2011. Available on http://www.pbs.org/newshour/bb/world/jan-june11/frontline_02-22.html
12 'Egypt: Senior Figure Says Muslim Brotherhood Ready for Sacrifices', BBC Monitoring Middle East, 3 February 2011.
13 Egypt's Muslim Brotherhood insists Mubarak must go. Al-Hayat. 3 February 2011. BBC Monitoring. 3 February 2011 (notes p. 18)
14 'Will Egypt's Government Now Strike a Deal with the Muslim Brotherhood?' in *Christian Science Monitor*, 6 February 2011.
15 Statement issued by Muslim Brotherhood, Ikhwanonline, 6 February 2011.
16 Amani Tawile. *Al-Ikhwan Wal Thawra Misria A Mostaqbel?*
17 'Muslim Brotherhood Says won't Bid for Presidency in Egypt,' *RIA Novosti*, 4 February 2011.
18 'Egypt Opposition Say Mubarak Must Go before Talks,' Reuters, 1 February 2011.

19 'Mubarak "fears chaos" if He Steps Down,' AFP, 4 February 2011.

20 'Egypt's Muslim Brotherhood Begins Dialogue with Government', in *Xinhua*, 6 February 2011.

21 'Egypt Protests: Muslim Brotherhood's Concession Prompt Anger,' in *Christian Science Monitor*, 7 February 2011.

22 'Hossam Tamam. Al-Ikhwan Yemidoun Yeda Al-Hiwar Were Yerfahoun Riad Al-Usian Bil Yed Al-Okra' (Hossam Tamam: The Brotherhood Reaches Out for Dialogue with One Hand and Raises the Banner of Rebellion with the Other) Swiss Info, 9 February 2011. Available at http://www.swissinfo.ch/ara/detail/content.html?cid=29442394. 09

23 Ibid.

24 Quoted in Tadros, *The Muslim Brotherhood in Contemporary Egypt: Democracy Redefined or Confined?*, p. 37

25 'The MB Group Opposed the Theocratic State Because it is Against Islam,' Ikhwan Online, 10 February 2011.

26 Statement posted on Ikhwanweb, 7 February 2011.

27 *Al-Hayat*, 8 February 2011.

28 AFP Middle East news summary, AFP, 9 February 2011.

29 'Egypt: Islamist Muslim Brotherhood to JoinSsecond Round of Talks with Govt', Adnkronos International, Rome, 10 February 2011.

30 Statement posted on Ikhwan Online website, 13 February 2011.

31 'Egypt: Muslim Brotherhood Plans Political Party', The Associated Press, 15 February 2011.

32 International Crisis Group, 'Lost in Transition: The World According to Egypt's SCAF', Middle East/North Africa Report, No. 121, 24 April 2012.

33 Makeen F. Makeen, 'In Bed with the Brotherhood', Think Africa Press, 1 May 2011.

34 Sherif Tareq, 'Egypt's Muslim Brotherhood and Ruling Military: Deal or No Deal?', Ahram Online, 28 September 2011.

35 Quoted in International Crisis Group, 'Lost in Transition: The World According to Egypt's SCAF'.

36 Ibid.

37 Mustafa Lamel Al-Sayyed, Quoted in 'Muslim Brotherhood Plies Strategic Path in Egypt', Agence France Press, 24 November 2011.

38 International Crisis Group, 'Lost in Transition: The World According to Egypt's SCAF'.

39 Khalil al-Anani, 'Egypt's Freedom & Justice Party: To Be or Not to Be Independent', 1 June 2011. Available at http://carnegieendowment.org/2011/06/01/egypt-s-freedom-justice-party-to-be-or-not-to-be-independent/6b7p

40 Rashad Al-Bayoumi, for example, stressed that the Brotherhood was not studying existing models of the movement's political parties elsewhere in

the region and that whilst the party would share the Ikhwan's ideological framework, it would be completely separate. (Asharq Alawsat. 27 February 2011 A talk with Muslim Brotherhood's Rashad al-Bayoumi). Similarly, Brotherhood spokesman, Walid Shalabi insisted that the party and the movement might share the same Islamic ideals and would support each other when necessary, but that they would be completely separate in matters of management and finance (Freedom and Justice Party, *Jaddaliya*, 22 November 2011).

41   BBC Monitoring Middle East, 29 March 2011. Egypt's Muslim Brotherhood head discusses local issues in TV interview. Excerpt from report by Muslim Brotherhood website Ikhwanonline on 28 March. In order to demonstrate this division, the Freedom and Justice party took steps to differentiate itself from the Jama'a. It took as its slogan, 'Freedom is the solution and justice is the application' rather than 'Islam is the solution.

42   Nathan J. Brown, 'The Muslim Brotherhood as Helicopter Parent', ForeignPolicy.com, 27 May 2011.

43   Jeff Martini and Julie Taylor, 'Commanding Democracy in Egypt: The Military's Attempt to Manage the Future', Foreign Affairs, September/October 2011.

44   'Egypt's Muslim Brotherhood to Try to Win One Third of Parliament Seats', Al-Quds Press, 13 March 2011.

45   'Brotherhood Contests over 50 Percent of Parliamentary Seats', *Egypt Independent*, 25 October 2011.

46   'Violence In Cairo Pits Thousands Against Police', *New York Times*, 20 November 2011.

47   'In Egypt, an Islamist at Odds with his Party; Moderate's Presidential Bid Highlights Lack of Unity in the Muslim Brotherhood', *International Herald Tribune*, 21 June 2011.

48   'In Major Reversal, Muslim Brotherhood Will Vie for Egypt's Presidency', in *Christian Science Monitor*, 1 April 2012.

49   'Egypt's Brotherhood Defends Presidential Bid', *Al-Jazeera*, 3 April 2012.

50   'Muslim Brotherhood Conspired with Military Council to Field Presidential Candidate: Former Member', Al-Arabiya News, 2 April 2012.

51   'Stillborn Assembly', *Al-Ahram Weekly*, 5 April 2012.

52   Ibid.

53   'Egyptian Court Ruling Raises Stakes in Presidential Race', in *Christian Science Monitor*, 11 April 2011.

54   'Keeper of Islamic Flame Rises as Egypt's New Decisive Voice', *New York Times*, 12 March 2012.

55   Marc Lynch, 'Tunisia's New al-Nahda', Foreign Policy, 29 June 2011.

56   Mouldi Al-Ahmar, 'Tunisian elections: The Reasons Behind the Failure of the Modernists and the Problems Caused by the Victory of al-Nahda', Arab

Center for Research and Policy Studies, Doha. 25 December 2011.

57   Abdelatif al-Hanashi, *'Intikhabat al-Majlis al-Watani Ata Sissi Al-Tunisi: al-Ittar, al-Messar, wa Nata'ij'* ('The Elections to the Tunisian Constituent Assembly: Framework, Pathway and Results'), Arab Center for Research and Policy Studies, Doha, March 2012. http://www.dohainstitute.org/file/pdfViewer/7f78d9ff-7059-4df1-8d7c-7ab00fd15fbf.pdf

58   Libya Focus, Menas Associates, November 2011. Subscription publication available at www.menas.co.uk

59   Senussi Beseirki, *'Intihkhabat Al-Muatama Al-Watan Al-Libi Wa Khiyarat Al-Kutal Siasiya Al-Faiza'* ('The Election of the Libyan National Congress and the Choices of the Winning Political Blocs'), Al-Jazeera Centre for Studies, 23 July 2012. http://studies.aljazeera.net/reports/2012/07/201272311 2953432636.htm

60   Mary Fitzgerald, 'Introducing the Libyan Muslim Brotherhood', Foreign Policy, 2 November 2012.

Conclusion

1   Sayyid Qutb, *Milestones*, New Delhi, 1998 edition.

2   Dr Abdullah Nafisi, *Al-Haraka al-islamiya: thakart fy altariq* (The Islamic Movement: Cracks Along on the Way), self-published and undated. Available in Arabic on http://www.alnefisi.com/f_s_v/alharaka_aleslamiah_thakart_fy_altariq.pdf

3   Azzam Tamimi, *Rachid Ghannouchi. A Democrat within Islam*, New York, 2001, p. 91.

4   Magdi Khalil, 'The Muslim Brotherhood and the Copts', Threats Watch, 20 April 2006. Available on http://threatswatch.org/commentary/2006/04/the-muslim-brotherhood-and-the/

5   'Tunisia's Islamists Hail Arrival of the "Sixth Caliphate"' in *The Telegraph*, 16 November 2011. http://www.telegraph.co.uk/news/worldnews/africaandindianocean/tunisia/8894858/Tunisias-Islamists-hail-arrival-of-the-sixth-caliphate.html#

6   Michael Emerson And Richard Youngs (Eds), *Political Islam And European Foreign Policy Perspectives From Muslim Democrats Of The Mediterranean*, Brussels, 2007, p. 70.

7   Ibid, p.70

8   'Muslim Brotherhood Initiative on the General Principles of Reform in Egypt', Cairo, 2004. Obtained from the Brotherhood's headquarters in Cairo

9   Ibid.

10   Ibid.

11   Quoted in Dr Abdullah Nafisi, *Al-Haraka al-islamiya: thakart fy altariq*

12   Mustafa Mashour and Maimoun al-Hodeibi, for example, both held the reins of power from behind the scenes for many years before becoming Murshid.

13   Interviews with An-Nahda members and former An-Nahda members, London, Paris and Tunis, 2007.

14   Hossam Tamam. *Tahawilat Al-Ikhwan al-Muslimoun* (The Transformation of the Muslim Brotherhood), Cairo, 2006, p. 46.

15   *Fi Istishraf Al-Mostaqbal ... 5. Al- Gharb, Al-Houkumat Al-Arabiya Wal Islamiyoun* (Foreseeing the Future ... 5. The West, Arab Governments and Islamists), Alasr, 6 June 2006. Available at http://www.alasr.ws/index. cfm?method=home.con&contentID=7857.

16   Hossam Tamam. *Tahawilat Al-Ikhwan al-Muslimoun,* p. 46.

17   Ibid. p. 51.

18   *Political Islam and European Foreign Policy: Perspectives from Muslim Democrats of the Mediterranean*, Centre for European Policy Studies, 2007.

19   Azzam Tamimi, *Rachid Ghannouchi. A Democrat within Islam*, New York 2001, p. 103.

20   Richard P. Mitchell, *The Society of the Muslim Brothers,* New York, 1969, p. 2

21   'Muslim Brotherhood Initiative on the General Principles of Reform in Egypt'.

22   'Muslim Brotherhood Statement on Islamic Law and National Identity', Ikhwanweb, 4 November 2012. http://www.ikhwanweb.com/article. php?id=30353

23   'Egypt's Salafi Surge', Foreign Policy, 4 January 2012. http://www.foreignpolicy.com/articles/2012/01/04/ egypt_s_salafi_surge?hidecomments=yes

24   'Salafi Cleric's "Coffin Campaign" Goes Live on Tunisian TV', *Al-Bawaba*, 7 November 2012. http://www.albawaba.com/entertainment/ salafi-tv-interview-tunisia-449923

25   'The MB's Relations with the US', in *Al-Ahram Weekly*, No. 1104, 28 June–4 July 2012.

26   'Foreign Policy in Morsi's Presidential Election Platform', Ikhwanweb, 5 May 2012. http://www.ikhwanweb.com/article.php?id=30004

27   Ibid.

28   Bassem Sabry, 'A Guide to Egypt's Challenges: Subsidies & the Budget', Al-Ahram Online, 16 August 2012. http://english.ahram.org.eg/ NewsContent/1/0/49605/Egypt/Subsidies--the-Budget-.aspx

29   'Analysis: Egypt's Mursi Dogged by Own Promises in First 100 days', Reuters, 5 October 2012. http://www.reuters.com/article/2012/10/05/ us-egypt-mursi-idUSBRE8940FB20121005

Bibliography

Books

A'asaf, Mahmoud, *Ma' imam shaheed Hasan Al-Banna* (*With the martyred Imam Hasan al-Banna*), Cairo: Ain al-Shamis, 1993

Abd-Allah, Umar F., *The Islamic Struggle in Syria*, Berkeley: Mizan Press, 1983

Abdelhalim, Mahmoud, *Al-Ikhwan al-Muslimoun. Ahdath sunat al-Tareeq. Ru'iah Min al-dakhil* (*The Muslim Brotherhood. The Events that Made History. An Insider's Vision*), Vols. 1, 2 and 3, Alexandria: Dar al-Dawa, 2004

Abu Amr, Ziad, *Islamic Fundamentalism in the West Bank and Gaza*, Bloomington: Indiana University Press, 1994

Al-Awadi, Hesham, *In Pursuit of Legitimacy: The Muslim Brothers and Mubarak, 1982–2000*, London: Tauris Academic Studies, 2004

Ayoubi, N., *Political Islam: Religion and Politics in the Arab World*, London: Routledge, 1991

Barot, Mohamed Jamal, *Yathrab al-jadida, alharakat alislamia alrahna* (*The New Yathrab, The Current Islamic Movement*), London: Riyadh El-Rayyes Books, 1994

Besson, Sylvain, *La Conquête de L'Occident: Le Projet Secret Des Islamistes*, Paris: Seuil, 2005

Burgat, François and Dowell, William, *The Islamic Movement in North Africa*, Austin: University of Texas Press, 1993

Cesari, Jocelyne, 'Islam in France: The Shaping of a Religious Minority', in Yvonne Haddad-Yazbek (ed.), *Muslims in the West, from Sojourners to Citizens*, Oxford: Oxford University Press, 2002

Diyab, Muhammad Hafiz, *Sayyid Qutb: Al-khitab wal ideologia* (*Sayyid Qutb: Discourse and Ideology*), Cairo: Dar al-Thaqafa al-Jadida, 1988

Eddine, Adnan Saad, *Mesirat jama'at al-Ikhwan al-Muslimeen fi Suria* (*The Journey of the Syrian Muslim Brotherhood*), Private publisher: undated. Copy given to author.

Emerson, Michael and Youngs, Richard (eds.), *Political Islam and European Foreign Policy. Perspectives from Muslim Democrats of the Mediterranean*, Brussels: CEPS Paperbacks, 2007

Fisk, Robert, *Pity the Nation*, Oxford: Oxford University Press, 1990

Hawa, Said: *Said Hawa hathihi tajrubati ... Wa-hathahi shahadati (Said Hawa: This is my experience and this is my testimony)*, Cairo: Maktabat Wahba, 1987

Kepel, Gilles, *Allah in the West*, Cambridge: Polity Press, 2004

Kepel, Gilles, *Les banlieues de l'Islam*, Paris: Seuil, 1991

Kepel, Gilles, *Muslim Extremism in Egypt: The Prophet and the Pharaoh*, Berkeley: University of California Press, 1993

Kepel, Gilles, *The Roots of Radical Islam*, London: Saqi Books, 1985

Landau, Paul, *Le sabre et le Coran*, Monaco: Editions du Rocher, 2005

Laqueur, W., *No End to War*, New York: Continuum, 2003

Lia, Brynjar, *The Society of the Muslim Brothers in Egypt: The Rise of an Islamic Mass Movement 1928–1942*, Reading: Ithaca Press, 1998

McGoldrick, Dominic, *Human Rights and Religion: The Islamic Headscarf Debate in Europe*, Oxford: Hart Publishing, 2006

Mitchell, Richard P., *The Society of the Muslim Brothers*, Oxford: Oxford University Press, 1993

Moaddel, Mansoor, *Jordanian Exceptionalism*, New York: Palgrave, 2002

Nafisi, Abdullah (ed.), *Haraka alislamia: Ruiat mustakablia, iwarq fi alnaqd althati (The Islamic Movement: Future Vision. A Working Paper in Self-Criticism)*. Self-published by Dr Abdullah Nafisi, Kuwait, 1989

Perrotin, Claude, *Qu'est-ce que l'UOIF?*, L'Archipel, Paris, 2006

Peters, Rudolph, *Jihad in Classical and Modern Islam*, Princeton: Markus Wiener, 1996

Qutb, Sayyid, *Milestones*, New Delhi: Islamic Book Service, 1998

Ramadan, Abdelaziz, *Jama'at al-Takfir fi misr. Al-oosoul tarikhia wa fikeria (Takifiri Groups in Egypt: Intellectual and Historical Origins)*, Cairo: Al-Haya Al-Maseria Al'Ama Lilkitab, 1995

Ramadan, Tariq, *Aux sources du renouveau Musulman*, Paris: Editions Tawhid, 2002

Roy, Olivier, *Afghanistan, from Holy War to Civil War*, Princeton: Princeton University Press, 1995

Rutherford, Bruce K., *Egypt After Mubarak. Liberalism, Islam and Democracy in the Arab World*, Princeton: Princeton University Press, 2008

Said, Rifat, *Al-irhab al-mutaeslim (Islamicised Terrorism)*, Vol. 1. Cairo: Akhbar Al-Youm, 2004. Second Edition.

Sardar, Ziauddin, *Desperately Seeking Paradise. Journeys of a Sceptical Muslim*, London: Granta Books, 2004

Sayed Khatab, Sayed, *Al-Hudaybi's Influence on the Development of Islamist Movements in Egypt. The Muslim World*, Vol. 1, Wiley-Blackwell, 2001

Shadid, W. A. R. and Van Koningsveld, P. S., *Political Participation and Identities of Muslims in Non-Muslim States*, Leuven: Peeters Publishers, 1996

Tadros, Mariz, *The Muslim Brotherhood in Contemporary Egypt: Democracy*

Redefined or Confined?, London: Routledge, 2012

Tal, Nachman, *Radical Islam in Egypt and Jordan*, Brighton: Sussex Academic Press, 2005

Tammam, Hossam, *Tahawilat al-Ikhwan al-Muslimoun (The Transformation of the Muslim Brotherhood)*, Cairo: Maktabat Moudbouli, 2006

Tamimi, Azzam, *Rachid Ghannouchi. A Democrat within Islam*, Oxford: Oxford University Press, 2001

Ternisien, Xavier, *Les Frères Musulmans*, Paris: Fayard, 2005

Ternisien, Xavier, *La France des mosquées*, Paris: Editions Albin Michel, 2002

Weaver, Mary Anne, *A Portrait of Egypt: A Journey Through the World of Militant Islam*, New York: Farrar, Strauss and Giroux, 2000

Wickham, Carrie Rosefsky, *Mobilizing Islam: Religion, Activism and Political Change in Egypt*, New York: Colombia University Press, 2002

Journal Articles and Papers

Abedin, Mahan, 'The Battle within Syria: An Interview with Muslim Brotherhood Leader Ali Al-Bayanouni', in *Terrorism Monitor*, Jamestown Foundation, Vol 3, No. 16, 11 August 2005

Al-Shobaki, Amro, *'Mustakbal jamat Al-Ikhwan Al-Muslimeen' (The Future of the Muslim Brotherhood)*, in *Al-Ahram Strategic File*, Year 16, No. 163, May 2006

Amghar, Samir, 'Les mutations de l'Islamisme en France. Portrait de l'UOIF, porte-parole de l'Islamisme de minorité', in *Vie des idées*, No. 22–3, October 2007

Batatu, Hanna, 'Syria's Muslim Brethren', in *Merip Reports*, November–December 1982

Belén Soage, Ana, 'Faraj Fawda, Or the Cost of Freedom of Expression' in *Middle East Review of International Affairs*, Vol. 11, No. 2, June 2007

Brown, Nathan J. and Hamzawy, Amr, 'The Draft Party Platform of the Egyptian Muslim Brotherhood: Foray Into Political Integration or Retreat Into Old Positions?' in *Carnegie Papers*, No. 89, January 2008

Centre for European Policy Studies, 'Political Islam and European Foreign Policy. Perspectives from Muslim Democrats of the Mediterranean', Brussels, 2007

Drysdale, Alasdair, 'The Asad Regime and its Troubles', in *Merip Reports*, November–December 1982

Gambill, Gary, 'The Syrian Muslim Brotherhood', in *Mideast Mirror*, Vol. 1, No. 2, April–May 2006

Hatina, Meir, 'Restoring a Lost Identity: Models of Education in Modern Islamic Thought', in *British Journal of Middle Eastern Studies*, Vol. 33, No. 2,

November 2006

'Islamism Digest: The Muslim Brotherhood in Afghanistan', in *CFSOT*, Vol. 2, No. 10, October 2007

Leiken, Robert S. and Brooke, Steven, 'The Moderate Muslim Brotherhood', in *Foreign Affairs*, March–April 2007

Sinha, P. B., 'Threat of Islamic Terrorism in Egypt', in *Strategic Analysis*, Vol. 22, No. 8, November 1998

Stacher, Joshua A., 'Post-Islamist Rumblings in Egypt: the Emergence of the Wasat Party', in *The Middle East Journal*, Vol. 56, No. 3, Summer 2002

Utvik, Bjørn Olav, 'Hizb al-Wasat and the Potential for Change in Egyptian Islamism', in *Critical Middle Eastern Studies*, Vol. 14, No. 3, Fall 2005

Vidino, Lorenzo, 'The Muslim Brotherhood's Conquest of Europe', in *Middle East Quarterly*, Vol. 12, No. 1, Winter 2005

Zollner, Barbara, 'Prison Talk: The Muslim Brotherhood's Internal Struggle', in *International Journal of Middle East Studies*, No. 39, 2007

Unpublished Theses

Khadija, Darif, 'Bricolages identitaires des Musulmans dans l'espace politique français: cas de UOIF', Institut d'Etudes Politiques d'Aix-en-Provence, 2004

Official Muslim Brotherhood Documents and Memoirs

'Muslim Brotherhood Initiative: On the General Principles of Reform in Egypt 2004'

'The Political Project for the Future: Syria, A Vision of the Muslim Brotherhood Group in Syria. 425 AH–2004 AD'

Abul Futuah, Abdel Moneim, '*Shehadat Abul Futuah*' (Abul Futuah's Testimony), on Islam Online, 15 July 2009. Available in Arabic on http://islamyoon.islamonline.net/servlet/Satellite?c=ArticleA_C&cid=124818730 0655&pagename=Islamyoun%2FIYALayout

Shahid Alla Aser, '*Al-Ikhwan al-Muslimoun Kama Yrahm Farid Abdul Khaliq*' (A Witness in Time, The Muslim Brotherhood as Seen by Farid Abdul Khaliq), on Al-Jazeera, Episode 1, 7 December 2003. Available in Arabic on http://www.aljazeera.net/NR/exeres/BF012F78-FC05-4E7B-839C-67E94CF195BA.htm

'*Ali Al-Bayanouni: Al-Ikhwan al-Muslimeen fi Syria*' (Ali al-Bayanouni: The Muslim Brothers in Syria), on *Special Visit*, Al-Jazeera, November 2005. Available in Arabic on http://www.aljazeera.net/NR/exeres/B990668B-5CA6-4DC9-B16A-6828149AE0EA.htm

'*Al-ilakat Al-dowlia kama yaraha Al-Ikhwan*' (International Relations as seen by
  the Ikhwan). interview with Youssef Nada on Al-Jazeera.net, January 2005.
  Available in Arabic on http://www.aljazeera.net/NR/exeres/BFC52150-
  5FCA-48F3-8E15-7080405A641C.htm
'*Dr Hassan al-Huwaidi, naib al-musrhid al-am yekshif al-mujtamaa: Kusat
  al-Ikhwan al-muslimeen fi Suria ... min an-nasha hata al-manfa*' (Dr Hassan
  al-Huwaidi, the Deputy of the Supreme Guide Reveals to Al-Mujtamaa: The
  Story of the Muslim Brotherhood in Syria from the Beginning until Exile),
  in *Al-Mujatmaa*, No. 1741, 3 March 2007
Kamel, Abdelaziz, *Muthakarat Dr Abdelaziz Kamel, Uthou fi al-Nizam al-Khass*
  (The Memoirs of Dr Abdelaziz Kamel, member of the Nizzam al-Khass),
  July 2007. Available in Arabic on http://www.paldf.net/forum/showthread.
  php?t=120458

Newspapers and Press

Akhbar al-Youm
Al-Ahram Weekly
Al-Arabiya
Al-Diyar
Al-Ghad
Al-Sharq al Awsat
Associated Press
Campione
Crescent International
Deutsche Welle
El Watan
Foreign Affairs
Front Page Magazine
Impact International
Khaleej Times
Le Monde
Le Monde Diplomatique
Strategic Analysis
Terrorism Monitor
The Chicago Tribune
The Daily Mail
The Daily Star
The Financial Times
The Jerusalem Report

The Middle East Journal
The Middle East Reporter
The New Humanist
The New Statesman
The New York Sun
The New York Times
The Observer
The Sunday Times
The Wall Street Journal
The Weekly Worker
Time Magazine
Washington Post
World Tribune

Websites

Al-Ahram: www.alahram.org.eg
Al-Hewar: www.alhewar.com
Al-Jazeera: www.aljazeera.net
Al-Motamar: www.almotamar.net
Al-Minhadj Forum: www.alminhadj.fr
BBC Online: www.bbc.co.uk
Ikhwanweb: www.ikhwanweb.com
Ikhwan Online: www.ikhwanonline.com
Islam Memo: www.islammemo.info
Islam Online: www.islamonline.net
Jyllands-Posten: www.jyllandsposten.dk
Memri Special Dispatch: www.memri.org
Radio Free Europe, Radio Liberty: www.rferl.org
Religioscope: www.religion.info
Simon Wiesenthal Centre: www.wiesenthal.com
Threats Watch: threatswatch.org
Ummah.net: www.ummah.net

Index

9/11 events 10, 17, 18, 54, 95, 105, 118, 130, 137, 138, 166, 178, 180, 182, 209, 213

Aachen, Bilal mosque 164
A'asaf, Mahmoud 28
Abbas, Mohamed 216
Abd al-Karim, Salah 50
Abd Al-Maqsud, Salah 51
Abd al-Raziq, Ali 20
Abdel Latif, Mahmoud 34, 41
Abdel Rahman, Sheikh Omar 255
Abdelbaqi, Hosni 37, 40
Abdelhadi, Sheikh 149
Abdelhalim, Mahmoud 19, 26, 30
Abdelkader, Suleiman 241
Abdu, Muhammad 9, 189
Aboul Fotouh, Dr Abdul Moneim 17, 38, 40–1, 41, 42, 43–4, 45, 52–3, 53, 55, 59, 61–2, 104, 115, 197–8, 202, 203, 206, 207, 217, 218–19, 220, 232, 247
Abu Ghuddah, Sheikh Abdul Fattah 73, 85
Abu Ismail, Hazem 235
Abu Nasser, Mohamed Hamed, Murshid 48–9, 50, 114, 121, 155, 192
Abu Nizar 82
Abu Sen, Haj 205
Abu Zeid, Sana 41

AEIF (*Association des Étudiants Islamiques en France*) 140
al-Afghani, Jamal al-Din 20
Afghanistan 13, 54, 117, 189–92, 193–5, 206
Afghan mujahideen 117, 126, 180, 189, 190, 191–2, 192, 193–4
Ahl al-Dhimma (Christians and Jews) 127
Ahmed Sheikh 159, 160, 162, 178
Ahrar party 46
al-Ahsan, Sheikh Ahmed 153
Akef, Mehdi 46, 51
    appointed Murshid 28, 55, 111, 132, 133, 134, 182, 196, 226
    resigns ofice of Murshid 60
    friction with Guidance Office 61
    visits Munich 165, 169
    support for Hizbullah 201
    corruption from the West 206
    US as Satan 206
Al Droubie, Riad 154
Al-Azhar University 20, 68, 151, 153, 181, 189, 191, 234, 253
Al-Gomhuriya (Egyptian newspaper) 180, 181
Al-Haqq magazine 142
Al-Hayat newspaper 220
Al-Jazeera TV 89, 97, 217
Al-Murabitoun magazine 192
Al-Youm Al-Sabi'e 63

Alaoui, Fouad 145, 146, 150, 151
Alawites 66, 76, 77, 87
Aleppo 86
Aleppo Artillery Schoolm 83
al-Alfi, Hassan 104
Algeria 116, 118, 128, 145, 189, 225
Algerians in France 145
Amal party 46
Amin, Giuma 62
Amnesty International 89
al-Amoush, Bassam 121, 131
An-Nahda party 7, 11, 12, 140, 149,
    237–40, 244, 245, 247, 248, 252,
    254, 257
Anglo-Egyptian Treaty 1936 24
Aqla, Adnan 82, 83, 89
Arab Ikhwan 71
Arab Spring 8, 11, 211–12, 237, 244,
    245, 246, 250, 253
al-Ariyan, Issam 17, 38, 39, 41, 44, 52,
    53, 57, 60, 61, 62, 206, 218, 221,
    225–6, 226
al-Asal, Fathi 31
Ashwami, Saleh 27, 28
al-Assad, President Bashar 96, 132
al-Assad, President Hafez 86, 97
al-Assad regime 98–9, 132, 197, 204
al-Athaum, Yousef 124
Atta, Mohamed 180
al-Attar, Issam, Syrian Guide 70, 71,
    74, 77, 82, 88, 259
    while in exile 72–3, 107, 109, 140, 141
    at Aachen 110, 112, 138, 164
Ayuobi, N 186
Azami, Mustafa 153
al-Azzam, Hudaifa 191, 193
Azzam, Sheikh Abdullah 180, 190–2,
    191–2, 195

Ba'athist regime 66, 67, 71, 76, 77, 88
    siege of Sultan mosque 72
    attack on Sūltan mosque 80

campaign to root out Brotherhood
    83–4
    death for Brotherhood members 86
    razes Hamah to the ground 89
    in Iraq 203
Badie, Mohammed, Supreme Guide
    62, 62–3, 218, 227
Bahrain 111
al-Banna, Hassan 16
    founds Muslim Brotherhood 18, 182, 251
    struggles for balance 18
    personality cult 19
    ideology 20
    anti-imperialist views 21
    concerns about Westernisation 21,
        204, 206
    organising ability 21
    untouchable legacy 22, 153
    demonstrates expediency 23
    pragmatism 23, 25
    fields parliamentary candidates 24
    makes deal with government 24
    unilateral decisions 25
    adapts leadership style 26–7
    struggles to control Nizzam al-Khass 29
    assassination 30
    distances himself from violence 30, 185
    loses control of movement 30–1
    Qawl Fasl 30
    international outlook 106
    committed to jihad 189
    Ikhwan and the Palestine cause 198–9
    criticises political violence 208
    anxiety over public morality 222
    autocratic style 223
Barot, Mohamed Jamal 44–5, 84, 88
al-Bayanouni, Abu Naser 86
al-Bayanouni, Ali Saddredine 81, 82,
    86, 89, 92, 93, 96, 97, 98, 99, 121,
    123, 131, 178, 203–4
    criticises reform programme 94
al-Bayoumi, Rashad 62, 215, 220

al-Beltagy, Mohamed 217, 232–3
Ben Ali, President Zine El Abidine
    211, 213, 238
Ben Mansour, Abdallah 142, 143
Bensheikh, Soheib, Mufti of Marseille
    147
bin Laden, Osama 208
al-Bishri, Tariq 222
al-Bouazizi, Mohamed 211
Bourgiba, President Habib 238
Breeze, Lhaj Thami 145, 146–7, 148,
    150, 150–1, 151, 175
Brooke, Steve 202, 211–12, 214
Bush, President George W 179, 207, 225
Busuleimani, Sheikh 128

Cairo 15
CFCM (*Conseil Français du Culte
    Musulman*) 149, 151
Collectif des Musulmans de France 151
Cologne, mosque at Marburg 166
Coptic Church 234, 252

Da'bul, Muwafaq 73
Dandelle, Osama 82
al-Dari, Harith 133
al-Dawa 39, 69, 75, 79, 85, 106, 107,
    152, 153
Democratic Alliance for Egypt 229
al-Dhunaybat, Abd al-Majid,
    Jordanian Guide 104, 197, 199–200
al-Din al-Alawi, Nasr 254
Dulaimi, Adnan 133
al-Dwaila, Mubarak 123, 124

ECFR (*European Council for Fatwa
    and Research*) 164, 170
Eddine, Adnan Saad 73, 74, 75, 79,
    80, 82, 84, 85, 86, 90, 90–1, 92, 98,
    106, 109, 123, 259
    *The Journey of the Syrian Muslim
        Brotherhood* 91

Egypt, Day of Rage 212, 213, 214
Egyptian Ikhwan
    evolution 8–9, 11, 12
    state repression 16, 106
    broad based appeal 17
    internal divisions 17, 233
    resistance to al-Banna 25–6
    leadership contest 31
    becomes weakened 33
    hopes of Nasser regime 33
    crushed by regime arrests 34
    dissolved by Nasser 34
    Qutbist elements breakaway 35–6
    hawks seize control 37
    recruits students 37–8
    accepts use of force 42
    empowered by students 43
    attract the middle classes 44
    become political activists 44–5
    calls for political freedom 44
    aversion to party politics 45
    alternative entry into political system 46
    wins election seats 46
    wins more seats 46
    reformist revival 54–5
    ambiguities of reform initiative 55–6
    Muslim Brotherhood: Principles of
        Reform 2004 55, 198, 248
    draft policy platform 57–8
    internal hostilities 57
    limits rights of women and Copts 58
    platform calls for council of clerics 58
    locked in competing struggles 60
    conservatives in control 62
    elections fatwa 63
    hawkish rebuilding 108
    inflexible control causes losses 117
    call for new international *tanzeem* 135
    Afghan training camps 191–2, 193
    support for Palestinians 198
    reform platforms emerge 222, 225–6
    dilemma of opposing views on

constitution 252
willing to meet US officials 255
see also Muslim Brotherhood
Egyptian Medical Syndicate 194
El Baradei, Mohamed 214
Erbakan, Sabiha 166
Erbaken, Necmettin 124, 166

Facebook generation 213
Faisal, King of Saudi Arabia 72
Faraj, Mohamed Abdelsalam 224
Fares, Adel 87
Farhan, Dr Kamal 215
Fateh 80
FEMYSO (*Forum of European
    Muslim Youth and Student
    Organisations*) 166
Fighting Vanguard (al-Tali'a
    al-Muqatila) 79, 80, 81, 82, 82–3,
    87, 92, 208
Financial Times 97
FIOE (*Federation of Islamic
    Organisations in Europe*) 175–6
FIS (*Front Islamique du Salut*) 128,
    145, 146
Foda, Faraj 208
FOSIS (*Federation of Student Islamic
    Societies*) 152, 153, 154, 155, 156,
    157, 158
Freedom and Justice Party 7, 226–7,
    229, 231, 234, 236, 257
Front Page Magazine 179

al-Gannouchi, Rashid 238, 239, 240,
    246, 248, 250–1
Ganzouri, Prime Minister Kamal 232
Gaza Strip 98, 99
Geneva, Islamic Centre 110
Gerecht, Reuel 224
Germany 72, 162–70
al-Ghannouchi, Rashid 117, 122, 124, 128,
    140, 144, 147, 171, 219, 221–2, 232, 242

al-Ghazali, Imam Sheikh Mohamed
    38, 147, 205, 208, 225
Ghazlan, Mahmoud 38, 41, 221, 250
Ghoul, Moulay Abderrahmane 147
Ghozlan, Mahmoud 62
Ghuraiyba, Ibrahim 116
GIF (*Groupement Islamique de France*)
    140, 141
Guidance Office 16, 24*bis*, 25, 32, 34,
    37, 44, 50, 60, 62, 74, 113, 249
    intervenes in Syrian dispute 107
    appoints Secret Murshid 109
    dominates national branches 114–15
    denies Nada has official position 115
    woos Sudanese dissidents 116
    weak statements on Kuwait 121
    does not oppose Mahfoud Nahnah 129
    prefers Syrian regime to opposition 132
    troubled by Iraqi Islamic party in
        elections 133
    spiritual reference for IGD 169
    retains control of reformist ideas
        220, 223
Gulf states 76, 108, 111, 115, 116, 199
Gulf War crisis 105–6, 121

Habash, Mohamed 96
Habib, Mohamed 59, 60–1, 105, 115,
    131, 134, 177–8, 200, 207, 217, 226,
    227, 247
Hadid, Marwan 72, 79–80, 80–1, 82,
    83, 186, 208
al-Hafez, President Amin 80
Hamah 73, 75, 76, 90
    attack on the Sultan mosque 72, 80
    general strike 86
    insurrection 88–9
Hamas 98, 99, 132, 173, 180, 199, 201,
    202, 213, 215, 256
al-Hamid, Sheikh Mohamed 75–6, 80
Hamidullah, Professor Muhammad
    140

Hamoud, Abdelrahman Qura 85
Hanafi, Hassan 20, 21
Harbah, Mohamed Khalid 88
Hashemi, Tariq 133
Hashish, Usam 41
Hasnawi, Sheikh Mohamed 71, 72, 74,
    83, 84–5, 85, 87–8, 92, 259
Hassanein, Ahmed 37, 40
Hawa, Sheikh Said 73, 75, 75–6, 78,
    79, 86, 87, 91, 92
    *Soldiers of Allah: Culture and
    Manners* 78
al-Hawari, Sheikh Mohamed 73, 164, 171
Helal, Mohamed 60
Helbawy, Dr Kamal 103, 112, 120, 122,
    126, 129, 130, 130–1, 137, 153, 154,
    156, 157, 158, 159, 161, 166, 169, 191,
    192, 193, 194, 195, 209, 215, 223,
    233, 259
hijab affair 143, 150–1
Hijazi, Sofwat 135
Himmat, Ghaleb 115, 118, 119, 163, 165,
    166, 168, 173
Hizb al-Tayyar Al-Masri (Egyptian
    Current Party) 227
Hizb al-Watani (Nationalist Party) 23
Hizb ut Tahrir 225
Hizb al-Wasat party 51
Hizbullah 132, 201
    Al-Manar TV channel 200
al-Hodeibi, Hassan, Murshid 22, 31–3,
    34, 35, 36, 37, 44, 109, 186–7, 223
    Preachers Not Judges 36, 186–7
    plans for Arab executive office 107
al-Hodeibi, Maimoun 32–3, 48, 49, 50,
    51, 55, 114, 129, 130, 149–50, 159, 208
Howells, Kim 214
Huber, Thomas 173
al-Husayni, Musa Ishaq 20
Hussein, Mahmoud 234
Hussein, Saddam 90, 120, 122, 123,
    202–3, 204, 219

al-Husseini, Saad 62
al-Huwaidi, Dr Hassan 73, 85, 87, 89,
    90, 91, 103, 123, 131, 150, 155, 164
al-Huwari, Muhammad 87

Ibn Taymiyyah 66, 78, 184
IGD (*Islamische Gemeinschaft
    Deutschland*) 164, 166, 166–7,
    168–70, 173–4, 174
    Vice President is a woman 170
IICO (*International Islamic Charity
    Organisation*) 173
International *Tanzeem*
    secretive and decentralised 103–6
    Guidance Office in Cairo 105
    opportunity to control other
        branches 108
    The Internal Statute document 113
    controlled from the Cairo centre
        114
    uses global networks 117
    The Project document 119–20
    limits of Cairo's power 128
    advisory body only 131, 169
    decline follows demise of Mashour 134
    uncertain future 134–5
    annual meetings with other
        branches 150
    groups in Europe less important 157
    financial flows 165
International Union of Islamic
    Scholars 238
Iranian revolution 1979 43, 118
Iran–Iraq war statements 158
Iraq
    refuge for Syrian Ikhwan 90
    volunteers to fight occupation 197
    support for armed resistance 203
Iraqi Islamic Party 133, 134
Iraqi Muslim Brotherhood 133
    Iraqi Islamic Party 204
Irsheid, Zaki Bani 183, 227, 228

al-Islam, Saif 155
Islamic Conference, Berlin 2006 172
Israel 199, 202, 203
Izzat, Mahmoud 48, 59, 61, 62

Jaballah, Ahmed 140
Jaballah, Mokhtar 143
Jaballah, Sheikh Ahmed 143, 146, 148
Ja'far, Sheilk Idris 154
Jaj, Adeeb 92
al-Jama'at al-Islamiya
    enforces Islamic morality 38, 166
    popular Islamist movement 38
    umbrella for University groups 38
    contacts with Muslim Brotherhood 39
    becomes part of the Ikhwan 41, 188
    jihadists separate 41–2
    condemns Ikhwani unwillingness
        192
Jamiyat al-Sharia 57
Jamour, Riyath 82–3, 92
Jasmine Revolution 237
Jibali, Hamdi, Prime Minister 247
Jibril, Mahmoud 242
al-Jihad group 42
Jordan, refuge for Syrian Ikhwan 90, 93
Jordanian Ikhwan
    spread from Egypt 9
    denies international organation 104
    connections with monarchy 108
    supports Mashour's international
        ideas 112, 116
    support Saddam Hussein 123, 124
    Islamic Action Front 183, 228
    radicalisation 186
    support for Palestine 200–1
    objects to peace with Israel 201
Justice and Construction Party 7, 241,
    242, 243

kafir, definitions of 142, 171
Kamel, Dr Abdelaziz 25, 28

Kanan, Abdel 85
al-Katatni, Saad 218, 220, 225, 226, 234
al-Kebti, Bashir 241
Kember, Norman 203
Kepel, Gilles 187
Khaddam, Abdul Halim 97, 98, 99,
    132, 133, 219
Khalifa, Mohamed Abdelrahman 112,
    124
Khaliq, Farid Abdel 19, 21, 23, 24, 29,
    44, 188
al-Khatib, Hassan 160
al-Khazindar Bey, Judge Ahmed 29,
    208
Khomeini, Ayatollah 239
Kurds, reservations about Syrian
    Ikhwan 102
Kuwait 111, 112
    Saddam Hussein's invasion 120–1
Kuwaiti Ikhwan
    feel betrayed by the Brotherhood 125
    freezes membership of movement 126
    forms Islamic Constitutional
        Movement 127

Larayed, Ali 254
Le Monde Diplomatique 130
Leiken, Robert 202, 211–12, 214
Lia, Brynjar 21, 28
Libya 7, 135, 212
Libyan Ikhwan 232, 240–4, 252, 257
Limdaris, Falah 126
Livingstone, Ken 162
London
    Islamic Centre 110, 154
    Muslim Brotherhood media office 129
    Muslim Welfare House, Finsbury
        Park 154, 157
    Muslim Brotherhood office 158
London meeting, criticises draft
    platform 59
Londonistan 152

MAB (*Muslim Asociation of Britain*)
159, 160–2, 167
Madani, Abassi 225
Madhi, Abu Ala 38, 40, 41, 43, 44, 45,
47, 49, 57, 114
leads al-Wasat reformist group 51,
51*bis*, 52, 104
al-Mahgary, Mohamed Ali 163
Majid, Abdul 156
Makri, Yamin 151
Maktab al-Amm (General Office) 107
Maktab al-Khadamat 191
al-Malat, Dr Ahmed 37, 40, 48, 74,
108, 109, 112
Mandela, Nelson 202
Mashour, Mustafa 37, 40, 44, 45,
46–7, 48, 223, 246
appointed Murshid 50, 114
comments on Christians 51
international aspirations 108, 111–12,
116, 134
encourages Sudanese break up 116
ties with the Kuwaitis 123, 125
turns attention to Egypt 129
disowns Helbawy 130
visits to Europe 155, 156, 164, 169
denies violence 181
visits Afghanistan 191, 192, 194
doubtful acceptance of democracy
217, 221
*The Path of Al-Dawa: Between Reform
and Deviation* 220–1, 250
Maududi, Abu Ala 36, 78, 184, 187
Mawlawi, Sheikh Faisal 110, 141, 142,
144, 147, 149, 171
Meshal, Khalid 132
Meskine, Dhaou 149, 175
military training camps 90, 197
Millî Görüş 167, 168, 172
Mohamed's Youth 27
Moral Behaviour, Society for 251
Morocco 215, 228

students in France 145
Morsi, Mohamed 213, 218, 226, 232
declared President 235–6, 247, 255,
256, 257
MSS (*Muslim Students' Society*) 153,
154, 155, 157, 167
MTI (*Mouvement de la Tendance
Islamique*) 140, 149, 238
Mubarak, President Hosni 45, 112, 212,
220, 221
Electoral Law 1983 45
Mubarak regime 213, 214, 215, 216–17
Mufti of Jerusalem 198
al-Mujaddidi, Sheikh Haroun 190
Munich, Mosque and Islamic Centre
110, 111, 163, 165
Murshid (Supreme Guide) 15, 18, 29,
113, 223, 232
Muslim Brotherhood
roles 7
wins Egyptian elections 7
behaviour during Arab Spring 8, 13
political role 9–10
reactionary force 9
spreading ideology 9
in Europe 10, 12–13, 110, 136–7
movement in stasis 11, 16
international organisation 12
ideology of violence 13
state repression 16
reformists 17
loses all election seats 63–4
against presence of US in Kuwait 122
unwilling to condemn Saddam
Hussein 125
fears labelling as terrorist group 130, 137
pragmatic working with
establishment 137
reticent about links to Brotherhood
137, 138
need to dissociate from leaders'
proclamations 138–9

informal links to UOIF 147
links to MAB 161
denies allegations of using violence 181
jihad as a duty 182–3, 197, 198
limited action in Afghanistan 192
supports Iraq bombings 196
supports Palestine bombings 196
military struggle against US and
    British in Iraq 201
repressed in Iraq 203
anti-Western discourse 206–7
accused of terrorist ideology 207–8
ambiguity towards violence 209
failure to address violent past 210
welcomes dialogue with the West 212
reluctant to be involved 213–15
becomes arch organiser 216
joins call for regime change 217
participates in dialogue 218
protestations of moderation 218
accused of betraying the revolution
    219
declares not hungry for power 221
joins legal committee 222–3
works with Supreme Council for
    Armed Forces 222
eager for amendments referendum
    223–4
accused of plot with SCAF 225
youth elements break away 227
expels 'errant youth' 228
presses SCAF to allow party lists 230
returns to street demonstrations 230
fields presidential candidate 231–2,
    232–3
packs constituent assembly with
    Islamists 233–4
not Islamic enough 254
expected to deal with poverty and
    injustice 256–7
see also Egyptian Ikhwan; Syrian
    Ikhwan

Muslim Council of Britain 160
Muslim Welfare House, Finsbury Park
    154

Nachatt, Ahmed 147
Nada, Yousef 45, 104, 110, 118–19, 119,
    120, 165
al-Nadwi, Abu Hassan 78, 184, 185
Nafisi, Sheikh Abdullah 56–7, 115–16,
    219, 246
Nahas, Obeida 81, 87, 97
al-Nahas, Prime Minister Mustafa
    Pasha 24
Nahnah, Mahfoud 128–9, 147
Namangani, Nurredine Nakibhodscha
    163
Nasreddin, Ahmed Idris 118
Nasser, President Gamal Abdel 33, 70,
    152, 190, 205, 229
    attempted assassination 34
al-Nasser, Saud 126, 127
National Salvation Front 97, 98, 213
New York Times 235
N'Gazou, Mohsen 147, 176, 177, 178
Nizam al-Khass (military wing)
    formation 27–9
    political violence 29, 30, 182, 208
    dominates movement 32–3
    prison releases 37
    recruits student leaders 40
    militants flee abroad 45
    hardline group returns 48
    curbs reformists 49
    core principle obedience 117
al-Nour party 231, 254
Nuqrashi, Prime Minister 30

Obama, President Barak 213, 226–7
Organisation 1965 35, 67, 188
Osman, Dr Alamin 116, 153, 156
Oubrou, Tareq 147

Pakistan 117, 193, 195
  Jama'at e-Islami 153, 156, 168, 194
Palestine 198–201, 202
Palestinians 98–9, 124, 132, 256
Paris mosque 143
Plumbly, Sir Derek 214

Qadhafi, Colonel Mu'ammar 197, 212, 240, 242
al-Qa'ida 10, 48, 118, 166, 180, 183, 190, 192, 208
al-Qaradawi, Sheikh Yusuf 38, 51, 117, 119, 147, 153, 162, 170, 172, 177
Qasir al-Aini Hospital, Cairo 39
Qur'an 20, 143, 148, 189, 217
Qutb, Sayyid 13, 22, 35–6, 39, 63, 67, 80, 91, 147, 183, 191, 208, 250
  In the Shade of the Quran 155
  Milestones 155, 186, 187, 205, 207, 246
  emerges as radical scholar 184–6, 187–8, 195, 205, 220

al-Rab'i, Dr Ahmad 207
Ramadan, Said 109–10, 136, 140, 154, 162–3, 168, 198, 219
Ramadan, Tariq 110
al-Rawi, Ahmed 175–6, 196
Rice, Condoleeza 213
Rida, Rashid 9, 20, 189
Riddah (apostasy) 78
Rifat, Ahmed 25, 26
Riyadh, World Assembly of Muslim Youth 111
Roy, Oliver 194

Sadat, President Anwar 37, 39, 45, 108, 112, 219
Sadeq Abdelmajid, Sheikh 116
Said, Dr Rifat 115, 165, 180
Said, Mohamed 87
Salafists 39, 73, 149, 229, 231, 233, 252, 253, 253–4

Saleh, Sobhi 222
al-Sanadi, Adel Rahman 29
Sananiri, Kamel 37, 40, 41, 48, 108, 190–1
Sardar, Ziauddin 153, 155
Sarkozy, Nicolas 151
Saudi Arabia 10, 39, 72, 78, 99, 110, 117, 118, 163, 168, 194
Saudi monarchy 110–11
Sawan, Mohamed 241
SCAF (*Supreme Council for Armed Forces*) 212, 222, 223–4
  limits party lists in elections 229
  proposes Supra-constitutional principles 230–1
  refuses to dissolve government 232
  dissolves parliament and bars entry 235
Schadlow, Nadia 259
Secret Murshid (Supreme Guide) 109
Setmariam, Mustafa (aka Abu Musab al-Suri) 180
Shabab Mohamed groups 68, 70
Shafiq, Ahmed 236
Shamis, Ashur 153, 155, 186
al-Shaqfa, Mohammed Riad, General Guide 101
  no objection to women or Christians 101–2
Sharia law 17, 38, 45, 54, 56, 58, 59, 93–4, 176, 179, 211, 216, 218, 219, 224, 243, 246, 248, 251, 252, 253
al-Shater, Khairet 48, 231, 232, 233, 235
Shati, Ismail 126
el-Shayyal, Jamal 161
Shobaki, Amr 53, 56
Shukri, Mustafa 36, 208
al-Sibai, Mustafa, Syrian Guide 68, 68–70, 75, 77–8, 92, 199
  Islamic Socialism 78
Siria, Saleh 225
Smith Richardson Foundation 12, 259
Soltani, Sheikh 225

Sudanese Ikhwani 116, 154
Sufists 73
suicide operations 171–2, 180, 196,
    197, 200
Suleiman, Omar 218, 219, 220, 235
Sultan, Issam 47, 50, 51, 52–3
Sultani, Sheikh Abu Jarrah 147
al-Suri, Abu Musab (aka Mustafa
    Setmariam) 180
al-Swaidan, Tariq 126
Syria, Islamic Front 86–7
Syrian Ikhwan
    spread from Egypt 9
    uprising against Ba'athist regime 10,
        67, 182
    shift to violence 12, 13
    reformist programme 18
    Aleppo wing 65, 66, 73, 74
    Damascus wing 65, 66, 73, 74, 77,
        79, 164
    Hamah massacre 1982 65–6, 67
    radicalisation 67, 76
    weakness of leadership 67
    movement in exile 67–8, 85
    becomes Muslim Brotherhood 68
    accepts secular constitution 69
    anti-feudal agenda 69
    submits to al-Banna's authority 69
    forced to dissolve 70
    gains seats at election 71
    given ministries 71
    al-Attar's banishment creates
        vacuum 73
    division into competing wings 73–4
    Adnan Said Eddine elected General
        Guide 74, 109
    Cairo organises election 74
    regime reforms threaten social
        balance 76–7
    call for jihad 79
    absence of leadership 84
    weapons training 85
    leads Islamic Front 86
    Damascus wing rejoins 87–8
    attempts to evaluate Hamah 91–2
    civil democracy platform 93–4
    National Honour Charter 93
    ignores non-Arab minorities 94
    alternative to Ba'athist regime 95
    courts Western audience 95
    attempts to reach out to regime 96,
        226
    joins Abdul Halim Khaddam 97, 133
    joins National Salvation Front 97, 213
    leaves National Salvation Front 98
    reformist platforms as opportunism
        99
    supports Syrian uprisings 100
    Pledge and Charter 101
    defends Saddam Hussein 127
    sheltered by Saddam Hussein 204
    see also Muslim Brotherhood
Syrian National Council 100, 102

Tahrir Square 213, 215, 216, 217, 219,
    220, 224, 230
Taibah (Albanian charity) 173
al-Takfir wal-Hijra jihadist group 36,
    188, 208
Talat, Yousef 33
al-Talia (the Vanguard) 74, 164
Tamimi, Azzam 129, 160, 161, 196, 201
Tammam, Hossam 117, 220, 250
Tantawi, Sheikh Abdullah 92, 151
al-Taqwa bank 45, 104, 118–19, 165,
    166, 173
al-Taweel, Sheikh Abdul Rahman 171
Tayfour, Mohamed Farouk 98, 100–1
Tikriti, Anas 161
Tikriti, Osama 154, 161
al-Tilimsani, Omar, Murshid 19, 22,
    41, 42, 109, 156, 187
    urges entry to the political arena
        44–5, 46

death 47, 114
Tunisia 7, 211–12, 237–40, 252, 254, 257
Tunisian Islamists stamped out 144
Tunisians in France 141
al-Turabi, Dr Hassan 107, 116–17, 117,
    124, 154
    rejects Egyptian leadership 128, 232
    in Europe 155, 156

Üçüncü, Oğuz 167–8
UK Ikhwan 241
United Arab Republic 70
UOIF (Union des Organisations
    Islamiques de France) 140, 141,
    142–3, 144–6, 161, 166, 175, 177
    denies link to Brotherhood 146
US, financial aid and support to Egypt
    255
US Treasury, Terrorist Finance Unit
    214
Utaiki, Abdullah 126

al-Wafd party 46, 64, 218
WAMY (World Assembly of Muslim
    Youth) 167, 173
al-Wasat party 51–3, 104, 130
Weekly Worker magazine 161
Western forces, prepare to liberate
    Kuwait 121–2
Western values, contamination by 176
Westernisation 20, 204–5, 204–6,
    206, 251

Yemen 118
el-Youssef, Ibrahim 89

al-Zaim, Dr Abdel Sattar 83, 92
al-Zarqawi, Abu Musab 183
al-Zawahiri, Ayman 48
    Knights under the Prophets Banner 190
El-Zayat, Bilal 166
El-Zayat, Farouk, Imam 166

El-Zayat, Ibrahim 166–7, 168, 169–70,
    172, 174, 178
el-Zayat, Muntassir 166
Zidanai, Sheikh Abdulmajid 195
Zouheir, Mahmoud 142, 175